# The Argument for
# **Acceptance**
# in Zoroastrianism

# Dr. Kersey H. Antia

Expanded version of the paper *The Argument for Acceptance – A reply to the three High Priests*, Parsiana Publications, 1985.

Twilit Grotto
Kasson, MN 55944
USA

ISBN-13: 978-1466363335
ISBN-10: 1466363339

# FOREWORD

The crux of the religion propounded by Prophet Zarathushtra is "Asha," *i.e.* Righteousness, or Truth. But ironically enough, amongst the followers of this great Prophet, whenever Truth is propounded, many followers become hysterical because Truth, which at times is stranger than fiction, does not suit the followers. So they come out with puerile theories which, to say the least, are not in conformity with the old religion as propounded by the Prophet, nor in tune with the current times, which have compelled the followers of every faith to change the time-honoured traditions.

Our community is a community full of contradictions, and in no other community will you find thousands of people claiming to be orthodox side-by-side with an equal number – sometimes more – crying for reforms. But their cries are unfortunately drowned in thin air.

Dr. Kersey H. Antia, the writer of the article, whose family I knew long before he was born, hails from a priestly class. In 1983, he performed the "Navjote" ceremony of one Joseph Peterson who was a keen student of the Zoroastrian religion. Peterson was converted to the Zoroastrian faith by donning him with "sudreh" and "kusti," and a lot of fuss was made about this. The Zoroastrian religion preaches love, but can sow hatred. If one analyses carefully, one will find what drives one to religion is misery or disease. The path of escapism is found only in one's own religion or one's own faith.

The way in which Dr. Antia has critically analysed the issue of conversion demands an objective probe by the authorities. He has come to the inevitable conclusion that Zoroastrianism ordained conversion.

Unfortunately, the leaders of the community have a mentality of an ostrich. They are not prepared to face the problems which are confronting it. No controversial question is to be discussed at any conference or meeting. Grave problems facing the community are shelved. Social gatherings arranged. A computer study is made of fire-temples, their funds, number of persons visiting the fire-temples, etc., but no one is prepared to come forward and solve the issue of "Kathi" without which fire-temples cannot survive. Likewise, no one is prepared to solve the issue of maintenance of Parsi priests. We have problems of grave character, which, if not solved, will gradually erode the community. We are however wasting our time in running after rainbows. Does it matter whether a person puts on a "sudreh" and "kusti"? We are more interested in the magic of bull's urine than in the study of our old religious books and scriptures. We are more interested to ensure that dead bodies of Parsis in Bombay are not allowed to be seen by non-Parsis. We have greater sanctity for the dead than the living.

One zealous writer had the audacity to suggest in the Press that Parsis in India have to ignore the Parsis abroad and have their own creed, have their own faith, have their own religion untouched by foreign hands, and unpolluted by Parsis abroad.

I would very earnestly appeal to members of my community to study the accompanying thesis carefully and objectively, and come to their own conclusions.

The issues raised by Dr. Antia cannot be dismissed as piffling or frivolous. In my view, Dr. Antia has exhibited singular moral courage in controverting the views of leading Dasturjis of India and I am sure that after reading this article, those of us who have fossilized views will spare time to re-think. No community can be strong and healthy unless it realises its own weaknesses, and seeks to remove them.

Let Divine Light shine on the noble teachings of our Prophet, and let providence guide the destiny of the community.

January 8, 1985.                                                                                          (S.R. VAKIL)

P.S.

As I finished writing this Foreword, I was informed that though Dr. Antia desired to read a paper at the Fourth World Zoroastrian Congress, a diplomatic letter was sent by the Chairman of the Reception Committee, Mr. J.N. Guzder, virtually barring him from reading the paper. The community is not composed of fools and nincompoops; the community fully realises why Dr. Antia was barred from reading the paper. A day will dawn when posterity will not forgive this lapse on the part of the self-appointed leaders of the community who wish to avoid discussions on controversial issues.

# Contents

# INTRODUCTION

There have been few developments so striking and significant in the religious history of mankind as the rise and fall of Zoroastrianism. While Zoroastrianism has been unanimously acknowledged by religious scholars and historians in our times as the faith that has influenced the ideology as well as eschatology of other major religions more significantly than any other religion in the world, few in our times have even heard about it, and fewer still know what it is all about. One cannot help but wonder how did such a fascinating and unique religion meet such a tragic and undeserving fate!

There could be various reasons for this unprecedented tragedy in the religious history of mankind, and at times the reasons for this tragedy may depend upon one's own background and vantage point. However, most scholars attribute its downfall, among other things, to brutal attempts at extinguishing its ancient flame by various conquerors from Alexander the Great to Tamerlane, as well as to its ultimate confinement to the race of its original adherents despite the ardent plea of its founder, Prophet Zarathushtra (whom the Greeks and Europeans later came to call Zoroaster) to spread his teachings among ALL mankind. In view of the latter, these people who would have very much wanted to believe in its basic tenets had no choice but to adopt other religions that welcomed them with open arms.

We have it from one of the most learned scholars of Judaism and Zoroastrianism, Prof. Shaul Shaked of Hebrew University, that "Jewish Iranian history provides us with one of the longest and most fecund cultural encounters between two divergent cultures in human experience. The fruits of these contacts have been of far-reaching significance not only for the formation of Jewish thought and religious faith, but also for that of Christianity and subsequently of Islam, thus affecting the course of the whole intellectual development of Europe and of the Islamic world. May this book serve as a reminder that world civilization would have been so much the poorer but for the fruitful encounter between these two peoples, and that neither Judaism, nor Christianity or Islam, would be the same without the mutual openness displayed by Jews and Iranians towards each other in the past."[1] It seems so improbable that a religion which has been so interwoven into the fabrics of other major religions could have been originally conceived and preached as a regional religion meant for only one race, as claimed by some of its present adherents, Parsis of India.

Zoroastrianism is such an ancient faith that we have little evidence as to when its founder, Prophet Zoroaster lived, though most scholars seem to place him prior to 1200-1500 B.C. in ancient Persia. Today it is practiced by only a handful of people – about 25,000 faithful followers in Iran, 75,000 staunch adherents in and around the city of Bombay in India, and a few thousand others scattered all around the world in recent times.

The Zoroastrians in India, also called Parsis (meaning Persians), are descendants of the Zoroastrians who migrated from Iran about 1200 years ago to pre-

---

1  *Irano-Judaica*, Ben-Zvi Institute, Jerusalem, 1982, pp. IX and XIII.

serve their faith in the land of the tolerant Hindus and prospered there due largely, rather solely, to their tolerance, but those who remained in Iran, millions at the time, met a tragic fate.

Scholars and historians have often noted, with great surprise, that the Zoroastrians in Iran and India differ so little in their religious beliefs and practices despite being separated from each other for nearly 1200 years. However, there is one area, namely the acceptance of genuine believers from other faiths, in which they have differed sharply from each other over the centuries.

Nothing, therefore, seems to divide them so sharply, since the time of a brutal clash over the issue of their ancient calender in 1745, as the acceptance in their fold of an outsider, however devoted and self-taught, who happened to discover and follow the teachings of Prophet Zoroaster entirely on his/her own. A noted author and scholar found it necessary to write a booklet, "Concerning Emancipation and Universal Propagation of Zoroastrian Religion" in order "to emphasize the glad tidings of acceptance into Zoroastrianism." The Zoroastrians of Iran believe "that the Good Mazdean Religion belongs to all humanity, and should be shared by all peoples inhabiting the globe. However, a few misguided, misinformed, and ignorant leaders claim that Mazdean religion belongs only to their race. If these leaders truly believe in Zoroastrianism, and have understood the ethical teachings of Mazdaism, then why do they want to prevent humanity from becoming Zoroastrian? If they know something is good for all, and they deprive them from partaking in such goodness and excellence, then such leaders are sadist and masochists that prevent the non-Zoroastrians to share the Good Religion. Thus, we Zoroastrians of Iran and also the Parsis believe that Zoroastrian religion has been held hostage by a few, so that the Good Religion must be emancipated and made a universal medium for the brotherhood of man and the salvation of humanity.... Consider all the different races that have embraced Christianity but none has changed his race by becoming a Christian. Hence, it is a misunderstanding, ignorance, and confusion that the Parsi clerics mix or exchange religion with race.... Therefore, it is a sin against God, against self, and humanity not to propagate Zoroastrianism and not to fulfill one's duty by promulgating the teachings of Zoroaster and not proselytizing the Dean-e Mazdayasna."[1]

The Irani Zoroastrians almost unanimously welcome outsiders as a living proof of the greatness of their ancient faith for which they had spared no sacrifice, and the devotion to their faith seems to make them feel that their sacrifices for the preservation of their faith over 1400 years were not in vain. But the Parsis see in them a grave threat to their very existence. Their example, they feared, will lead to massive influx in their tiny but affluent and highly educated community and disintegrate it beyond recognition, though they have often admitted it was dying out already because of inter-marriages, late marriages, no marriages, birth control, etc. One can therefore either abide by the Parsi tradition of not accepting outsiders in its fold, or abide by the teachings of the Prophet, which adds cogency to what a great Zoroastrian scholar, R. C. Zaehner, has charged: "Of all the great religions of the world, Zoroastrianism was the least well served. Zoroaster himself has every

---

1    Pp. 1-4 and 28.

right to the title he claimed ... but his successors never fully understood his message.... It clearly shows how ... even a great religion with a vital message for man ... (can) turn into something wholly different from what the founder intended."[1]

Unfortunately, however, enough has been written on this subject yet that keeps the Parsis in the dark about the universality of their religion. Often enough very plausible attempts have been made to negate the universal character of the Prophet's Revelation and teachings in order to justify the exclusiveness and parochial practices.

The abysmal ignorance of the modern-day Zoroastrians about their ancient faith make them so vulnerable to such sophistry. Time has come, therefore, when they need to realize how much at variance they are from their Prophet's own teachings in this regard. This book is therefore sincerely dedicated to this purpose. Let the Parsis rediscover the universal basis of their Prophet's teachings and learn to survive in this changing world instead of going against the teachings of their Prophet and adopting, thereby, a course of self-destruction.

We have it upon the authority of one of our most learned scholars, Ervad She-riarji Dadabhai Bharucha that "any single priest may convert. He is not under any obligation to take anybody's permission."[2] Some may not readily accept this scholarly statement and may try to defend their strong prejudices on this subject, but history is replete with such cases of priestly initiatives and *Parsiana* details some of them in its series on The Parsi Punchayet Case. In view of the recent trend toward deriding and undermining the honesty of those scholars who maintain that Zoroastrianism enjoins conversion, it is worthwhile to note that Sir Jivan-ji J. Modi who opposed Ervad Bharucha's views on conversion found it fit to dedicate one of his publications, "Lectures and Sermons on Zoroastrian Subjects, Part IV," in 1909, "as a token of my admiration for him as an industrious, honest, bold and learned preceptor.... As a teacher, preacher, priest, and author, you have displayed courage. You have always spoken out what appeared to you to be true and good without caring for public odium or applause; and by your own example you have taught much good to many in this direction." The well-known scholar, late F. Rustomjee of Ceylon goes so far as to maintain that "If a priest were to refrain from performing the Navjote of any child of an inter-communal marriage, then a Parsi Zoroastrian layperson (note the word "layperson" [vis-a-vis the regular word 'layman'] which implies either man or woman) can undertake to invest the child with a Sudreh-Kusti if he is satisfied that the child is conversant with the Kusti prayers.... Our religion allows any Zoroastrian to perform the Navjote ceremony for a child born of a Zoroastrian mother and father. Such a Parsi Zoroastrian may also invest *ANY* person above the age of 15 with the Sudra and Kusti if the person is conversant with the prayers. These are not reforms but the legitimate rights of every Zoroastrian mother and father and such rights cannot be taken from them by priests.... The children having committed no wrong by being born (of inter-communal marriages), cannot be denied the rights of a Navjote by a Mobed or

---

1    *The Dawn and Twilight of Zoroastrianism*, pp. 170-1.
2    *Parsiana*, March 1982, 4(9), p. 37

Dastur"[1] The famous Bansada case is another illustration. This is not to imply that a priest should not care for the demands and dictates of the community. But, above all, a priest must care for the demands and dictates of his own conscience and ensure that the former are not so woefully in conflict with the teachings of his Prophet. Even those that initially supported such Navjotes, but later on suddenly rallied against it, had readily conceded earlier that "Neither the Prophet Zoroaster, nor the priests of the early times would have denied (such) individuals … the right to live as a true Zoroastrian."[2]

Nothing could be more worthwhile and productive for the survival of Zoroastrianism than the work undertaken by the Fourth North American Zoroastrian Congress held on April 11, 1982 in Montreal, when "The Zoroastrian Association of Quebec (ZAQ) was charged with the responsibility of doing the spadework into the question of "Acceptance" into the social fabric of religion, the individuals of non-Zoroastrian origin. ZAQ distributed its first communique in this regard on July 29, 1982, "to generate and survey a well-informed opinion on the question of conversion/acceptance of non-Zoroastrians into the Zoroastrian religion." The communique observes that "diagnosing a prolonged malaise, and not making an effort to cure it, is in fact euthanasia. *THAT CANNOT AND MUST NOT BE AL-LOWED TO HAPPEN TO ZOROASTRIANS.* (Italics are not my own.) It faithfully concludes: "To talk about the same issues over and over again every two or three years will slowly but surely sow the seeds of stagnation which in time can lead to irreparable damage to this invaluable heritage that *once was a way of life of a majestic civilization*."[3] Such discussions are being held since· 1903 when Mr. R. D. Tata married a French lady, but the community has not resolved this issue yet.

Moreover, as Dr. Lovji Cama revealed long ago in 1978 at the Third World Zoroastrian Conference held in Bombay, "The children of mixed marriages have a right to be Zoroastrian irrespective of the sex of their Zoroastrian parent and will be assimilated into the fold if they so wish.... The liberal priests have no objection to performing the Navjotes of children of mixed marriages irrespective of which parent is Zoroastrian.... A majority of the Zoroastrians here do not consider the acceptance of children of mixed marriages or of non-Zoroastrian spouses as active conversion of aliens to the faith. It is more adjustment to the realities of our new homeland and a necessity for our survival." And yet today we are still talking about the same subject, and so when will we be able to resolve this problem?

I had in the past often discussed this problem with the visiting high priests from India and they had realized the need for us to be more liberal about inter-marriages than we have been in India, and one of them even advised another priest who performed one such Navjote with me to perform the Navjote of non-Zoroastrian spouses first, and thus accept them in our fold before doing their wedding ceremony.

---

1   *Parsiana*, March 1978, 2(3), p. 7.
2   *Parsiana*, 1983.
3   All italics in this text are mine unless stated otherwise.

## Opposite Viewpoint

No significant references are made to Avestan or Pahlavi passages bearing on this question by those who oppose acceptance. Is it possible that these people have not studied them or do not realize what they say do not support their arguments? It seems clear that the two sides of this debate arise from basic theological differences: one is ethnocentric, and the other is based on scripture. As Zarathushtra exhorts us in Yasna 30.2, 45.2, etc., one must examine and choose carefully for oneself.

What instead does the opposing view allude to? They talk about "subtle esoteric arguments against initiation of a person not born in the faith," "an irreversible step with regard to the unique genetical pool some of us associate closely with our religious heritage," "preservation of ethnic purity," "youngsters of other faiths would be attracted to ours and cause ill feelings between us and their communities," "Conversion of our religion is not a number game," "religion and community (are not) at the brink of "extinction" as we hear about it so often," "We shall vanish, if we mix up genetically," "The father gave away his rights and automatically became a non-Parsi the moment he married a non-Parsi lady," "These newly-born 'Conference-Zoroastrians,' if I may call them, sitting in their own ivory towers and trying to thrust their own definition on the community are blissfully unaware of the feelings and thinking of their common Zoroastrian brothers and sisters back in Bombay, Udwada, Navsari, Surat, etc.," "What good there is going to be in just affixing a mere 'external stamp' of a Zoroastrian on a total outsider," "Attempts are made to quote Gathas and other ancient Zoroastrian scriptures are referred to by twisting and perverting the texts so as to render them suitable to their own views," (but no example is generally cited for such a distortion), " 'Bunyad Pasbani' (preservation of genetical heritage) was the motto (of our forefathers), the objective and the very purpose of their lives," "Teach the religion first to members of your own community" (though proselytes are entirely self-taught Zoroastrians), "a very strong feeling of "displeasure and disapproval" about such Navjotes exists and on behalf of several such members we have spoken with, *"we appeal and urge the aspirants of such Navjotes to reconsider their decision* and not hurt our feelings and split our community which has been so far a harmonious, peace-loving, and a cohesive group of people,"[1] "The repercussions and effects of your Navjote would be very serious in and on our community throughout the world wherever Zoroastrians live and set up a precedent which – would be someday responsible for the dilution of our community, disappearance of our proud heritage and downfall of our community," "Call --- our community members and speak with them personally on a one-to-one basis to convince yourself what they think," *"We very sincerely urge you to reconsider your decision and spare our community from a probable split."*

## The Response of Ervad Noshir Hormuzdiar

It would be worthwhile to review the views of another Parsi priest, Ervad Noshir Hormuzdiar, who is in favor of Acceptance:

---

1    Italics are not my own.

Let's face it, we Zoroastrians do not have a "Recognized communal authority" per se, nor is there such a thing as Zoroastrian "Tradition of long standing" not to accept others in the religious fold. It may be a Parsee "Tradition of the last two hundred years or so" but definitely not the Zoroastrian tradition. Irrespective of present Parsee tradition, I have asked myself what is the right thing to do in such a situation and have come to the firm conclusion that the prophet indeed would prefer such a Navjote ceremony. If I would feel that my performing such navjotes is going to hurt or harm Zoroastrians or non-Zoroastrians as individuals or as a group, then I would have declined. I know that the only difference is in ideology, the way of thinking and that this whole process of initiation intends no malice or hurt.

I believe that my performing such a navjote is an act of serving my religion in my own way. I consider it an act of merit. A navjote or NOZUD – a new spiritual birth – may not change a thing on this earth, but the navjotees' own outlook towards life. Their desire to go through the ritual of Navjote is their deep-rooted feelings for the sense of belonging as a part of this sacred religion. Who am I or anyone else to deny them this God-given right? This nation of America believes in the freedom of religion. To such devoted navjotees, Zarathushtra's teachings are a revelation and I feel that this one act may change the outlook towards religion of our whole community for the better.

Time and again I have asked people to give me one reason, "Why I should not perform such Navjotes?" I have not gotten one single satisfactory or intellectually appealing answer from them or anyone else. I have been searching for anything different in our sacred books that I might have missed and the more I have looked the more I am convinced that all they give is a simple message, "Humata, Hukhta, Huvarshta".

I do not wish to do such navjotes privately unless the initiate so desires. Why should anyone have to smuggle someone into the religion? Why should a non-Zoroastrian have to go through a molten-metal test? Let's be open and candid in our thoughts, words, and actions. If there is a split on this issue – and there has been a split in the Parsee community for the last hundred or so years – then so be it. It is healthy. It gives people a choice, a kind of check and balance. *It will lead an individual to seek scholarship of their faith*. It will be a true testimony of Zoroastrian faith and a test of endurance leading to unity in diversity. It will help each to respect the other more, and accept the views of the other.

The reader may find the following excerpts from three chapters (Ch. XXIII-XXV) from late Dasturjee Maneckjee N. Dhalla's book *World's Religions In Evolution*" (Karachi, 1953) very illuminating in this context:

The one inalienable function of orthodoxy is never to tolerate any change in the matter of belief. It asserts a claim to belief and authority. It insists upon conformity to beliefs and customs that have been accepted by a people and opposed any reform or change in the matter. It is a consummate fidelity to tradition. It insists that the dogmas and doctrines that a people has inherited are unchangeable under any circumstances. The established views of life are fixed and right. It is rank obstinacy to forget anything old and to learn anything new. The average man being temperamentally timid and conservative, dislikes to be disturbed in thoughts and views he has inherited from the time past. Orthodoxy's safe refuge is in tradition. It longs to live content and secure in the dead past. Tradition is sacred to it. Being jealous of the views it holds, it vehemently opposes any change in them. It clips the wings of thought, gags speech, and cripples action. Free thinking is taboo to orthodoxy. It is impervious to the influence of changing times. It tolerates not intellectual dissent from established views. The collective orthodox mind drives the free thinking dissenters to secrete their differing thoughts in the lowest depths of their souls. Orthodoxy blindly opposes and prevents free thinking and high thinking. It is heterodoxy to dissent from the established dogmas and doctrines, customs, and beliefs. Orthodoxy has numbers on its side. It is the ingrained spirit in mankind. It still prevails all throughout the world in spite of the unprecedented progress of learning and cultural advancement. *Very few priests are fortunate to be free from the fetters of orthodoxy. They are blatantly branded by the zealous orthodox as infidels and heretics.*

No wonder, indeed, Hormuzdiar and I were branded as heretics by those who opposed such Navjotes.

## The Response of such Navjotees

Even when they come to learn of the strong opposition to their initiation into the fold, that does not seem to dampen their desire for the Navjote ceremony as that is all they want. One such Navjotee, Joseph Peterson, wrote:

I am only beginning to realize the complexity of the issue of performing Navjote ceremonies for outsiders. I suspect though that there is more involved than just community acceptance. I already feel accepted by many good people; but I doubt if I would ever be accepted by some others even if I were to pass a molten-metal ordeal. I don't believe however, that Zoroastrianism is as fragile as many people seem to believe, or that it should be subject to the changes in the Parsi cultural identity however fragile that may be.

Please understand that ritual is very important to me. Like language itself, I believe it is a medium which gives us unlimited potential for growth. I am genuinely disturbed at the scorn with which it is frequently treated by many westerners. I view Zoroastrian ritual as one of the greatest possessions of mankind. I highly commend your devotion to it.

I was told that my main authority, J. J. Modi, was inaccurate in his de-
scriptions. Even the texts of the rituals, as they appear in Geldner and
other versions, are not accurate it appears.

His address to the Fourth North American Zoroastrian Congress at Montreal on
April 10, 1982 speaks volumes for the universal appeal of this ancient religion.

It is also interesting to note what he had to say about Zoroastrianism at his
Navjote ceremony: "When I first started to learn about the teachings of Zarathushtra, it was a lot like when I got my first pair of glasses. I remember looking out a
window and being able to see all the leaves on the trees for the first time. And that
is how Zoroastrianism was and is to me. It answered my questions about life in a
very clear and logical way. This happened when I was fifteen."

## Is Zoroastrianism an Iranian Manifestation?

Such initiates should also inspire us to lay down strictest possible standards for accepting any converts. We will meet these standards even if we expect from new
converts only half of what they offer us in terms of knowledge, devotion, and
commitment, though most of our own children here or for that matter in the Old
World may not themselves be able to meet these standards.

Their devotion has clearly demonstrated that by parting with the ethnic basis
of Zoroastrianism and its Iranian manifestation one does not necessarily alter the
religion in a significant way, as claimed by their detractors. They have transcend-
ed those outer, man-made limitations, and touched the very spirit of Zoroastrianism. Their example suggests that not having an Iranian origin and background,
however desirable and helpful, is not an insurmountable barrier for a true follower
of Zarathushtra. However rooted our religion is in the pre-Islamic Iranian milieu,
its original roots were in the east of Iran. The spirit of Zoroastrianism is in no way
shackled by its historical rooting in Iran, which in reality is a direct consequence
of our ancestors not following the Prophet's precept of proselytizing once the faith
was well established in Iran. Iran was known as Elam when the Iranians began to
settle there, and ultimately Elamites too adopted Zoroastrianism, which I have detailed elsewhere at length.

Some of our own prayers belie the fact that Zoroastrianism is an Iranian manifestation. Thus, in Sarosh Yasht Vadi's Nirang a reference is made to 'TAZIYANE
BASTEKUSTIYAN,' that is, 'the Kusti-wearing Arabs.' Since Sir Harold Bailey
has conclusively proved that the Taziyans were Arabs, it is evident that Zoroastrianism was not confined to Iranians in the olden times. Attempts are often made to
explain away the real meaning of the word Taziyan, but the exhaustive research by
Sir Bailey leaves no doubt as to the meaning of this word. "In the Zoroastrian
Pahlavi Bundahishn there is a reference to 'hač matan i tačikan,' 'from the coming
of the Arabs.' The origin of the name of Arabs whom the Syrians called tayaye …
is from the Arab tribe Tai, in Byzantine Greek Tainvoi, Taivoi. The tribe Tayy is
also named on a magic bowl with other ethnic names Aramaic, Persian, Indian,
and Roman.[1] The Iranian name tačik is then from an older taičik.... The Tai were at
first in South Arabia but migrated to Syria and Iraq in the 4th century A.D., and

---

1    E.M. Yamauchi, JAOS 85, 1965, 523.

were in Babylon, according to Jewish evidence, from 150 B.C. to the 7ᵗʰ century
A.D., especially in Ktesiphon[1].... The Arab horse is the asp-i tačikik in Zoroastrian
Pahlavi and the Chorasmian t'čyk, and has survived in Turkish tazi. The Persian
Gulf was called the var-i tačikan ..., and there is also the dast-i tačik ... An epony-
mous ancestor Tač was read out of the name tačik. Hence there is in the *Denkard*
(253.16) tač tohmak 'the lineage of Tač, and (ibidem 597.20) tač-i tačikan sah
'Tač the king of the Tačiks.' In the *Bundahishn* (106.9), it is written ... 'the man
from the Tač woman by name Tačak' ... There is a phrase (ibidem 208.14)
hunusk-i tačikan 'evil sons of Arabs.'"[2]

   In 1882, Dastoor Jamaspji Minocherji, "who, everyone of the witnesses who
were asked about it, say, was a man of the highest integrity, honor, and truthful-
ness" ... "converted nine persons from Mazgaon, Bombay who had Parsi fathers
and non-Parsi mothers, whose age ranged from 35 to 77, in the presence of a large
number of leading Parsis."[3] In our own times, the late Mr. Burjorji F. Bharucha, a
great disciple of Mahatma Gandhi and one of the greatest Parsi social workers of
all times, was highly distressed by the fact that children of Parsi fathers and non-
Parsi mothers were denied admission into the faith despite their fervent desire to
be invested with Sudreh and Kusti. So he got their Navjotes done by one of the
most learned Dasturs of our times, Dastur Dr. Framroze A. Bode of Bombay.
Years later when Dastur Bode presented these converts who were then quite
grown up at a lecture in K. R. Cama Oriental Institute and challenged the audience
to find them to be any different than an average Parsi, I happened to be present
there as an early teenager. However, he was so much maligned and even physically abused by the orthodox of the community that I hope posterity will appreciate
the sense of justice he showed in this case, besides a true understanding of the religion. See my brief biography of Bode in *Parsiana* and *Hamazor*.

## Dasturji Dabu's Views

I was very impressed by a proper perception of this problem by my guru, Dasturji
Khurshed S. Dabu, who was undoubtedly the most respected of Dasturs of his
time in Bombay. Thus, Dasturji Dabu observes: "Those who left their homes and
possessions in Iran in order to follow their inner promptings of conscience, and remain loyal to Zarathushtra, came in small batches.... They were however so few,
that could not have preserved their distinct identity in the midst of swarming alien
masses. They were afraid they would be easily swamped and lost – as was the
case with refugees that went north. The bitter memory of sacred fire-temples having been destroyed by fanatics was fresh in their minds. Fear and doubts must
have assailed them. *So they decided to isolate their small community as a distinct
racial* unit." Dasturji Dabu thus makes it very explicit that it was "*they*," the Parsi
immigrants, who "*decided*" to isolate themselves racially as a religious unit because of very special circumstances they found themselves in, but not at all because of the teachings of the Prophet. Again, Dasturji Dabu adds: "All these cir-

---

1    JAOS 95, 1975, pp. 184 ff
2    *The Culture of the Sakas in Ancient Iranian Khotan*, Caravan Books, Delmar, New York, 1982, p.
     88.
3    *Parsiana*, 'The Parsi Punchayet Case' series

cumstances led them to 'remain aloof' as a special race.... One has to be born into this race. It was a case of survival against heavy odds." Most of the Parsis seem to have forgotten that closing our doors to others was "a case of survival" and not an injunction enjoined by their Prophet. Dasturji further observes: "Many verdicts have been pronounced by high courts ... that those who are not Parsis by birth and Zoroastrian by faith have no right to communal privileges; e.g., entry into temples, and benefit of charitable institutions and funds. If, however, new temples or towers of silence are dedicated by fresh trust-deeds, for the benefit of *ALL*, there may be no legal bar. Law respects the wishes of donors, who have a right to lay down the scope of beneficiaries of a trust." Thus, it is the law of the land and not any canonical requirement which governs the rules of entry into our sacred places. In North America, the late Arbab Rustam Guiv built many Darbe-Mehers with a clear exhortation to be broad-minded and keep the doors of the Darbe-Meher open to all. "Be broad-minded and welcome newcomers who desire to know and study Zoroastrianism," urged Arbab Guiv at the inauguration ceremony of his Darbe-Meher in New York. "Our Prophet did not ever put restrictions on anyone who willingly wanted to follow his principles"[1] He was very much distressed when some of us went against his wish and there were often times when he advised me not to be restrictive like them. How offended he would have been had he been alive to know of court injunctions being sought by some of us to stop the performance of a Navjote at his Darbe-Meher in New York. When a Zoroastrian donated money for the inner chamber of Arbab Guiv Darbe-Meher of Chicago, some orthodox talked about not letting non-Zoroastrian spouses in the inner chamber, though the wife of the donor himself happened to be a non-Zoroastrian. To them, not to do so will be going against their religion, but if we care to study our religion, we will not make a mockery of our religion and confuse race with religion. For, as Dasturji Dabu further observes: "It should, however, be conceded that each man is free to profess any religion of his choice. But there has to be a clear distinction between a *religion* (as a matter of personal interest) and a *community* that can lay down rules for admission to their fold.... So *Navjote* may initiate one to our religion; but that cannot confer communal rights and privileges also."[2] Thus, proselytes are free to profess Zoroastrianism and may be initiated into our religion through Navjote, though the Navjote cannot confer communal rights and privileges on them, a fact that should leave little ground for the traditionalist to protest against such Navjotes.

In another book, Dasturji Dabu observes:

(1) Truth has no limitations of time and space. The eternal verities are the same at all places and in all ages. The message preached by Zarathushtra embraced immutable Divine Laws applicable to humanity. For example: the law of Adjustment of Retribution has a universal application (VIZ., "As you sow, so shall you reap."). Therefore, in Avesta

1   *Parsiana*, December 1980, 3(6), p. 43).
2   Dabu, Khurshed S. *A Hand-Book of General Information Containing Significance of Zoroastrian Terms Pertaining to Religion, Customs, Rituals, Etc. and Answers to Some Important Questions.* Bombay: Sorab F. Ranji, 1976.

(Haftan Yasht), there is a very remarkable statement which every Zoroastrian makes openly: "We (the Zoroastrians) are lovers and acceptors of all good thoughts, words, and deeds, whether performed here or elsewhere, now or at any other time in the future, because we are ever the supporters of goodness!" Thus because we support goodness in all it aspects, we cannot restrict our faith to affixed time and place. If a thought, to be proclaimed five centuries hence, is to be pure and beneficial, it cannot be excluded from the purview of Zoroastrianism.

(2) In the longer declaration (from Yasna 12) we promise to praise all good thoughts, words, and deeds. The same declaration is made in "Frastuye" (Part of "Ahuramazda Yasht"), that we would uphold all good thoughts, words, and deeds, and renounce all evil ones.

(3) In the past we rejected all such speculative dogmas as were not good for the world at large; for example: the doctrines of Mazdak and Mani.

(4) In India, Parsis have been living, for over twelve centuries, in the midst of numerous races and creeds, with a tolerant feeling towards all good principles and practices of life. There is now in vogue, considerable exchange of comparative study of all religions between the Parsis and others.

(5) Zarathushtra, in the Gathas, enumerates some Divine laws and adds: "This shall be the truth-prevailing, right up to the end of the world." The catholicity of our religion is calculated to promote universal peace, amity and brotherhood."[1]

In his book *Message of Zarathushtra*, Dasturji Dabu further maintains:

The exclusiveness of Parsis with regard to aliens (dislike for mixed marriages, non-admittance to temples and to holy sacramental rituals) should be properly understood. Parsis are a microscopic minority, there being rarely 100,000 in India. Their racial characteristics are hereditary, and preservation of their blood from getting mixed with that of other races is a necessity. They are afraid that the progeny of mixed blood may not retain the original type of those that migrated from Iran twelve centuries ago, and that their racial identity or uniqueness may be lost and lead to racial suicide. But they have always provided facilities for aliens to study their scriptures. In fact a large number of scholars who have translated and interpreted these books are non-Parsis (e.g. *Sacred Books of the East* Series). *Zoroastrianism has no copyright. There is nothing to prevent anyone not born a Parsi from professing his spiritual allegiance to Zarathushtra* and adopting his message as it is the privilege of each soul to accept truth from any source. Thus Zoroastrianism is still open to adoption by the world to which the religion was offered. But, if an alien embraces Zoroastrianism, he or she cannot claim ameni-

1   *Zarathushtra and His Teachings*, New Book Co., Bombay, 1966, pp. 15-17.

> ties of the community, founded under trust-deeds with definite injunc-
> tions.... But there is no bar to an alien having his separate temples and
> other facilities for a new community or sect that he may form, while
> observing the tenets of Zoroastrianism. The admission to the Parsi com-
> munity is impossible as an alien cannot change his blood, and a Parsi
> has to be born of Parsi parents.... Then there is the lurking fear of fanat-
> ics (based on historical facts) who demolished numerous Zoroastrian
> Fire-temples in Iran, thus demanding great circumspection on the part
> of those who stuck to ancient forms in the face of persecution which
> naturally led to a sort of secret fraternity for some time.

See my two articles on Dabu in the *Fezana Journal*, beginning with Autumn issue,
2010 for more on this subject.

It is worth noting that in their preface to Rustomjie's book, *Daily Prayers of
the Zoroastrians* (1976), various High Priests have recognized the universality of
our religion. Thus, Dastur Bode refers to the "World Teacher Zarathushtra" (Part I,
p. ii), Dastur K. M. Jamasp Asa refers to "The Prophet of Ancient Iran who
preached a new World-Religion" (Part II, p. ii) and Dastur N. D. Minocheher
Homji maintains that Zoroastrianism "is founded on the bed-rock of Reason for
the welfare of all mankind" (Part III, p. 396). Dasturji Dr. Hormazdyar K. Mirza
points out the catholicity of our religion by quoting Yasna 1.16, Yasna 68.4, Yasht
11:16, 21, Vendidad 5.20, Patet, and Pazand prayers for "prosperity and welfare of
all peoples of the country and of all mankind," "of human species," "of all
species," and concludes: "Here all races of mankind are clearly mentioned."[1] Dasturji Mirza, however, makes no inference at all of the prophet's desire to teach his
religion to all mankind, for which then we must turn elsewhere. However, one
may be inclined to believe that the above examples of the catholicity of our religion are not just stray or unrelated instances of important civic duties of a Zoroastrian, etc., but are stray remnants and reminders of what little is left today of the
prophet's original vision of spreading his religion to the seven continents of the
world.

At the Third World Congress held in Bombay in 1978, it was maintained by
the leader of the orthodox views: "One must bear in mind the two aspects of the
matter, namely, Zoroastrianism is a religion whilst the Parsis are a race. You can
convert a person to any religion, but you cannot convert a person to a race. *No one
can have any objection to a person converting himself to the Zoroastrian religion
but it must be clearly understood that he will not be entitled to the benefit of any
of our Trusts.... The problems of the Zoroastrians residing outside India, stand on
a different footing* as they live at such places where there may not be Fire Temples, Dokhmas, and Mobeds" (*Parsiana*, 1978, pp. 33-34). *There was no objection raised to these remarks then*, but to the contrary, the speaker received the
loudest applause in the entire Congress, as per *Parsiana*, March 1978, p. 25. (Italics mine.)

---

1   *Parsi History*, Bombay, 1974, pp. 403-4.

## A Young Parsi Lawyer's Views

While the older generation of Parsis in India may find it hard to accept converts in view of their centuries old aversion to acceptance, some Parsis have shown remarkable insight in accepting them. An article written in the *Bombay Samachar* by a young lawyer-journalist, Mr. Berjis Minoo Desai, deserves to be quoted in full as it may come to represent the views of the future generations on this subject. He commented on the Navjote of such an initiate, the most fervently debated in the Parsi media, as:

> The Navjote of Joseph Peterson is one of the best things ever to have happened to Zoroastrianism in this country. From the entire episode, two conclusions emerge. One, that Peterson is a better Zoroastrian than most of us. Two, that this is historically the right moment for the so-called 'silent majority' of the community to publicly declare that they will not tolerate the tyranny of the fanatics.... Why is Joseph Peterson a better Zoroastrian than most of us? The answer is self-evident. We are Zoroastrians by *accident of birth*, Peterson is a Zoroastrian by *rational choice*. Born in Parsi and Iranian homes, we underwent the Navjote ceremony, mechanically and at an age when we were not capable of making any rational choice. We were mentally conditioned to emulate adult behaviour in matter of religion. We donned the Sudreh-Kusti, we visited fire temples, we participated in rituals, we recited prayers by rote in a language we did not understand, *only* as a matter of habit and imitation. In other words, most of us never even gave a thought as to why and what it was being Zoroastrians. But birth was not the factor in case of Peterson. We understand that he painstakingly studied Zoroastrian scriptures and the teaching of our Prophet, learnt Avesta – prepared his own Sudreh and Kusti and felt an all-encouraging *inner fascination* for this Ancient Religion. Peterson is not a stunt-man seeking publicity, nor is he a seeker of doles from our communal charities. He has chosen the Faith after active contemplation, long study, and as a matter of finding his true Self. For the above reasons, Joseph Peterson is a better Zoroastrian than most of us, Parsis and Iranians.... It is the second conclusion which is more fascinating. The entire episode has turned the spotlight on the issue of conversion as never before. All Zoroastrians who have welcomed Peterson's Navjote, should realise that little is achieved by copiously citing passages from the Scriptures, court judgements and genetical research reports indicating that Zoroastrianism *enjoins* conversion, and it is totally Universal in approach. For the fanatical sections it can also do exactly the same indicating that Zoroastrianism *prohibits* conversion. The net effect is to confuse the common man. The correct strategy is to totally ignore the verbose and long-winded arguments of the fanatics and pay no heed to their emotional outbursts or their ravings and rantings in public meetings and the Parsi daily. Instead, the supporters of Peterson's type Navjotes should only spread one clear and simple message that Religion, by its very na-

ture, is a matter of individual belief and rational choice (after all, the word itself derives from the Latin "religare" that is, to bind, or to de-scribe Man's *attitude* towards God). Every Religion is Universal in its approach and cannot be the private property of any ethnic or tribal group. One must not confuse the performance of rituals in temples or homes as "Religion." Zoroastrianism, with its special emphasis on Man's goodness to his fellowmen, cannot be anything but open-door. A faith, as ethical and ancient as Zoroastrianism, can never close its doors to any human being only on grounds of *race and accident of birth*.... In order to allay the fears of the common man, which are deliberately whipped up by the fanatics to cleverly confuse *Issues Spiritual* with *Issues Material*, it must be repeated again and again that the *Parsi-Irani-an* community is legally entitled and completely free, if it so wishes, to prevent any non-Parsi, non-Iranian Zoroastrian from entering the fire temples, burial grounds, and from allowing them the benefits of Par-si-Iranian charitable trusts and funds. However, this does not mean that the *Parsi-Iranian community*, even if it is unanimous, can prevent the Navjote being performed of any human being in the world, whether he be Aryan, Negro, or Mongol, nor can it prevent such person from wear-ing the Sudreh and Kusti, nor can it prevent him from believing in Zoroastrianism and living his life in accordance with Zoroaster's preachings.... The non-Parsi/Iranian Zoroastrians, like Peterson, should *never make the mistake of* attempting to enter fire-temples or applying for Parsi charitable aids or benefits. With the passage of time, the as-similation of the non-Parsi, non-Iranian Zoroastrians with Parsi-Iranian Zoroastrians shall be so gradual and imperceptible, that the physical barriers shall collapse. In the meanwhile, Navjotes like Peterson will continue without hindrance, as only the genuinely convinced persons will want their Navjotes performed in a scheme of things where there is no question of gaining any material advantage or satisfying any sense of curiosity as to what goes on behind the closed doors of Parsi-Iranian fire temples.... Of course what is there to prevent the *NEW ZOROAS-TRIANS* from consecrating their own Fire-temples, from building up their own Charitable Funds and from *ordaining* their own Priests? As a matter of fact, the next logical step, is to perform the '*Navar*' and '*Maratab*' ceremonies of Joseph Peterson, and initiate him as a full-fledged Zoroastrian High priest.

## The Parsi Punchayet Case

In 1903, Mr. R.D. Tata, a cousin of Mr. J.N. Tata and the father of Mr. J.R.D. Tata, married a French lady according to proper Zoroastrian customs and rites. After having her Navjote duly performed by a Parsi high-priest of Bombay, Mr. R.D. Tata then claimed that his wife "had become a Parsi professing the Zoroastrian re-ligion, and therefore was entitled to participate in all the charitable and religious funds and institutions of the Parsis." I had prepared my view of this case in 1983-

84 by collecting whatever information I could then about the Bombay Parsi Pan-
chayet case (also known as Petit vs. Jeejeebhoy 1908 case) and Saklat vs. Bella
1925 case. However, during my trip to India in 2010, I found an excellent book on
this subject, *Judgments – Petit vs Jeejeebhoy 1908, Saklat vs Bella 1925 – Reprint
of original judgments with explanatory articles* published by Parsiana Publications
in 2005. I see therefore no need to present my own findings, and urge the reader to
peruse this book and come to his/her own conclusion. However, as I find Justice
Beaman's judgment so adroit in exposing the cognitive fallacies in the arguments
of the orthodox Parsis then (and as now) that I find it proper to present it below,
along with Davar's judgment as it represents the Parsis' cognition of Acceptance. I
may, however, add that there are some new research findings in the Saklat vs. Bella 1925 case, which suggests that Bella was not really the person made out to be in
this court case, but was illegally sired by a Parsi father with a non-Parsi woman
whom he passed off as a Parsi. Whereas this finding seems quite plausible, nevertheless, it does not seem to affect the legal consequences and judgments in this
case in my humble opinion, though I would leave it to the legal experts to decide,
as I purport to keep the legal issues separate from religious issues involved here.

Justice Beaman's judgment exposes our cognitive rigidity and dissonance regarding Acceptance that does not allow us to perceive the real truth:

> Speaking here with the utmost deference and respect, I think that that
> consideration had some weight with my learned brother (Justice
> Davar). With me it carries absolutely none. What is the position? The
> Defendants admit that their religion enjoins the making of Converts.
> But they say that, since the Parsi emigration from Persia some twelve
> hundred years ago, the Indian Zoroastrians, commonly known as Par-
> sis, have never carried out that religious precept. And they rely on the
> absence of all conversions, in the proper sense of the word, to prove a
> custom abrogating one of the fundamentals of their religion.

> There is a perfectly plain and intelligible distinction between a positive
> or affirmative, and so-called merely negative custom or usage. The lat-
> ter is not, in strictness, a usage or custom at all. It is, as soon as the
> proposition is fairly stated, clearly absurd to reason from mere non-use
> to the contrary affirmation.

> The Zoroastrian religion enjoins making Converts. But for many years
> we have not made Converts. Therefore, although we still profess that
> religion and revere all its essentials, we rely on a custom of NOT
> MAKING CONVERTS, to abrogate the positive commands of our reli-
> gion. That is what the Defendants would say on this point, and it only
> needs to be stated to be set aside as absurd. There cannot be a custom
> of not doing a thing. Circumstances may have combined to render it un-
> desirable or impossible, and so a practice may have fallen into desue-
> tude. But as long as the cardinal dogmas of the religion itself have re-
> mained unchanged, their efficacy, where, as here it is freely admitted,
> cannot be impaired, much less destroyed, by inability or unwillingness

to obey them. It is as much the duty of every pious Zoroastrian to-day to make Converts as it was in the remote past. As a general abstract proposition, I think that is self-evident.

Now, let us look a little closer into the origin and justification of the alleged negative custom. The most orthodox, the most biggoted, champions of the Defendants' case are agreed here. We did not make Converts, they say, since we came to India, because we could not. That naive explanation is, of course, perfectly true. *But what of its effect upon the use to which this inability is now sought to be put?*

Look at the facts. The Zoroastrians were expelled from Persia, or fled from Persia. Those who reached India were a scattered remnant. They were only too glad to receive an asylum, to be allowed to live in peace and profess their ancient faith. In such circumstances, the idea of proselytising was impolitic and impracticable. They had enough to do to preserve their own faith, their own little society, against the impact of great surrounding forces, which, if not actively hostile, were not altogether sympathetic, religious, and social.

(I beg to differ here from the learned judge, as the Hindus have been singularly tolerant towards the Parsis through the ages, and we cannot possibly thank them enough for it.)

The danger which the early Indian Zoroastrians had to face, was the danger of being absorbed into the masses among whom they sojourned: their chief care must have been to maintain the purity of their own faith and the traditions of their own people. Any attempt at proselytism in those days would have invited reprisals. It would have been – regarding them as a body politic – politically suicidal. They were the strangers: they were the weak and broken fugitives. Of course; they did not seek to make converts: all they desired was that their own people should not be converted. Because, under these conditions, there is no trace of any proselytising actively for centuries – until owing to the influence of many other evident causes, the *essentially religious had been superseded by an essentially caste spirit* when another and equally potent explanation begins to emerge – *no inference can fairly be drawn that a local custom against making Converts had grown up.*

*Yet*, in the records and documents before us, *there is ample evidence*, I think, to show *that*, although no practical effect was given to it for reasons of policy, *the idea of conversion was quite familiar to the whole Indian Zoroastrian community, and frequently formed the subject of elaborate references, hypothetical cases, and controversial treatises.* I shall have a word or two to say on that later. I will now dismiss the point I have been discussing with this observation, that ... the *absence of any well-accredited instance of a genuine conversion has*, in my opinion, *little or no bearing – as usage or custom negativing the canon law – in this case.*

It may at once be said that *the Zoroastrian religion does admit – even does enjoin – conversion. That cannot be and has never been categorically denied.* It is true that the so-called learned men who have come before us to support the Defendants' case have wasted hours of our time in puerile attempts to gloss away the plain letter of the law. But that must be attributed partly to invincible bigotry which proverbially dulls the sharpest wits, and partly to a natural stupidity and want of training in clear thought, which prevented witnesses of the type of Mr. J. J. Modi from disentangling his own revelled thoughts and opinions. Passing over these interminable silly sophistries, and admitting that Zoroastrianism enjoins conversion, we are only a step on the way to our conclusion.[1]

Even the judgment of Justice Daver, whom Dasturji Dhalla described as "the leader of the orthodox party"[2] is very educative in this case as representing the Parsi view on conversion/acceptance of the time, which, however, is at variance with that of the trio and Z.S.[3] in our own times. His views also represent the Parsis' anxiety about the converts claiming entitlement to Parsi trusts and charities:

It appears that the main reasons which actuated those who advocated the admission of these children born of Parsi fathers, was that persons in whose veins Zoroastrian blood flowed should not be allowed to live and die without having the benefits of the religion of their fathers, and that a Zoroastrian's offspring should not be allowed to be buried or burnt after death as a Durvand (lower caste, non-Parsi). It was felt that this course appeared to lend countenance to immoral connections, but that was a lesser evil compared to the sin of allowing a Parsi's child to go through life without Sudra and Kusti and be burnt or buried after death.

When the controversy consequent on the Navjote ceremony of the French lady arose, there was intense excitement amongst the Parsi community. Meetings were held (in 1903). Committees were appointed, and learned men from the community were selected as experts, to report on the various religious controversial questions that arose. The Committee of Experts made their report. On this report, the Plaintiffs, has placed great reliance. This report says that not only is there nothing in the sacred books to prohibit persons professing other religions from being admitted into the Zoroastrian religion, *but that the Zoroastrian religion enjoins such conversions. I have proceeded throughout this judgment on the assumption that this is correct,* and I purpose to consider the questions before the Court on that basis.

---

1    *Parsiana*, August 1982, pp. 67, 69, and 71.
2    *Parsiana*, November 1982, p. 7.
3    Namely the three Parsi High Priests, and the Zoroastrian Studies organization. See below, pp. 1 ff.

The Zoroastrian religion is a revealed religion. It was revealed by the Supreme Being Ahura Mazda to Zarthost. The religion revealed to Zoroaster was by him communicated to King Vishtasp, who promulgated it amongst his people. It seems to me that all revealed religions must necessarily enjoin proselytisation, for otherwise how is the religion to progress beyond the prophet to whom it is revealed?

During the first century of their settlement in India, the emigrants who settled in India had great difficulties in preserving their own people from going away from their own religion – they had great difficulty in preserving their religion and performing their religious rites and ceremonies, and safe-guarding their religious books.... It was felt besides that it would have been ingratitude towards the Rana who had given them refuge to try and convert his subjects.[1]

The only question of importance on this part of the suit that now remains to be considered is the general question raised by the Plaintiffs, *as to who are the parties entitled to the benefits and uses of the Charitable Funds and Institutions now in the possession and under the management of the Defendants*. The contentions of both sides are fully set out in the pleadings. The Plaintiffs say: "There exist numerous rich endowments consisting of property, both moveable and immoveable, devoted to various charitable and religious purposes for the benefit of *persons professing the Zoroastrian religion.*

They say that the Trusts declared by the Trust Deed of the 25th of September, 1884 are in terms "at variance with the Trusts and purposes for and to which the same were originally provided and dedicated."

The Plaintiffs believe that, "at the time the said Deed was prepared and executed, there was no intention by the terms thereof to exclude from the benefits of the said Trusts *any person* professing the Zoroastrian faith." They complain that the Defendants had interpreted the Trusts in a manner which would exclude from the benefits of the Trusts persons born in other religions and subsequently admitted into the Zoroastrian religion; and they pray that, in so far as the Trusts declared by the Deed of the 25th of September, 1884, differ from the original Trusts, they may be declared *ultra vires* and void; that the true Trusts on which the charitable properties are held may be ascertained and declared; that the Deed of 1884 may be construed; and that it may be declared who are entitled to the benefits of such of the Trusts as may be held to be valid.

The Plaintiffs say: Every Juddin[2] admitted into the Zoroastrian religion is entitled, as a matter of right, to all the benefits of all the Charitable Funds and Institutions in the Defendants' possession.

---

1   *Parsiana*, February 1982, pp. 3, 4, and 5.
2   Juddin: non-Zoroastrian.

The Defendants say: The parties entitled to the benefits of the Funds and Institutions under their control are persons who are Parsis who are the descendants of the Zoroastrian emigrants from Persia; their Iranee co-religionists who may come and settle either temporarily or permanently in India; and the children of Parsi fathers born of alien mothers, if they are admitted in, and profess, the Zoroastrian religion.

A great deal of time and energy were expended on the argument as to the exact meaning and significance of the word Parsis, and as to whether the words *Parsis* and *Zoroastrians* mean the same thing and designate the same persons, or whether there is any distinction in the individuals designated by the terms Parsis and Zoroastrians.

I confess this question has never, at any time, presented any difficulty to my mind: a Zoroastrian is a person who professes the Zoroastrian religion. A Zoroastrian need not necessarily be a Parsi. Anyone who professes the religion promulgated by Zoroaster – be he an Englishman, Frenchman, or American – becomes a Zoroastrian the moment he is converted to that Faith. *But how can he become a Parsi?* It was argued that the 6th Plaintiff's wife was now a Parsi. Supposing a Parsi lady becomes a Christian and marries a Frenchman, can it be said that she had become a Frenchwoman? And if she adopts Christianity and marries an Englishman, does she become an Englishwoman? One has only to see how the word Parsi came into existence, and what it was meant to designate to realize that the word Parsi has only a racial significance and has nothing whatever to do with his religious professions.

*The word Parsi, when used in India, could only mean the people from Pars.* When the emigrants from Persia settled in India, the people around them probably knew little of their religion but they knew they came from Pers or Pars, and they called them Parsis. Thus, all the descendants of the original emigrants came to be known as Parsis. A Parsi born must always be a Parsi, no matter what other religion he subsequently adopts and professes. He may be a Christian Parsi, and he may be any other Parsi according to the religion he professes; but a Parsi he always must be. The word Zoroastrian simply denotes the religion of the individual: the word Parsi denotes his nationality or community, and has no religious significance whatever attached to it.

To my mind, the distinction between the two terms, Zoroastrian and Parsi, is most clearly defined when one sets about carefully examining the real meaning of the two expressions. *Surely, there is no Parsi religion in existence.* What, however, was intended to be conveyed by the expression was the religion generally professed by the Parsi community. To my mind, the expression "Parsi religion" is as meaningless as the expressions: "English religion," "French religion," or "Dutch religion."

Before the controversy in connection with the French lady arose, no one had the remotest idea that a Zoroastrian could be anybody other than a member of the Parsi community. For centuries, the only people who in India professed the Zoroastrian religion were the members of the Parsi community born in the religion of their forefathers. No one had for twelve centuries ever made an attempt to convert persons professing other religions. Proselytising was wholly unknown amongst them. No one preached the religion or attempted to teach it to an alien. There was not an instance known either in modern or ancient times, of anybody but a Parsi who professed the Zoroastrian religion. The Zoroastrian religion was professed by the Parsis alone in India; and small wonder, therefore, if the expressions Zoroastrians and Parsis came to be loosely used, as if the two words meant one and the same thing.

In 1884, it was not within the contemplation of any one that, in the near future, converts to Zoroastrianism would come into existence, and neither the English Solicitor who drafted the Deed of the 25th of September, 1884, nor those who instructed him to prepare the Deed, and who subsequently executed the same, had the remotest conception of such a class or such an individual as an alien Convert to Zoroastrianism coming into existence; and therefore there could be no possible object in intentionally declaring wrong Trusts or Trusts at variance with the intentions of the donors and founders. In fact, the Plaintiffs themselves say that, in declaring the trusts as they are declared in the Deed of 1884, there was no intention "to exclude from the benefit of the Trusts any person professing the Zoroastrian faith," meaning thereby Juddin converts to Zoroastrianism. This, at all events, is an admission that there was no intentional wrong declaration of Trusts in the Deed of 1884.

Till 1903, the two expressions, Parsis and Zoroastrians, were used most promiscuously to mean one and the same thing. When the members of the Parsi community professing the Zoroastrian religion were sought to be designated, some used the word Parsis and some used the word Zoroastrians.[1]

Even though Davar's judgment made it explicitly clear one hundred years ago that the converts will not be legally entitled to the Parsi trusts for the reasons well explained by him, Parsis' opposition to conversion seems to be still fueled by their anxiety about it.

## Opinions of Scholars in 1903 on Conversion

When the controversy was raging in the Parsi community over the issue of conversion in 1903, the community was fortunate enough to have the best of its savants, including the Guru of them all, Mr. K. R. Cama, alive then. Their learned views on conversion were published in Gujarati by an anonymous Zoroastrian in 1909. I am grateful to Dasturji Framroze A. Bode and Mrs. Homai Bode for taking

---

1    *Parsiana*, May 1982, pp. 14 and 15.

the trouble of finding out my whereabouts in the United States in order to send me this rare manuscript. I am also grateful to Ervad Noshir Hormuzdiar and his wife Marion for translating it into English as best as they can. Since most of the schol-ar-priests in 1903 maintained that Zoroastrianism did enjoin conversion, and since most of the scholar-priests eighty years later vehemently oppose such a view in our own times, one may want to enlighten himself or herself by reviewing the views held by illustrious scholars in 1903. I therefore find it worthwhile to present them in their entirety in Appendix I for the benefit of the reader.

## Dasturji Dhalla on the Vansada Case

The orthodox Parsis were in furor when Dasturji Framroze Bode performed the Navjote of the children of Parsi fathers and non-Parsi mothers in Vansada, a vil-lage near Bulsar (Valsad) in the State of Gujarat in 1942. The reader may find the following extract from the book Dastur Dhalla – *The Sage of a Soul*, and pub-lished by *Parsiana* (November, 1982 and February, 1983) very enlightening:

> A great book like the *Dinkard* states that the most virtuous deed a 'Jooddin' can perform is to relinquish his own religion and embrace the Zoroastrian faith. Moreover, it is written in the *Dinkard* that with the assistance of the learned Dastur Adarbad, King Shapur II performed memorable deeds to revive and radiate his religion. The *Dinkard* further adds that if persuasion and placation do not prevail, then it is correct to convert non-Zoroastrians into Zoroastrianism forcefully. Even a ritual-istic document like the *Aerpatistan* gives evidence of conversion, *Madigane hazar dadistan* which relates to legal and constitutional mat-ters informs us that if the Christian slave of a Zoroastrian master aban-dons Christianity and becomes a Zoroastrian, he should be set free.

## Genetical Frequencies of Parsis vis-a-vis Iranian Zoroastrians

Since an issue is often made of the unique genetical pool, genetical purity, Bun-yad Pasbani, etc. of the Parsis, and since Dr. Undevia and his colleagues have done exhaustive study on this subject, I would like the reader to acquaint himself or herself with their scientific findings, and let the reader decide for himself or herself the truth in the matter.[1]

Another study by Steinberg et al., published in *The American Journal of Hu-man Genetics* (May 1973, pp. 302-09) has established that "The presence of $Gm^{1,5,13,14}$ haplotype among the Parsi and Irani (in India) suggests that they have some African or Indian "Tribal" (that is, noncaste) admixture. The presence of the $Gm^{1,3,5,13,14}$ haplotype, which is common among Orientals, Melanesians, and Mi-cronesians, also suggests admixture.... The lower frequency (of these two) haplo-types among the Irani as compared with the frequency among the Parsis suggests lesser admixture.... These haplotypes are not likely to have been present before migration from Iran.... This conclusion is reinforced by the observation that the sickle-cell trait, present in some Tribal Indian populations, occurs among the Par-

---

1   Dr. Undevia's 1972 and 1973 findings are discussed in more detail below.

sis.... The ancestors of these populations originated in Iran, but these people have some haplotypes not found in Iran, and have different frequencies of those they share in common." This finding falls in line with the observations made by Amir Taheri, consequent to his visit to the fire-temple in Yazd: "But the claim of racial purity and Aryanism advanced by some Mazdean hotheads has no basis in fact. Many Negro slaves and Turkish servants of the Zarathustrians were converted to the religion centuries ago adding their own racial characteristics to the blend."[1]

In a research paper, entitled "The Distribution of Some Enzyme Group Systems Among Parsis and Iranis in Bombay" published in *Human Heredity*, 1972, pp. 274-282, Dr. Undevia et al., observe:

> There are a number of differences which are suggestive of divergent evolution between the Parsi and Irani populations and further research on the Zoroastrian Iranis in Bombay and in Iran will be justified. Of special significance is the occurrence of the $Phs^C$ allele in the red cell acid phosphatase system among the Iranis, but not among the much larger sample of the Parsis sampled. Conversely, the Parsis have a high frequency of the LDH 'Calcutta-l' variant, whereas it was absent among the Iranis. Frequencies of alleles in the phosphoglucomutase and adenylate kinase systems were similar in the two populations, and in a number of other systems no variation was found in either population. In the 6PGD system the absence of variants in the Iranis is due possibly to the small size of the series investigated.
>
> From what is known already about the different distribution of alleles for some of the blood group systems, G6PD deficiency and HbS, as well as for the enzyme systems noted above, *it is clear that the Parsis and Iranis as a result probably of a combination of genetic drift, selection and hybridization with neighbouring groups, have become genetically differentiated from one another.*

In another genetical study, entitled "Serum Protein Systems among Parsis and Iranis in Bombay" published in *Human Heredity,* 1973, 23, pp. 492-498, Dr. Undevia et al., conclude: "The $Hp^1$ gene frequency was significantly different for the Parsis and the Iranis.... The present study supports previous work on blood group antigens and red cell enzymes (by Undevia, et al.) which indicates genetical differentiation between Parsis and Iranis in Bombay. Our results show a significant difference for the haptoglobin system.... In the case of haptoglobin system, the Iranis have a similar gene frequency to Zoroastrian population still residing in Iran, whereas the Parsis have a markedly lower $Hp^1$ gene frequency."

These findings have been supported by various case histories and facts listed in the series entitled "The Parsi Punchayet Case" started by *Parsiana* in October 1981, p. 11, and *Parsiana*, Nov. 1981, p. 3. Further we learn that "the mere performance of the Navjote ceremony – by a priest, without any other ceremonies, was considered sufficient to let them in."[2]

1   *Parsiana*, September 1974, p. 29.
2   *Parsiana*, October 1981, p. 11.

These findings seriously undermine the validity not only of the genetical purity of the Parsis, but also of the inseparability of Zoroastrianism from the pre-Islamic Zoroastrian ancestry and culture.

When we meet in large numbers, such as at the Third World Zoroastrian Congress, our euphoria invariably seems to turn to the topic of our genetical pool, or purity with its ramifications of genetical superiority, etc. We unfailingly wax so eloquent on this subject, so easily forgetting the oft-repeated Gathic admonition of our Prophet that only those that fight evil and pursue the path of righteousness in every way have a claim to the everlasting fame and bliss. Thus, as *Parsiana* faithfully chronicles, one of "the two speakers who received the loudest ovations" at the above Congress was the one "who espoused the orthodox point of view" on this subject (March 1978, p. 25). In the same issue, however, *Parsiana* (pp. 31-32) depicts the pensive musings of A. D. Moddie, who read a paper at the Congress:

> Ironically, after the ... Congress I found myself taking a train to Cochin – the home of the last remnants of endogamous Jews and also of the Syrian Christians. The Jews ... are now a pale handful, reflecting a major concern of ... the Congress ... survival; the second are confidently growing with faith, with inter-marriage, with conversion.... There was a sense of euphoria at the Congress.... The euphoria fed on things such as ... But euphoria went a little too far beyond that. There were impassioned pleas for the purity of the racial stock, the "Aryan" stock. Never did so little genetics go so far! For a moment one wondered whether one was at a Zoroastrian Congress or at a stud farm. No one seemed to remember a man who made the same claims only a generation ago: Adolf Hitler. No one remembered one of the greatest biologists of the age, Sir Julian Huxley, who quite apart from the terrible consequences of Nazi genetical claims, disproved them on scientific grounds.... The path to hell is paved not only with good intentions, it is also paved with extremism."

Let us then avoid extremism in this regard and let us take a more rational and intelligent approach that measures up to the teachings of our great Prophet.

## A Concluding Prayer

I have found it my bounden duty to write this treatise, though in doing so, I find myself at odds with best of my friends, relatives, teachers, and well-wishers. Painful though it was to respond to this call, I shall feel rewarded if this treatise will inspire our children to remain Zoroastrian, and raise their progeny as Zoroastrian despite the ultimate and sad eventuality of their marrying outside the community for reasons so peculiar to the North American milieu. As I conclude my treatise, I clearly recollect the sense of trepidation that overcame me as I undertook this project, because I had no time or literature to fall back upon. With the grace of Ahura Mazda, I feel I have done as good a job in this regard as was possible for someone with my background and circumstance. I hope someone else will have more time, energy, devotion, resources, and knowledge to enlarge upon it, whenever necessary. I also hope and pray that my work will not be used to justify indiscriminate inter-marriages or conversions. *I have always emphasized the need to preserve our identity in every way that we possibly can. Such an earnest attempt should precede any sanction for inter-marriages or conversions.* Nor do I recommend conversion as an easy safeguard or buttress against our dwindling and diminishing numbers, though I would readily endorse it for the right reasons even if we were teeming with millions. I approve of it simply because the teachings of the Prophet are very clear on this subject. I am afraid it is rather too late to recommend conversion as a panacea for our rapidly eroding numerical strength, as we failed to take care of it earlier. But Zarathushtra has given us no right to slam our doors shut on others and those that do so will surely be accountable to him and to God.

While our co-religionists in the Old World still have time to resolve this crisis, those of us in North America do not have such a grace period. For us it is an extremely painful situation of seeing our religious and racial heritage almost totally wiped out in a generation or two thanks to the unique melting-pot phenomenon here. If we follow the old Parsi tradition in this regard, we will lose both race and religion to this melting-pot. But if we follow the eternal and universal teachings of our great Prophet, then we will continue to be Zoroastrian and even swell our ranks with worthy and qualified aspirants who could be nothing but an inspiration to our progeny that our faith is catholic and worthy of their allegiance in the New World. Joe Peterson's example should serve as a beacon light to our children who are dissatisfied with our religion and are turning to other faiths to satisfy their spiritual hunger, because we have often failed in inspiring them to the basic teachings of our religion in this regard. Joe's example should beckon them back to our faith as well as those that have already become Christians, etc. Joe's Navjote has done more to highlight this problem, as also to bring us nearer to its solution at least in North America than hundreds, nay, thousands and thousands of meetings, discussions, conferences, reports, symposiums, etc., held in this regard ever since 1903 when the great debate started with full force in India. The solution for this crisis has always been there, if we follow the ancient wisdom contained in the Pahlavi scripture, *Shayest Ne-Shayest*, which admonishes us to retain the fundamentals of our religion and cling on to them even when it becomes almost impossible to do so due to the circumstances beyond our control, by keeping the basic beliefs and shedding the non-essentials one by one, but only as the tyranny of the time dictates. The time will come, it says, when a Zoroastrian praying one Ashem Vohu will get the benefit equal to praying, say, the whole *Yasna* or *Avesta*. Unfortunately, that time has come for our children here, even as the traditionalists turn blind eye to this danger-signal, essentially because of their own cognition and psychological make-up and rigid, dogmatic personality, rather than because of the teachings of Zarathushtra. Few people in our generation can claim to have been raised in a more orthodox and traditionalist atmosphere than this author, a fact which I have enjoyed and savored more than the present predicament we find ourselves locked in. It will be so nice if we could survive another 1300 years without making any changes. But we simply cannot. I have tried, however grudgingly, to open my eyes to the horrifying situation we are in now. As children we all basked in the glory and greatness of our illustrious community. Our children in North America, however, have no such edge here, and God only knows what predicament our grandchildren will find themselves in, that is, if somebody will even be able to find them except in places of their major concentrations. I had never anticipated that such a calamity will hit us in my lifetime and to my own children. My hands tremble, my heart aches, and tears roll from my eyes as I pen these words and peep into the future. I wish at times I had retained the old traditionalist in me and refused to face the future.

I hope that this treatise has been of some solace and guidance to open-minded Zoroastrians in general and particularly to our future generations for whom especially I have toiled so hard and weathered severe storms of criticism to complete this work. Let us conclude, as all our Nyaeshes and Yashts conclude:

> Dad Din beh Mazdayasni: Agahi ravai go Afargani bad. Hafta-Keshwar Zamin. Aedun-bad. Man Ano Awayad Shudan.

> May the knowledge, spread, and fame of the commandments of the Mazdayasni religion be established over all the seven continents. May it be so (as I wish). May I attain my goal there. Amen!

This book is an earnest attempt at responding to the urgent plea made by the Zoroastrian youth in North America at the Fourth North American Zoroastrian Congress:

> What are we, the younger generation supposed to do, when Zoroastrian immigration to North America falls to zero? If official changes are not begun now, then when? When you are gone, we the younger generation will be left high and dry. We will be the last, and without experience as to how to handle these changes on our own. When you are gone and we are totally lost as to what to do, where does it leave our great religion? Leaving behind those least prepared to deal with change, would be the ultimate disservice to Ahura Mazda and, most simply, to us.

> We young Zoroastrians are disillusioned; we have few hopes left for a religion which preaches free will and the tolerance of others' beliefs, but which allows our spouses and friends only peripheral involvement in Zoroastrianism; we are disappointed in a community which complains constantly of extinction, but which regards as marginal Zoroastrians those of mixed-marriage parentage; we are confused by rituals and customs which no one can explain to us. Most of all, we are defeated by our fellow Zoroastrians who will not stand behind us – who refuse to open the gate and use their collective strength to preserve our religion – for the road not taken leads nowhere.

This book is a humble attempt at responding to the crisis facing our youth here as elsewhere.

Now I would like to present my arguments for acceptance in the following chapters in response to their rejection by the three most learned Parsi High Priests of our times, who happened to be my esteemed professor and classmates, and by the Zoroastrian Studies (Z.S.) organization, which jumped into the fray to reject my responses to them, as if they were not able to do so themselves, even though I had not involved Z.S. in any way in my responses to the trio, which speaks for itself.

# THE ARGUMENT FOR ACCEPTANCE

The views of those opposed to Acceptance are so different from other savants, that a meaningful and dispassionate dialog does not seem possible at this stage. I shall therefore try to fulfill my responsibility as an advocate for acceptance by taking time to explain what really our Prophet and scriptures say on this subject, and let the reader and posterity be the judge. As it happens so often in the field of Zoroastrian studies, the views one represents may not be acceptable to all. However, despite an acute shortage of reference materials on this subject, I have tried to provide as much evidence as was possible in my circumstances in order to inspire readers to decide on the whole of this manuscript rather than any portion of it with which he may not agree.

## Other Opinions in Contrast with the Orthodox Views

The 1903 opinions of such stalwarts as S. D. Bharucha, E. K. Antia, T. D. Anklesaria, etc., and their revered Guru, K. R. Cama, differ radically from this triad's. Camaji then declared: "It is the duty of every Zoroastrian to accept (non-Zoroastrians).... If we create difficulties and delay in the process of initiation of these people who request to become Zoroastrian, then this is comparable to stopping someone from correcting his path of wrong deed to changing to good deeds." T. D. Anklesaria has written a book in Gujarati on "The Evidence in Support of Accepting non-Zoroastrians into the Mazdayasni Religion" and so has Dasturji Jamaspji Minocheherji who publicly performed the Navjote of nine Mazgaon Juddins, which was attended by distinguished Parsis and applauded as adding "prestige to the community."[1] Dasturji Kaikhusru Jamaspaji of Anjuman Atashbehram therefore concluded in 1903: "from the examples of the above booklets ... one can say that for any new student there is nothing left to search for." Kaikhusru Jamasp Asa, the present Dasturji of the Anjuman Atashbehram, one of the triad himself, along with Helmut Humbach, the world renowned linguist, has established the validity of *Vaetha Nask* which provides the clearest proof possible of Iranians admitting aliens ardently avowing on their own to accept our faith. "Conversion and especially reconversion of former Behdins was discussed and to a certain extent admitted among the Zoroastrians of Iran."[2] Jamasp Asa himself describes Zoroaster as "the Prophet of Ancient Iran who preached a new *World Religion.*"[3]

In our times Dasturji Dabu has maintained: "There is nothing to prevent anyone not born a Parsi from professing his spiritual allegiance to Zarathushtra and adopting his message.... Thus Zoroastrianism is still open to adoption by the world to which the religion was offered."[4] The triad's views are thus sharply in contrast with these views of one of the most dedicated Dasturjis of our times.

The liberal milieu in North American, true to its melting pot, would lead the

---

1    Pangborn, Cyrus R. *Zoroastrianism: A Beleaguered Faith*. New York: Advent Books, 1983, p. 144.
2    *Vaetha Nask – An Apocryphal Text on Zoroastrian Problems*, 1969.
3    F. Rustomji, *Daily Prayers of the Zoroastrians*, Colombo, 1976, Part II, p. 11.
4    *Message of Zarathushtra*, p. 16.

Zoroastrians there to study what our Prophet actually taught about conversion and be guided by it, though it may unfortunately be contrary to the present opposite views or politics. This is not to suggest that some of the Parsis in India have not reached the same conclusion on this subject as the Parsis in North America have. The views of the illustrious Parsi M. P., the late Mr. Piloo Mody, as detailed in his Introduction to Mr. Pastakia's book on Zoroastrianism, are far bolder than those of the North American Parsis. The views of one of the most illustrious Parsis of our times, Mr. Nani Palkhivala, the former Indian Ambassador to U.S.A., are so strong and sincere on this subject that he boldly chose to express them on an occasion least conducive to hearing liberal views, as when he was honored by the Bombay Parsi Punchayet on December 21, 1982: "First I have always thought that the teaching of Zarathushtra was not intended merely for 1,20,000 out of a total world population of 4-½ billion. It is a universal teaching. Like all great philosophies of life, like all great religions, it is a religion which transcends religions in the narrow sense. Universality is the one element which Rabindranath Tagore noted about Zarathushtra's teachings. He said he was the earliest and the greatest of the Prophets who raised religion above the level of the pagan God, above the religion of the tribal God. I am afraid this is one lesson we cannot afford to forget. Zoroastrianism is not for a tribe only.... I can end no better than with the prayer that "May the Great Spirit of Zarathushtra abide not only with our community but with the human race always."

In answer to a question "did the author of Yasna 31, (Zarathushtra), have in mind a hope for universal conversion of mankind?", Dr. Mills replies: "It is impossible to doubt that the gifted composer (Zarathushtra) must have known that his words could bear that interpretation."[1] In a letter dated July 18, 1903, to the Anjuman Atashbehram Trustees, Dr. Mills who later worked on the above BPP publication further maintained: "The main question which should come before us is whether the original Zoroastrian religion discouraged the admission of proselytes.... To that point I would answer that this is to the last degree improbable as a fact, while it is positively contradictory to the letter and spirit of the original documents." Prof. Wm. Jackson and others shared this sentiment in 1903 with these Trustees.

## Reasons that Led to Rejection of Conversion later by Zoroastrians

I hardly know of any impartial western scholar who has opined otherwise. One can view almost any western scholar's research on this subject, such as the one very much in vogue now, Dr. Mary Boyce, the teacher of Kotwal, who has praised her works "as authoritative and learned," as well as "a number of other serious scholars" (Kotwal) also have, such as R. C. Zaehner and whom the orthodox writers also quote to support their argument. Boyce describes Zoroastrianism as "the oldest of the dogmatic, proselytizing world religions."[2] *She also provides us a clue as to why and how we ceased to convert others*: "How, or exactly when, the religion then reached western Iran (from which Parsis claim their origin), where it

---

1    *An Exposition of the Lore of the Avesta*, Bombay Parsi Punchayet, 1961, p. 164.
2    *Zoroastrians*, 1979, p. 99.

first enters recorded history, remains unknown. It seems, however, that by the time it did so, Zoroaster's great vision of a world faith had been largely lost, and his religion had come to be regarded as specifically that of the Iranian peoples. There must have been a number of reasons for this. In any case, Zoroastrian missionaries would plainly have found it easiest to work among fellow-Iranians, both because of the absence of a serious language barrier, and because the common religious heritage provided a basis for acceptance of the new faith. These considerations must have been reinforced by inherent pride of race, which was naturally strengthened in the case of a conquering people. To Iranians in general the non-Iranian, the 'anarya' (Pahlavi 'aner') was as much a creature to be despised and disregarded as was the 'barbarian' to the Greeks; and so might be left to follow what religion he pleased, provided only that it was peaceable. As the numerous Iranian peoples were brought gradually to accept Zoroaster's teachings, they came accordingly to regard these as part of their own racial heritage, to be treasured accordingly, rather than as a universal message of salvation for all mankind."[1] As per, K. M. Jamasp Asa's own translation of Duchesne-Guillemin's *Religion of Ancient Iran* (p. 251), the Irani Zoroastrians "considered it a sin to refuse anyone all the benefits of the Good Religion."

*Boyce gives another reason why Zoroastrianism later became confined to Iran*: "The basic doctrine is simple and attractive, and it involves every member of the community in fighting the good fight unceasingly through the ordinary tasks of daily life. This is one of the great strengths of Zoroastrianism.... but Zoroastrian rules regarding daily living can be shown to have proliferated down the centuries, and they created eventually an iron code of conduct which had the effect of raising a barrier between Zoroastrian and unbeliever almost as rigid as that which separates the caste Hindu from the rest of humanity.... The existence of the developed Zoroastrian code must have contributed to the failure of the Good Religion to gain converts beyond Iranian borders; for its stringency it makes demands of a kind to which it is better to grow accustomed from earliest childhood, so that acceptance of them becomes instinctive. Otherwise the requirements may well seem too irksome, the self-discipline needed too strict."[2]

*In Volume II* (p. 189-90), *Boyce provides yet another clue to this problem*: "Zoroastrianism itself had long had this double character, being both universal in its message and yet special to the Iranian peoples.... Down the centuries the Zoroastrian priests elaborated rules in defense of both actual and ritual purity ... indeed the existence of this code must have been a major factor in preventing the spread of Zoroastrianism as a coherent faith beyond the Iranian peoples themselves.... After years of necessary keeping of the Zoroastrian purity code (which has nothing in it repugnant to Jewish laws) it is hardly surprising that Nehemiah, although a layman, should have concerned himself in Jerusalem with questions of purity among the Jews. Nor does it seem overbold to suppose that it was Zoroastrian example, visible throughout the Empire, which led to the gradual transformation of the Jewish purity code from regulations concerning cultic matters to laws

---

1    Op. cit., p. 47.
2    *A History of Zoroastrianism*, Vol. I, p. 294-5.

whose observance was demanded of every individual in his daily life, their setting being no longer only the Temple, but 'the field and the kitchen, the bed and the street,' and their keeping a matter which set the Jews in their turn apart from other peoples, in self-imposed isolation."

In *The Dawn and Twilight of Zoroastrianism*, Zaehner laments: "Of all the great religions of the world Zoroastrianism was the least well served. Zoroaster himself has every right to the title he claimed: ... *but his successors never fully understood his message, nor had they a living and authentic tradition to guide them*.... in the Sassanian period, they ... tried to impose a strict orthodoxy which few could tolerate.... One is tempted to say that all that was vital in Zoroaster's message passed into Christianity through the Jewish exiles, whereas all that was less than essential was codified and pigeon-holed by the Sassanian theologies so that it died of sheer inanition.... All this does not detract one whit from the stature of the Iranian Prophet himself, who remains one of the greatest religious geniuses of all time. It merely shows how ... even a great religion with a vital message for man ... can turn into something wholly different from what the founder had intended" (p. 170-1). This is especially true of what became of Zoroaster's original teachings on converting all of mankind to his faith. Similarly, Darmesteter observes: "(Zoroastrian) principles required an effort too continuous and too severe to be ever made by any but priests, who might concentrate all their faculties in watching whether they had not dropped a hair upon the ground. A working people could not be imprisoned in such a religion, though it might be pure and high in its ethics. The triumph of Islam was a deliverance for the consciences of many, and Magism, by enforcing its observances upon the nation, brought about the ruin of its dogmas, which were swept away at the same time: its triumph was the cause and signal of its fall."[1] May the present-day Zoroastrians learn to avoid such further falls which may prove very catastrophic for them.

## Parsis and Westernization

What Professor James E. Whitehurst observes in this regard is worth noting:

> Perhaps the greatest threat to the Parsi community comes in the form of a frontal attack on much that Parsis have considered sacrosanct. Parsis may manage to stem the population decline, but if the religious bond that has given them identity as a people crumbles, it is meaningless to talk about their survival as a historical community.... The advent of western education sowed the seeds of skepticism and radical questioning.... However much indebted the Parsis may be to the process of Westernization, industrialization and technology for their rise to prominence, they have become, in other respects, victims of that process.... *The full force of its disruptive power is perhaps more dramatically revealed in this tiny community than anywhere else in the world*.... Dissatisfied with the ancestral faith, Parsi youth seem to be drifting off into agnosticism and skepticism. The erosion of modernity has thus cut deeply into the community.... Nonetheless, as bleak as this picture may

---

1    *Sacred Books of The East*, 1980, Vol. 4, p. lvi.

seem, there is a hopeful, aspect that should be considered.... The secularization that is so rapidly encompassing the world is not a demon to be resisted but a potential good to be embraced; it is, he (van Leeuwen) believes, a child of the biblical heritage. Materialism, prosperity, technological advances, and creature comforts are not in opposition per se to the Kingdom.... Although not generally considered a part of the Judeo-Christian heritage, Zoroastrianism seems closer to this stream than to the "wisdom of the East." If not a daughter of biblical faith, it is at least a first cousin – or possibly one of its parents.... Whether or not cultural borrowing can definitely be established, there is certainly a basic parallel between Zoroastrianism and biblical faith at a number of points. Chief among these is perhaps the deep aversion on the part of the followers of Zoroaster to any kind of asceticism. Zoroastrianism is one of the few great religions that has never had any patience with monasticism. The celibate life is considered inferior to the married state (through which alone men and women can come to the maturity of self-sacrificing love). As corollary, Zoroastrians shun all oriental views that regard the world as maya or illusion. Instead, man is regarded as a co-worker with Ahura Mazdah; his clear duty is to multiply the race, subdue the earth, and overcome as much evil as possible. Indeed, man, according to one Zoroastrian myth, consciously chooses to enter life for this very purpose. Taking this world with utmost seriousness as a realm in which God's will is to be accomplished through struggle, gives Zoroastrianism a healthy secular thrust in just as radical a form as found anywhere in biblical tradition. If van Leeuwen is right, the radical process of secularization of society brings an end to "religion" as we know it.... There is no turning back; the process, according to van Leeuwen, is irreversible.... Hence if a spiritual view of life is to have any role whatever in mankind's future, it needs to refocus its concern from the transcendent world to the secular world; it must recognize man as a being who creates history through his existential choices. In particular, its concerns should be directed toward the production and distribution of the earth's resources so that the material potential of this plant might be used for the benefit of as much of mankind as possible. What is urgently required, says van Leeuwen, is "a theology of materialism, a theology of wealth." We must recognize the fact that "world peace and world prosperity belong inseparably together." Here, too, the Parsis are our kinsmen and may even have something to teach us. Their well-known charitable enterprises are a model of practical stewardship and evidence a deep concern for the well-being of their fellow men, Parsi and non-Parsi alike. This, coupled with their cosmopolitan spirit, puts them in the forefront of the type of spiritual leadership van Leeuwen contends is necessary for our time. Further, as a highly urbanized people for several generations, they know from experience the possibilities – and terrors – the "Secular City" holds for man. Having

once tasted its freedom and potential, most Parsis are unwilling to retreat into the past.... Their success in becoming westernized is perhaps
best symbolized by the Parsi-founded firm of Air India. The name itself, in English, combines the western achievement of aviation with the
eastern mystique of levitation – the trademark of the little turbaned
"maharajah" on the flying carpet. Hopping from city to city and continent to continent. Air India exemplifies the Parsi genius for world trade
and represents their mobility, urbanization and cosmopolitan spirit....
Parsis of recent decades have pioneered in the technocratic revolution,
supplying – at least as far as Asia goes – key leadership in aerodynam-
ics, engineering, and atomic physics.... The notable work of the Tata Institute of Science at Bangalore, founded in 1898 by J. N. Tata, is further
evidence of long-standing Parsi concern in this area.... Examples could
be multiplied to illustrate the way Parsis demonstrate the world-affirm-
ing, life-embracing aspects of their faith. In the light of this thesis, the
current pessimistic calculations about the future of the Parsi community
may be premature. Westernization has had its baneful influence; "reli-
giously" the Parsis may not be doing well. But, if they should follow
the implications of western thought to the finish and affirm, without
qualification, the secular note latent in their faith, Parsis may yet prove
to be one of the religious communities best equipped to enter the new
age.[1]

In this connection it is worth noting how the Parsis themselves have wittingly or
unwittingly begun to adopt these views and see the realization of their traditional
religious values in their efforts at industrializing India and providing jobs to its
poor. Thus, replying to a staunch critic of Mr. J. R. D. Tata's Parseeism and standing in the Zoroastrian faith, Mr. S. R. Vakil retorted that such critics "forget that
*the greatest cosmopolitan Fire Temple in the private sector has been kept burning
at Jamshedpur by the Tata's day and night. which is feeding half a million mouths*.
There are 66,400 men on the roll with a minimum (monthly) wage of Rs. 636.00
and a maximum wage of Rs. 2671.00." However, the best testimony to the transformation of ancient religious precepts and practices into serving the needs of humanity comes from the life and work of Mr. J. R. D. Tata himself. The *Reader's
Digest* (April, 1963, 248-252) sums up his philosophy admirably well: "We here
at Tata are so obsessed with our people's poverty that we don't deserve special
credit for having public service on our minds.... Whether or not we succeed in the
formidable task of converting our ancient land into a modern and prosperous nation," says J. R. D. Tata, "will depend largely on the extent to which we give of
ourselves in this struggle for revival and regeneration." ... "About 80 percent
(now it is even more) of the parent (Tata) company's profits go back to the people
in the form of trusts for medical research and the relief of human suffering.... This
man (J. R. D. Tata) who employs 135,000 people – shy villagers, scientists and
salesmen – takes seriously his own and Tata's duties to India."

---

1    "The Zoroastrian Response to Westernization: A Case Study of the Parsis of Bombay," *Journal of
the American Academy of Religion*, 1969, 37(3), pp. 231-6.

Moreover, as observed by Kotwal and Boyd in their notes:[1] "Among certain Zoroastrians today the very question of what constitutes the fundamental religious purpose of Zoroastrian ritual is also being raised." As they further observe: "It is not technically correct to say that 'Avestan, as the holy word, is held to have power er in itself.'[2] However, as Professor Boyce notes, the use of Avestan Manthra by some Zoroastrians verge on magic because of the beliefs that it has power in and of itself without qualification" (op. cit., p. 50). However, Kotwal and Boyd's own views seem to differ somewhat from this view as when they claim "miraculous influence" for the Avestan Manthras, which "becomes a shield against evil," "even if the Manthra is not quite properly pronounced by the priest but is said with devotion, in a physically pure place" (op. cit., p. 50), and Boyce does not seem to agree with them in toto. In reply to a question: "Is there also any truth that vibrations in the original recitations – the word Manthras might describe it – can bring in some divinity?" Boyce replied: "Vibrations are a thing that I personally cannot cope with. However, these words which one hears if one is a Zoroastrian from earliest childhood and which one knows have been used – all these – have their own depth of association and so become splendid vehicles for filling with devotional meaning. I think that's as far as I could go myself."[3] Most Zoroastrians in North America, if not in the old world, seem to echo Boyce's view on this subject. *To prove or disprove the efficacy of the Avestan Manthras is not the intention here*. We simply have to face the fact that "being a small and highly westernized community ... (Parsis) have not been exempt from the wave of secularism that once engulfed Europe and is now enveloping the whole world" (Zaehner, op. cit., 24). We will therefore be well advised and well prepared to offer our future generations something that will still rightfully secure their allegiance to Zoroastrianism, even though in so doing they will move further away from ritualism and purity laws.

### Evidence for Conversion in India

According to Boyce, "The Parsis had come to be regarded ... as a caste within Hindu society, and this together with their pride in their Iranian lineage led them to regard religion as a hereditary matter. This way of thinking was, as we have seen, a tendency in the whole Zoroastrian community from early times, but it had never been made a rigid principle; and when the Parsis consulted, the Iranis as to whether they should allow *their Hindu servants* who wished it to enter the religion, they received the answer" in the affirmative (op. cit., p. 174). The very fact that the Parsis asked the Iranis in *The Rivayat of 1778* (13th Question) "whether or not it is allowable to place their corpses into the Tower of Silence" suggests that without such conversions actually taking place, the necessity for raising such a question does not even arise. Few scholars have doubted that the servants or Gulams referred to in the Rivayats refer to non-Zoroastrians and we have no tradition of denying any Parsi, grave-digger or corpse-bearer, any religious privileges after taking proper Bareshnum. If anyone was denied such a privilege, it is very diffi-

---

1   *Journal of Mithraic Studies*, 2(1), 1977, Routledge and Kegan Paul, p. 50.

2   Boyce, 1971: p. 228 – *Zoroastrianism*, Historia Religionum, Leiden.

3   *Proceedings of the Second North American Zoroastrian Symposium*, ZAC, 1977, 58-59.

cult to conceive that they will continue to this day their surnames such as Ghorkhodu and not change it to avoid any discrimination to their progeny. It is possible that such surnames were often allegorical and not literal in their meaning, given the nature of Parsi humor. Since no other acknowledged scholars have to my knowledge ever doubted that the servants referred to in the Rivayat were non-Zoroastrians, including B. N. Dhabhar who translated it, it is difficult to accept the opposition view that they were Zoroastrians, unless they can document at least one case history to buttress their claim. Not only does Boyce refer to these servants as being Hindu, but Jamasp Asa's own translation of J. Duchesne-Guillemin's *Religion of Ancient Iran* (Bombay, 1973, p. 251) suggests their being "low-caste Hindus."

H. E. Eduljee quotes an European traveller Karsten Niebuhr (1733-1815) as saying that "they (Parsis) do not reject those of another religion like the Hindus, but they receive proselites. (*Kisseh-i Sanjan*, Bombay, 1996, p. 197.) Eduljee also quotes another traveler, S. Master, who arrived at Surat in 1656 and describes Parsism in depth, and adds: "They say ... all Nations shall be of their religion ere the world be ended." (p. 154).

Such a stalwart as S. D. Bharucha refers in the *Dastur Hoshang Jamasp Memorial Volume*" (Gatha Society, Bombay, 1918), to "Hindu slaves and slave-girls." Even if we discount the fact of these slaves being Hindu, the answer of the Iranian Dasturs in this volume makes it clear that "It is a deed of great merit to purchase children of *other* religions.... He who interferes in this matter and does not allow their corpses to be consigned to the Towers of Silence, that person is "Margazan" (a great criminal) according to religion and he shall be disgraced before Meher and Sarosh (while giving account of his deeds after death)."

Duchesne-Guillemin, as translated by Jamasp Asa himself (op. cit., p. 251), also makes it very clear in summarizing the Rivayats' response in this regard that the Iranian Zoroastrians "could not share the Parsis' anxiety to safeguard themselves from the influx of undesirable elements. They considered it a sin to refuse anyone all the benefits of the Good Religion." I wonder what they would have said about the Parsis' callousness and fanaticism about Joseph Peterson since they severely chastised the Parsis when they learnt after talking with the Parsi interpretor that "they have passed resolutions that the above-said children must not be taught Avesta and must not be brought into the good Mazdayasni Religion.... Most respected Sirs, (may God keep you safe), in the third Chapter of Vendidad, the Holy Creator of corporeal beings, has commanded to Lord Zarathustra, the descendant of Spitama of the immortal soul, that it is the duty of all to show the path of good religion to all mankind and to make them honoured and respected by its profits. Again, (it is our belief) that *in the times of Hoshedar Mah, Hoshedar Bami and Saoshane, all men of other religions will be brought into the Good Religion.* Therefore, according to this argument and proof, it is inculcated on us in the Good Religion that to convert the above-said children into our Good Religion is an act of great and permanent merit, and, therefore those who become objectors in this matter, help, as it were, to increase the religion of aliens. They have no knowledge of the essence of things (they are ignorant) and they go on the path of fault and error. It is impossible according to the religion, to call them Behdins. Who is a real Behdin, he will further the Good Religion."[1] When we had a tradition of accepting children of non-Zoroastrian mistresses into our fold in those days, it is difficult to believe, as the triad would have us believe, that the full-fledged Parsis who some-how happened to be grave-diggers and corpse-bearers or forgot their heritage, would not even be allowed to say the Avesta.

To quote Dasturji Dhalla from his autobiography: "Unbiased examination reveals that not only the offspring of white women wedded by the laws of 'Civil Marriage', but even the children of Bhils, destitute and untouchable Hindus and of wheat-complexioned Muslim as well as yellow-skinned Chinese mistresses of Parsi fathers have become cultured, adventurous merchants, industrialists, bankers, people of position and status, charitable and of noble character and religious-minded – in short, people whom everyone would deem it an honour to call their own. Such worthy sons of the soil have mingled with our community in fairly large numbers in every town and city and can be found living illustrious lives even today" (p. 711).

## Conversion in India Indicated by Genetical Research

That such Juddins as well as the children of Parsi father and Juddin mothers were received in the fold may be the reason why Dr. Undevia, et al, have found genetical differences between the Parsis and Irani Zoroastrians.[2] In another study in the *American Journal of Human Genetics*,[3] Steinberg, et al, have found certain "haplotype among the Parsi and Irani ... (which) suggests that they have some African or Indian (that is non-caste) admixture.... The lower frequency (of these) haplotypes among the Irani .... suggests lesser admixture.... These haplotypes are not likely to have been present before migration from Iran.... This conclusion is reinforced by the observation that the sickle-cell trait, present in some tribal Indian populations, occurs among the Parsis." Many other genetical studies on the Parsis have pointed to the same conclusion and deserve our attention.

## Was King Vishtasp Converted by Zoroaster?

Apropos *the opposite view that it "shows gross ignorance" to say that King Vishtasp was converted*, the evidence not only from Boyce, but also from almost all western and Parsi traditions (later so ably translated by Kotwal himself) point so conclusively to the contrary that it seems to be contradictory to all that is known to mankind on this subject. One of the foremost linguists of our times, H. P. Schmidt notes: "Zarathushtra was convinced that the age of truth was initiated with the conversion of these powerful patrons," namely, "Vishtasp, Frashooshtra, and Jamaspa."[4] A. T. Olmstead in his *History of Persian Empire*,[5] which has been described by M. Rostovtzeff as "the fullest and most reliable presentation of the

---

1   Bharucha, *Persian Rivayat of 1778*, Question and Answer 13th, op. cit.
2   *Comparison of the Genetical Characteristics of the Present Parsi Population with Its Ancestral and Affiliated Groups*, 1973.
3   May 73, pp. 302-309.
4   *Zarathustra's Religion and His Pastoral Imagery,*" Universitaire Pers Leiden, 1975, p. 8.
5   University of Chicago Press, 1970, p. 103.

History of the Persian Empire in existence" at the time, refers to King Vishtasp's "conversion." R.E. Hume writes about "the conversion of the king, Vishtaspa (Yasna 28:7; 46:14; 51:16; 53:2; also SBE, 47:50, 67, 72). Also the King's brother, son, a counselor, and the grand vizier were converted.... The names of eighty-nine early converts along with the king are recorded (SBE, 23:203-211)."[1] To quote Boyce: "*The conversion of Vishtaspa is traditionally* said to have taken place in Zoroaster's forty-second year.... It was probably through his wife that *the king was converted* .... Accepting his teachings involved Vishtasp in battles with neighboring princes, who seem bitterly to have resented the establishment of a new faith in their midst. Their names appear in various ... Yashts, notably in Yt. 5.109, where Vishtasp (prays): "I may crush Tathryavant of bad religion, the daeva-worshipper Peshana and the wicked Arejat-Aspa" (Arjasp). In these struggles he was valiantly supported by his (relatives).... The chief hero of these wars *in the religious tradition* is, however, Vishtasp's own son (Yt. 13.103), the Isfandiyar of Persian epic. The survival of Zoroastrianism is proof of the tradition that these early battles were fought triumphantly by the upholders of the new faith.... The account of the early days of Zoroastrianism thus furnished by the Gathas, in conjunction with the Yashts and the Pahlavi books ... appear wholly probable.... Once a ruler had been converted to the new faith it flourished and became firmly established. Casual details provided by the sources, ... give this account, ... an impressive reality.... The legends which remain best known and most current among Zoroastrians today are those concerned *with the prophet's conversion of Vishtasp.*"[2] Jamasp Asa's own translation of Duchesne-Guillemin[3] refers to "The three heavenly messengers sent by Ohrmazd to *convert Vishtasp.*"

As per Dhalla, "His victory was complete when ultimately he triumphed in winning as a convert Vishtasp."[4] *Denkard* books 7 and 8,[5] *Zadsparam*, 23.7 and *Bundahishn* 17.8 further lend support to it. Zaehner observes: "like Muhammad, Zoroaster relied on the sword to enforce the efficacy of his prophetic word."[6] "In his *Outlines of Parsi History*,[7] Dr. Mirza himself says: "King Vishtasp and the Iranian people accepted the religion of Zarathushtra." Professor John Hinnells also observes: "At first Zoroaster's teachings provoked great hostility, but the persecution ceased when he converted the king, Vishtaspa."[8] As per *The Cambridge History of Iran*, Volume 3 (I), "It is during the reign of Gushtasp that Zoroaster proclaims his religion. Gushtasp embraces the new faith and joins the prophet in proselytizing" (p. 376). In *Persia – Past and Present*, Professor A. V. William Jackson refers to "the conversion of King Vishtaspa, who became the Constantine of the faith." He adds: "Vishtaspa is converted only after a long struggle, hesitancy, and deliberation; but when once convinced, he exhibits all the zealous enthusiasm that

---

1    *The World's Living Religions*, 1959, p. 205.
2    Op. cit., Vol. I, pp. 187-9, 279.
3    Op. cit., p. 227.
4    *A History of Zoroastrianism*, p. 25.
5    Sacred Books of the East, Vol. 47, Book 7.74-,66, 5.12, 6.13, and Vol. 37. Book 8.11.2,3.
6    Op. cit., p. 36.
7    p. 375. See also p. 371.
8    *Spanning East and West*, The Open University Press, 1982, Unit 26, p. 10.

is characteristic of a new convert" (p. 64).

Even in Sasanian times when Shapur II revived Zoroastrianism, the *Denkard* says, he "summoned men from all lands to examine and study all doctrines so that all cause for dispute might be removed.... He issued a declaration to this effect: 'Now that we have seen the Religion upon earth, we shall leave no one to his false religion, and we shall be exceedingly zealous. And so did he do.'"[1] (The author regrets the impossibility of providing uniform spellings for the proper nouns, etc., for reasons well known to those familiar with the long linguistic history of Zoroastrianism.) As per Dr. Mirza's own rendition of the *Denkard* in his *Outline of Parsi History* (p. 287), Shapur "in order to make (it) faultless in disputation with *all peoples of the world*, brought all (religious) verdicts under deliberation.... Emperor Kushro I ... declared ... 'The truth of the Mazdayasn Religion is recognized; the intelligent ones can see it *in the world* with steadfastness by deliberation!" The *Denkard* praises the man who propagates the religion and "gives instructions to the sons of men" and not just the Mazdayasnans. Zaehner further observes: "after his *conversion of King Vishtasp*, his (Zoroaster's) whole tone changes, and he now sounds a note of exultation" (p. 73) and he dilates on that theme in his book. As per the *Shikand Gumanik Vizar*, Chapter 10, 64-68:[2] "(64) Zarathusht came alone, on a true mission, to the lofty portal of Kai Gushtasp, (65) and *the religion was taught by him, with a powerful tongue*, to Kai Gushtasp and the learned, through the speech of wisdom, through manual gestures, through definite words, through explanation of many doubts, and through presentation of the visible testimony of the archangels, together with many miracles. (67) And Kai Spend-dat and Zargar and other royal sons (zatak), instigating the many conflicts and shedding the blood of those of the realm, *accepting the religion as a yoke,* (68) *while they even wandered to Arum [Asia Minor] and the Hindus, outside the realm, in propagating the religion.*"

According to Bahman Yasht, Chapter 2, 16-17:[3] "(16) And that which was golden is the reign of King Vishtasp, when I and thou converse about religion, and *Vishtasp shall accept the religion* and shall demolish the figures of the demons.... (17) And that which was of silver is the reign of Artashir the Kayan (Kai), whom they call Vohuman son of Spend-dat, who is he who separates the demons from men, scatters them about, and *makes the religion current in the whole world.*"

*Denkard* Book 7, chapter 4, 74[4] maintains: "(74) Also to proclaim its truth intelligibly, and to make king Vishtasp and those previously learned men without doubt as to the truth of the religion, the creator Auharmazd sends some spirits, Vohumano, Ashavahishto, and the propitious fire, as a reminder to Vishtasp about the true prophesying of Zaratusht, *and the desire of Auharmazd for the acceptance of the religion of Mazda-worship by Vishtasp and for its propagation in the world.*"

These legends which Boyce expands in her Vol. I (pp. 279-81) are more or less corroborated by Kotwal and Boyd's translations in Meherjirana's *A Guide to the Zoroastrian Religion*" (pp. 22-30), such as:

1    Madan's *Denkard*, p. 412-5.
2    SBE XXIV, pp. 170-171.
3    SBE V, pp. 198-199.
4    SBE XLVI, p. 67.

"When Zoroaster planted the tree, every leaf had written on it "Vishtasp accept the Good Religion." Compare the *Shah-Nameh*. If Zoroaster could first convince the learned persons at the Court through miracles, *the people of the world* would automatically accept the religion. It was also the command of God that he should first ask Vishtasp to accept the religion. For that purpose God had given Zoroaster a book called the *Vaetha Nask*. In that Nask the acceptance of the religion by Vishtasp ... was stated. At present we have eight chapters of that Nask preserved. Q. Did Zoroaster want Vishtasp to accept his religion? A. Yes. Zoroaster had wished before God that Vishtasp would become his disciple, i.e., accept his religion (Yasna 28[.8]). Q. Did God tell Zoroaster that Vishtasp would accept the religion? A. Yes (Yasna 46.[.4]).... Zoroaster said: first accept my religion in good faith after witnessing this miracle; second, let your son Aspandyar accept it and explain it *to the people of the world* so that they will accept it; third, let your wife accept the religion and explain it to other women.... Four majestic horsemen ... appeared before the king (Vishtasp) and said: "We are four fireshtes; God has sent us to tell you that the religion of Zoroaster is genuine. Accept it.... compare the *Dinkard* and the *Zardusht Namag*.... Aspandyar propagated the religion.... When *Aspandyar proclaimed the religion throughout the world* a learned man named Tutianus came from Greece ... two learned men from India, Changraghach and Vyas, came for discussions ... and accepted the religion. Compare the *Dasatir.*" In the above *Guide*, Kotwal comments whenever and wherever he differs from the author, but the only comments made so far is about these learned men coming to see Zoroaster. "Such specific episodes seem very doubtful, since they cannot be verified in the earliest Avestan and Pahlavi sources...." However, Dhalla in *A History of Zoroastrianism* (pp. 455-6) narrates the same stories on the basis of *Dabistan*, I.276-2834, *Desatir*, 2.120-144, Bombay, 1818 and Jackson's *Zoroaster*, pp. 85-90 and observes: "He (Changranghacha) embraced the new religion, took a copy of the Avesta with him to India, and converted in a short time eighty thousand people to the religion of the Iranian Prophet." Although there is thus some basis in books for these stories, *the question is not whether they are true or not. The question is: how could such devout souls so conversant with Zoroastrianism as to write its sacred texts blaspheme their Prophet by saying Greeks and Hindus adopted his religion when only a Mazdayasni could become a Zoroastrian?* How could then we find recurring references in Avesta and Pahlavi about "spreading the Good Mazdayasnian Religion over all the zones that are seven" (Yt. 13.94 and the last-but-one para. of every Nyaesh and Yasht) over the whole world (Bar Khalk); or about Taziyane Baste-kustiyan (the Kusti-wearing Arabs), etc.?

Indeed, the most learned early nineteenth century "conservative priest" Dasturji Erachji Meherjirana, whose book Kotwal and Boyd translate, provides the answer: "Q. Did Zoroaster bring the religion only for those who lived in Iran? A. It is stated in the 5th Book of the *Denkard* that God had sent this religion for all the people of the world." In his learned comments Kotwal observes: "The lofty teachings of Zoroaster are universal. His teachings will remain forever and are a benefit to the whole of humanity. Parsi and Irani Zoroastrians, however, are the only followers of Zoroaster who have continuously maintained the traditions taught by

Zoroaster in the form of daily practices and ritual observances. Insofar as Zoroastrian practices are concerned, therefore, it is the Parsi and Irani people who possess the indigenous tradition. Hence, although everyone can advantageously follow the ethical principles, not everyone can become a part and parcel of this ethnic group" (p. 25), which may be tantamount to saying that one can become a Zoroastrian, but cannot become a Parsi. While this view differs from the broader views prevalent in (or up to) the 19th century, it is still quite broad enough to refute the contention that only a Mazdayasni could be a Zoroastrian (or the like). "In the catechism Erachji suggests that the most desirable goal for all good people of the world is to believe in the Zoroastrian religion" (p. xxxix). In answer to the question: Is there an injunction regarding preaching?, Erachji replies: It is a required duty to give information about the religion to everyone and explain it. Compare Yasna 53.5. Again, what benefit does a person who propagates the religion receive? Erachji's answer is: A person who gives strength to our religion and propagates it is much loved by God. Compare Yasna 45.11: "Ohrmazd becomes a friend, a brother and a father to the dastur or leader who is beneficent and promotes the religion." Kotwal comments: "To propagate means to teach those who seek knowledge of the religion. In the Avesta there is evidence that Zoroastrians of old used to do 'missionary' work in India and even China. Now it is more a matter of tending to our co-religionists. It is not necessary that our ceremonies (*kriyas*) be universally practiced. The truths we speak of are universal, but the ceremonies are part of our identity as a community. It is expressly stated in Pazand: 'May this good Mazdayasnian religion spread over the seven regions of the earth': that is, may God and his blessing bring progress to the entire world. But other religions may have their own ceremonies. Our ceremonies give us our identity. We are the continuation of an ancient culture which exists nowhere else in the world; we are the sum and substance of ancient Iran. We are preserving a nation, and like every nation. we have the right to exist" (p. 182-3). Here again there is no reference to Zoroastrianism being confined to the Mazdayasnis, but rather an evidence of "missionary work in India and even in China" which will contradict this thesis. The comments, however, elucidate his thinking for us, i.e., Zoroastrianism is universal but its ceremonies are not. Although one may find innate logical contradiction in such a position, he expounds the orthodox position admirably well, and everyone must readily concede the right to exist to the Parsis. However, such views will become anachronistic when we won't be able to survive, if we cannot follow all rituals and purity laws, a stage which we have almost reached in North America except for most basic rituals which too cannot be performed entirely in conformity with our Purity Laws. Such is the sad consequence of equating religion with ritualism. We will then perforce have to live by the ethical principles of Zoroastrianism, and since Kotwal concedes that "everyone can advantageously follow the ethical principles" and "the lofty teachings of Zoroaster are universal," logically there could be no objection to the proselytes sharing the basic Zoroastrian philosophy with us in North America.

As Zaehner wrote in 1961: "Faithful still to the basic injunction of their creed – 'good thoughts, good words, and good deeds' – they (Parsis) have long turned their backs on the observance of their rituals (irrational and repellent to the modern minds as many of them are).... Thus, though it is possible that Zoroastrianism will shortly become extinct as a cult owing to a death of candidates for a hereditary priesthood, its ethical values ... are likely to be retained."[1] It seems therefore that Zoroastrianism is headed to wind up ultimately as an ethical force, a stage we have more or less reached here already, and thus, as Kotwal maintains, "everyone can advantageously follow the ethical principles" of Zoroastrianism. In this regard Dhalla's advice is very relevant: "Zoroaster, the chosen of Ahura Mazda, does not belong to any single period and particular people, but to all ages and to all peoples.... Zoroastrianism will live by its eternal verities.... Dogmas and rituals are based upon the needs of the times.... They are the accompaniments of religion, but not religion itself. Man may fall away from dogmas and rituals, and yet he may remain religious. Righteousness rests on the individual's piety, and not on a scrupulous observance of ceremonials.... let the Parsi ... abide steadfast in the path of righteousness, and they will be practising true Zoroastrianism."[2]

Dhalla's old appeal was fully supported by Insler who has come closer to truth in translating the Gathas than any mortal so far. His erudite observations herald the return to the view represented by Dhalla:

"I have tried to emphasize the moral and ethical character of Zarathushtra's teachings, which, to my mind, has been seriously neglected in the recent misplaced fascination with the ritualistic background of these exalted lyrics.... the focus and emphatic insistence of the prophet's hymns are directed towards a purpose and unity of thought which oppose the empty, mechanical methods of the ritual. In contrast, I see the extraordinary contribution of Zarathushtra in the profound realization that man can both serve and honor god more meaningfully in the enactment of the lordly principles of truth and good thinking among his fellow men than in the awesome reverence founded upon fear and dread.... If the world is to be saved, this can only happen if man responds to man in accordance with those lofty principles which God founded."[3]

## Does One Have to be a Mazdayasni to Become a Zoroastrian?

The opposite view holds that Zarathushtra's only mission was to reform the Mazdayasni religion already in vogue before him, and so one has to be a Mazdayasni in order to be a Zoroastrian. However, Yima (Jamshed), "the first man, the first king,"[4] and a Mazdayasni prophet, is severely criticized by Zoroaster (Yasna 32.8). Zaehner explains the reason for Gayomard and Yima both being regarded as 'the first man': "Zoroaster's condemnation of Yima, however, was to change considerably the ancient myth of Yima's golden reign.... Thus rather than accept him as first man, they invented a first man of their own, ... Gayomart ... (who) inherited certain of Yima's characteristics.... In Avesta, however, we hear little of Gayomart.... In the *Bundahishn*, a Pahlavi text largely concerned with the creation of the world, we again meet ... Mashye and Mashyane, the father and mother of the

1   Op. cit., p. 24.
2   Op. cit., 509-511.
3   *The Gathas of Zarathushtra*, 22-23.
4   Darmesteter, op. cit. p. 10.

human race who themselves sprang from the seed of the dying Gayomart. Like Gayomart, Mashye and Mashyane are substitute figures for Yima.... The physical death of Gayomart made it possible for the human race to increase and multiply. From his seed the first human couple was born.... *And as mankind was created one and undifferentiated in Gayomart, so will it be resurrected one and whole.*"[1] It is for this reason that Zoroastrians repeatedly invoke "all the Fravashis of the holy from Gayomard to Saoshyant," from the first man to the last one, thus embracing the whole humanity. Linking Zoroastrianism with Gayomard thus seems to have been an attempt on the part of our ancestors to identify it with the whole humanity from its inception. *Denkard* Book 9, chapter 37, h[2] contradicts the Mazdayasni theory: "(h) Thou shouldst proclaim this to kinsmen and confederates, to priests and him who is most active in the country; as to *those who will dispute this thy religion of the Mazda-worshippers, thou shouldst proclaim this over the earth of seven regions*, unto that which is the furthest of houses, villages, communities, and provinces: 'Do thou openly curse these who are heretical towards me, thou united Mazda-worship of Zaratusht, opposed to the demons, which is the ordinance of Auharmazd!'" What *Denkard* Book 9, chapter 51, pp. 5-8 (SBE XXXVII, p. 285) says is again not in agreement with the opposition's contention: "(5) First, that which occurs when, *on account of the preservation of MANKIND from hell, they praise the religion of Mazda-worship*; and that which occurs when Zaratusht the Spitaman: whose guardian spirit is reverenced, came to the obedient king Kai-Vishtasp. (6) Second, when the power and triumph of renewed sovereignty are again connected with the religion, *and MANKIND, on that account, return to the good religion*; and this occurs on the near approach of Aushetar, son of Zaratusht, when the righteous Kitrag-miyan arrives. (7) Third, when *mankind* contentedly praise the religion of the Mazda-worshippers, and this occurs as Aushetar-mah, son of Zaratusht, arrives. (8) And fourth, that which occurs when *everyone shall practise the religion of Mazda-worship with eagerness*; at that time arrives the beneficial and triumphant producer of the renovation, Soshans, son of Zaratusht; and this becomes the consummation (sar-hômôndîh) and supreme triumph of the sacred beings." Again what the triad contends is at variance with what *Denkard* [Book 7, chapter 4, 18][3] exhorts: "(18) *If you attract him, O Zaratusht! and he believes in it and also gives currency to this religion of thine*, and sits before thee in discipleship, *this that one calls discipleship of thine he shall undertake*, and *the religion he hears fully he shall propagate (rubak vabidunyen)*." (I am grateful to Mr. Joseph Peterson for these references.)

Another name for the religion of Mazdayasnis is Pouryotkaeshi and it is by this name only that their Fravashis are invoked in the Afringans. Boyce translates Mazdayasni as "Mazda-worshipper" (Vol. I, pp. 253-4) and so do almost all scholars, including S. D. Bharucha (in his address to the World Parliament of Religions held in Chicago in 1893) who calls it "Mazda-worship," "Mazda being the name of God, and promulgated by Zoroaster.... It is clear that ... Zoroaster teaches the

---

1    Op. cit., pp. 130, 136-7, 275, 309.
2    SBE XXXVII, p. 271.
3    SBE XLVI, p. 54.

worship ... of the One True God, Mazda." "... Zi Mazdaonhodum," says Zoroaster, "Be you the worshipper of Mazda only.... Mazdayasno Zarathushtris," "I am a worshipper of Mazda as announced by Zoroaster." ... It is ... a similarity to the "Kalema" of the Mohammedans in later times which says "There is no God, but Allah, and Muhammed is the Prophet of Allah."[1] Geldner also translates Mazdayasni as "Mazda-worshipper."[2]

Moreover, Yasna 12 containing these declarations is regarded by many scholars as "the original avowal made by converts in the early days of the faith," "the oath which was required of someone being received into the faith ... which set the convert apart from unbelievers. The very first demand made upon him is that he should avow his worship of Mazda and allegiance to his prophet, Zoroaster.... the convert acknowledges his prophet's claim to divine revelation and authority by the repeated references to the "encounterings at which Mazda and Zoroaster spoke together" in which "Ahura Mazda taught Zoroaster." ... That Zoroastrians should have so suffered ... is no more remarkable than that the early Christians should have been persecuted, for the two faiths had evidently much in common with their missionary endeavors."[3] Jamasp Asa's translation of Duchesne-Guillemin[4] also indicate that the Fravarane (Yasna 12) "was perhaps a sort of *CREDO* employed by missionaries."

Thus, in this larger context of Yasna 12, Mazdayasno Ahmi does not relate to the Pouryotkaeshi religion as the pre-Zarathushtrian religion, but to the belief in One God as is evident in the use of Mazda in the preceding line, JASA ME AWANGHAHE MAZDA, which means "O Mazda! Come to my help!" Otherwise, how can we explain what soon follows after that, namely, Mazishtacha, Vahishtacha, Sraeshtacha...," "I pledge myself to the Mazda-worshipping religion, which of all (faiths) existing now and coming into existence in future, the greatest, the best, and the most excellent," (note the superlatives) "which is Ahuric, Zoroastrian." These three superlatives clearly denote the superiority of Zoroastrianism over other religious systems, past, present, or future, which along with other scriptural references to the superiority of Zoroastrianism, makes it so very hard, if not impossible, to believe that Zoroaster addressed himself only to the "Pouryotkaeshis" as defined by the triad. *Pouryo* means "first" and *tkaeshi* means "faith." As Fravardin Yasht celebrates the Fravashis of those who were the first to accept the religion during its crucial time, they are naturally adored and worshipped as Pouryotkaeshi, there being little reason to adore *here* those that preceded Zarathushtra. Just as the sea Vourukash is bigger than the rivers flowing into it, says the Avesta, just as a giant tree overshadows smaller ones, so does Zoroastrianism stand superior to other faiths. Hartman finds it hard to reconcile the Zoroastrian belief in supremacy of his religion with his present-day tolerance of other faiths. He observes: "There is an English translation of a book in Gujarati by J. J. Modi, namely *A Catechism of the Zoroastrian Religion* (1911 and 1962), in which one can observe the greatest points in common between Parsism and

1   *Zoroastrian Religion and Customs*, 1979, pp. 7-8.
2   "Zoroastrian Religion in the Avesta," *Journal of the K. R. Cama Oriental Institute*, 1933, p. 24, 25.
3   Boyce, *History* Vol. I, pp. 253-6.
4   Op. cit., p. 149.

Christianity.... But a Zoroastrian must also know the following: 'The Zoroastrian religion of Ahura-Mazda is the greatest, best, and excellent of all religions that exist and that shall, in future, come into existence (p. 39).... With a firm and earnest belief in our own religion (says Modi), we must behave with forbearance, toleration, and respect towards the professors of other religions' (p. 39). The last-mentioned is perhaps not directly inspired by Christianity but more probably by Hinduism.... Tolerance of faith in combination with exclusiveness of cult." The bias against conversion is thus colored more by the Hindu milieu in which the Parsi mind and attitudes have evolved over centuries than the attitude of the Iranian Mobeds Council towards conversion, as seen later. There are on the whole few religious differences between Parsis and Irani Zoroastrians, but an overwhelming majority of Iranis do not share the Parsis' repugnance to the acceptance of non-Zoroastrians in their fold and attribute it to the influence of the Hindu casteist sentiment on the Parsis, as does Boyce, as seen earlier.

The Prophet himself calls his revelation "Hatam Vahishta," "the very best for the living beings" (Yasna 44.10). As per Schmidt, "The verses (Yasna 33.3 and 4) apparently reflect the universal claim of Zarathushtra. Everybody beyond the Aryan fold is to enjoy the same privileges as the Aryan community, provided he dedicates himself to the cow or good religion. We know that one of the prophet's first patrons was a Turanian (46.12)." In a footnote to this he adds: "The fact that later Zoroastrianism became an exclusively national religion, has historical reasons which need not be discussed in our context." He defines "the pregnant cow" mentioned in Yasna 46.19 as "the community of good vision or religion that is ever to procreate and expand itself," as opposed to the suicidal course we are heading at present. He also opines that in Yasna 29.10 and 11, Zarathushtra seeks to teach his religion to "mortals in general."[1] Indeed Zaehner indicates that the term Mazda, "probably being his own creation," "was added to the divine name by the Prophet himself, and thus his religion thereby came to be called 'worship of Mazda' rather than worship of Ahura, the latter word having been used for a whole class of deity before his time." Humbach,[2] Duchesne-Guillemin,[3] and Kaj Barr[4] also tend to believe that Zoroaster might himself have created Ahura Mazda, while adopting Ahura from the older religion. While the antiquity of our religion does not allow us to be sure about such surmises, we have it on the authority of the prophet himself that what he had to say was "unheard of" (Yasna 31.1) and thus quite new for the Mazdayasnians themselves, which may then lend little basis for limiting his message to the Mazdayasnians only. It is for this purpose of reaching out to and reforming every soul in this universe that the prophet prays, as per Bulsara,[5] in the very opening line of his divine message: "That herewith may I spread Gladness in the Universe and Joy in all its Souls" (Yasna 28.1).

---

1    *Zarathushtra's Religion and His Pastoral Imagery*, Universitaire Pers Leiden, 1975, pp. 11, 12, and 18.
2    *Die Gathas des Zarathustra* 1, p. 74.
3    Op. cit., p. 120.
4    *Illustreret Religions historie*, p. 277.
5    "The Religion of Zarathushtra Among Non-Iranian Nations," *Journal of The K. R. Cama Oriental Institute*, 1942, pp. 35, 129.

In a very well-researched article entitled "Mazda Ahura – Ahura Mazda – Au-ramazda = Lord Wisdom," in *Iranica Antiqua*, XVIII, (pp. 199-220), B. W. W. Dombrowski seems to believe "that *Mazda* has been the real name Zoroaster experienced and professed in his messages" (p. 210). He further observes: "Surely Zoroaster did not 'distort' the name Ahura Mazda, he and his early followers created it like most other forms of god's name in a relatively short span of time through Zoroaster's repeated experiences of revelations of his god's messages, his theology (in the widest sense of the word), and the day-by-day use and practice of psalmodising in his congregation.... Zoroaster's 'true' god was what his name says: 'wisdom.' This explains the enormous preponderance of Mazda in the Gathas (which occurs 116 times in the Gathas). It suits also better to the leitmotiv of his theology than the ostensibly neutral term ahura, whose Sanskrit equivalent asura, by the way, was loaded with contents entirely different from Zoroaster's theology.... So the words daeva and baga were obviously considered unsuitable, though on different grounds, whereas ahura was chosen because of its meaning 'lord' and its background based on the idea of 'life, living, divine,' in order to emphasize what Mazda was supposed to be for Zoroaster's congregation and the world.... Important is, however, that Zoroaster's god was 'wisdom' or, much less likely, 'The Wise,' and this is seemingly further corroborated through the fact, that in the majority of references to his followers these were adduced as mazdayasna 'Mazda- worshipper.' Moreover, on coins of king Kanishka, Zoroaster's god is represented in the legend as MOZDOOANO that is 'Mazda-Besieger'." Thus, various research on this subject do not seem to support the Mazdayasna theory. Moreover, no reputable or impartial scholar has ever given any credence to this theory, which thus remains untenable and unacceptable to those that strive to seek the truth.

In the Gathas the word Mazda occurs 116 times, Mazda Ahura 28 times and Ahura 64 times. As Sven S. Hartman observes: "The name Mazdah, 'the Wise,' seems to be Zarathushtra's own designation for the supreme god, for this tallies excellently with the tendency that characterizes the names of the Gathas at large, that is, moralization and spiritualization. This tendency has resulted in the fact that those divine beings who surround Mazdah have received names that express virtues,"[1] such a tendency being more or less absent before Zarathushtra.

Zaehner explains that in adding "Mazda" to the ancient word Ahura, Zoroaster "purified the whole concept and quite changed the nature of the old religion." This "seems clear enough from the fact that in his own Gathas (this) double name is not yet fully fixed.... In the later Avesta, on the other hand, the order is almost always Ahura Mazdah," which later became Ohrmazd.[2] Pangborn implies his disagreement with the Mazdayasni thesis.[3] There seems to have been religious wars with Tanthryavant, Peshana, Ashta-Aurvant, the son of Vispa-thaurvoasti, Darshinika, Spinjaurusha, Pesho-chingha and Humayaka (Yasht 5:19 and 19). Many of these names seem to be of Indian origin. As per the *Denkard, the Prophet visited Baby-*

---

1   *Parsism, The Religion of Zoroaster*, Leiden, E. J. Brill, 1980, p. 3.
2   Op. cit., pp. 64-7.
3   *Zoroastrianism: A Beleaguered Faith*, p. 142 footnote.

*lon and "converted the city from sorcery"* (7:4:72). This is obviously an anachronism, but how could the learned Dastur say that if the Prophet confined the religion to Iranians only? Even an Arabic text of the tenth century, *Tathbīt* (fol. 87b, p. 185), notes that the Magians "do not discourage anyone from adopting (literally "entering") our religion, nor do we attempt to make him desirous of (doing) this, this being a religion with regard to which God has singled us out. But whoever adopts it is not prevented by us from (doing so).[1] Darmesteter refers to "the religious wars against Armenia."[2] "Vahram V entrusted Indian bride to the high priest ... so that she might undergo purification, including undoubtedly the barashnom, before entering his household."[3]

Boyce starts her book on Zoroastrians by saying "Zoroastrianism is the oldest of the revealed world-religions, and it has probably had more influence on *mankind*, directly and indirectly, than any other single faith" (p. 1). As I have extensively studied these influences since I won treatise-prizes on this subject at the age of 19 from K. R. Cama Oriental Institute, which inspired me to write a book on this subject, I find it very improbable that Zoroaster addressed himself only to the Mazdayasnis and not to the whole of humanity. Even such a "devout Christian" as Zaehner has boldly proclaimed: *"Christianity claims to be the heir of the prophets of Israel. If there is any truth in this claim, it is no less heir to the prophet of Iran, little though most Christians are aware of the fact."* And Boyce calls Zoroastrianism "the most influential single religion that the world has known."[4]

While this may be a rather indirect evidence of the universality of Zoroastrianism, its influence on other religions is so pervasive, profuse, and profound that one wonders if this could be at all possible had the prophet really intended to limit his faith to the Mazdayasnians. Rather, these influences seem to be an unfolding of the divine plan to make Zarathushtra's precepts reach mankind even when for various reasons seen above, the Iranians confined them to themselves despite the prophet's ardent desire to be the savior of mankind. The fact that neither any Sasanian king, nor Dastur Kirder ever refer to Zoroastrianism in their inscriptions, but only refer to 'Mazdesn' may suggest that Mazda-worship was synonymous with Zoroastrianism, and it had no other connotation whatsoever, as implied by the proponents of the Mazdayasna theory. This conclusion is supported by the concluding line of Jasa Me Awanghahe Mazda: "Such is my adoration for the Mazdayasni Din," which makes no reference to Zoroaster while talking about his own religion. Otherwise, it will be difficult to explain how such a Sasanian King as Anoshiravan 'the Just' (King Khosrow) encouraged his Turkish subjects to become Zoroastrian, as per Boyce: "These (Turks) he settled within his own borders, entrusting them with the defence of the area. And then, he says: 'I gave orders for the building of a temple by our priests. I gave them the mission of instructing the Turks who had put themselves under our authority in the immediate advantages which obedience to kings brings in this world, and the reward which follows in the life hereafter. I

---

1   See *Studies in Mysticism and Religion*, The Hebrew University, 1967, pp. 177-8.
2   Op. cit., p. c.
3   Boyce, *Zoroastrians*, p. 139.
4   *Proceedings of the Second North American Zoroastrian Symposium*; ZAC, 1977, pp. 53-4.

ordered them to inculcate in the Turks the duty to love us, to be just and faithful, and to combat our enemies; and [I bade them] teach the young people our beliefs and rituals.' Though this order was primarily political in motive, there was plainly no reluctance to accept these non-Iranians into the Zoroastrian fold, provided they were instructed and willing converts."[1] Boyce[2] and Benveniste[3] provide further proof of conversion in the Sasanian times.

In his latest research which Dr. Richard Frye of Harvard University acclaims as "significant contributions to the scholarship of the Avesta," Professor Malandra maintains: "It was, no doubt, partially his religious zeal, partially his visionary intellect, *partially his drive to proselytize*, which raised Zarathushtra from the anonymity of all his predecessors to a place in history as the prophet of what was destined to become the state religion of Iran and one of the most influential religions of the ancient world. It appears that these initial efforts at spreading the word and winning support for his views in his homeland were met with stiff opposition and ultimately failure .... Be that as it may, Zarathushtra eventually found a patron, the Kawi Wishtaspa, who not only espoused the new faith but protected it and *helped propagate it by force of arms*. Beyond *these few facts* little more can be said about the prophet's life."[4] Scholars often reject evidence from sources that do not conform to their bias or background, but I hope it may not be so in this case as Prof. Malandra expresses his gratitude to "Dr. Firoze M. Kotwal, who offered many constructive suggestions on the improvement of the text."[5] (Kotwal is an ardent supporter of the Mazdayasni theory.) Similarly, Dr. Kotwal's teacher, Boyce observes: "That in the end a fanatic should have slain the prophet seems wholly credible in the light of the fierce religious controversies and holy wars depicted in the Avesta; and before we press on to glean what can be learnt of the early history of the faith, we must first address ourselves to the major task of elucidating Zoroaster's own teachings and seeking to discover what was so new and challenging in them that they should have awakened either self-sacrificing devotion or deadly hate, so that Zoroastrianism received, like nascent Christianity and Islam, an early baptism of blood."[6]

As Hume observes under the heading, "The First Attempt at a Universal Religion, Now Abandoned":[7] "Prior to the emergence of a world-wide outlook and aim in the course of biblical history, Zoroaster was the first among the founders of the world's living religions who taught a religion which should be voluntarily and universally adopted. A form of confession of the Zoroastrian faith, which stands in the earliest of its canonical scriptures; and which is still repeated as part of the daily liturgy of its worship, asserts the belief that Zoroastrianism is permanently superior over all the religions of the world. Yea, I praise the Faith of Mazda, the holy creed which is the most imposing, best and most beautiful of all religions which

---

1    Op. cit., p. 134.
2    *History* Vol. I, p. 215.
3    *Journal Asiatic*, 1964, pp. 52-3.
4    *An Introduction to Ancient Iranian Religion*, University of Minnesota Press, 1983, p. 18.
5    Op. cit., p. vii.
6    *History*, Volume I, p. 191.
7    Op. cit., pp. 200-1.

exist and of all that shall in future come to knowledge – Ahura's Faith, the Zoroastrian creed.[1] Yet for at least the last 400 years Zoroastrians have lost their founder's vision and purpose, and have been maintaining a religion which is as narrowly hereditary as any in the whole world."

On the basis of various Sasanian texts, Zaehner asserts: "Zoroastrianism, like Christianity, lays great stress on individual salvation; yet the fate of the individual is ultimately seen in *the context of the whole of the human race.*"[2] He further observes: "In the *Denkart* it (Frashkart – the final Rehabilitation) is the natural culmination of the fructifying power of the Good Religion.... *The Good Religion can thus be seen as the religion of creative evolution, which culminates in the greatest possible growth of all, and the elimination of all that militates against life and happiness.* No wonder that the Zoroastrians could see nothing but evil in the non-Iranian religions which declared that the Creator and the Destroyer were the same. The Good Religion, however, is not only synonymous with God's omniscience, it is also the expression of his will, and his will is that all men should be saved from the Adversary.[3] The Religion is, then, his principal instrument for bringing about his will on earth."[4] Zaehner quotes from Madan's *Denkard* 268.3-8: "Since the Creator Ohrmazd created creation from one substance, he caused man to be born of one father, so that creation, being of one substance, one thing should sustain, provide for, and help another, and men being born of one father should esteem each other as their own selves. Like affectionate brothers they should do good to each other and ward off evil from each other. Thus unity is natural to man just as it is unnatural to the demons.... The union of the whole of mankind in brotherly love will spell the final defeat of the Lie. "When mankind achieves union firmly based on mutual love, the demons will lose all hopes of [ever again] being able to harm man.... At the final Rehabilitation the whole of mankind will be firmly and unchangeably linked in mutual love.... Then there will be a universal joy for the whole of creation for all eternity" (Madan's *Denkard*, pp. 9-18).

"*The solidarity of the human race which will ultimately defeat the Lie, will be achieved under the aegis of the Zoroastrian religion which at the end of time, all will confess* (Madan's *Denkard* 86.14-22).... This unity (of mankind), however, is only a reflection of the divine unity; and man, in achieving his own total integration, must also be integrated in God; and *God, to be loved, must be known, and he can only be known through the true Religion of Zoroaster* which alone confesses him to be all-good (Madan's *Denkard* 307.11-13).... *The Zoroastrian religion alone can do this, for it alone, among all the religions of the world, acknowledges God as all-good and devoid of evil in any form*[5].... God is the source of wisdom and reason, and wisdom and reason are identical with the Good Religion (Madan's *Denkard* 314.9-10). *The Zoroastrian religion, then, is itself God's eternal Wisdom.... In its extra-temporal essence, however, the Good Religion is identical with the Creator's Wisdom by which he creates and sustains the world.... The divine*

1    SBE, 31:250.
2    Op. cit., p. 302.
3    *Shikand-Gumanik Vichar*, 10.20 ff.
4    Op. cit., p. 296.
5    Op. cit., pp. 280-1.

*omniscience, which the Good Religion is, manifests itself in universal justice.*"[1]

There are evidences of non-Mazdayasnis embracing Zoroastrianism through-out the ancient times. "In Asia Minor ... Zoroastrianism flourish(ed) long after Alexander's conquest, rather as the country squirearchy in Iran itself maintained the old religion long after the coming of the Arabs.... Even stronger evidence for the Iranian religious presence in Asia Minor appears to be furnished by the Areb-sur inscriptions (which) ... provide evidence for the spread of Zoroastrianism among the *local* population of Cappadocia,"[2] and thus clearly not confining itself to the Zoroastrians settled there in the days of our Empire, as is often claimed. Again, "Syria was integrated into the (Achaemenian) Empire, and the Persians were able to induce a certain feeling of imperial patriotism.... The developments meant that the imperial faith, Zoroastrianism, was practised in Syria and was able to exert its influence strongly there."[3]

Boyce,[4] Darmesteter,[5] Zaehner,[6] and many others have established that the peo-ple of Pars, from which we Parsis (or the Irani Zoroastrians) hail, were converted to Zoroastrianism hundreds of years after Zoroaster taught. It is so very ironical therefore that had conversion been not allowed in Zoroastrianism, they would have never become Zoroastrians *even if* they were Mazdayasnis, as the zeal of spreading the faith would have subsided by then if Zoroaster had not kept his reli-gion open to mankind as well as not emphasized proselytizing. Professor Malan-dra elaborates on this thesis and concludes: "After having consolidated their posi-tion in the East, especially in Seistan, and bringing with them a sizable mass of texts in the sacred Avestan language, the Zoroastrians moved to the West, i.e., Me-dia and Persia. As they gained royal favor, the Magi, out of an instinct for sur-vival, converted (to Zoroastrianism), and in time they became a dominant force. Since Zoroastrianism already possessed, a sacred language, Median and Old Per-sian had to be abandoned and the Avestan scriptures learned. Evidently, Avestan was never well understood and fell into disuse in its new geographical setting. This accounts for the patchwork nature of many of the Yashts and other texts, as well as the terribly inept handling of the language in texts such as the Vendidad, which must have been substantially composed in Arsacid times. Before passing on to the texts themselves, I shall outline briefly the nature of the literary sources for old Iranian religion and then consider in some detail the problems of textual criti-cism."[7] To illustrate his point that the Magis (Mobeds) were not so familiar with Avesta as it was not their native language, Professor Malandra observes: "The mi-nor Yashts (e.g., Yasht 1) and texts like the Vendidad exemplify a degenerate state of the language, a dead, poorly understood ecclesiastical language. In certain cases like that of the Nirangistan (a ritual text), the language (aided by corrupt manu-script tradition) has often degenerated to the point of being unintelligible. Young

---

1   Op. cit., p. 295.
2   Boyce, *History of Zoroastrianism* Vol. II, pp. 274-5.
3   Boyce, *History* Vol. II, 188.
4   *History* Vol. II, 40-48.
5   Op. cit., xxxv-iv.
6   Op. cit., pp. 164-5.
7   Op. cit., p. 26.

Avestan texts, no matter how archaic much of their content may be, have not escaped the clumsy hand of latter-day redactors."[1] Professor Darmesteter also repeatedly maintains in his Introduction to the Avestan texts in the *Sacred Books of
the East* that the people of the Pars, including the Magis, converted to Zoroastrianism centuries after Prophet Zarathushtra preached his religion. The Avesta does
not at all mention Persia and Media from which the present Irani Zoroastrians
have originated. As asserted by Boyce, "there are not the slightest grounds (apart
from their own propaganda) for supposing that the Persians had any special lien
on Zoroastrianism, or that this great religion had to wait well over a millennium
after the life-time of the prophet for the Sassanians to create for it an orthodoxy."[2]
Moreover, Sir Harold W. Bailey's life-long research on ancient Khotan shows that
"before the coming of Buddhism older Iranian beliefs had dominated (in Khotan).
Of these older beliefs the Buddhist texts retain some traces of concepts which
could be taken over into the Khotanese Buddhism.... It has been a regrettable experience that Turkologists, Sinologists, Tibetologists, and Indianists have approached those different problems without an adequate preparatory schooling in
Iranica.... It is interesting that for the ancient Zoroastrian Avesta tradition a similar
survey was made by W. Geiger almost a hundred years ago (1882) in his valuable
*Ostiranische Kultur.*[3] Thus, Zoroastrianism got so deeply ingrained in areas
around Iran that when Arabs thrice converted the people of Bukhara to Islam, they
converted back to Zoroastrianism. The Arabs had to defeat them four times and
"make their religion difficult for them in every way" in order to make it impossible for them to remain Zoroastrian."[4]

Zaehner describes Zoroastrianism "at least as handed down in the Gathas," "as
a proselytizing religion." ... "In his war against the 'followers of the lie' Zoroaster
neither offers nor seeks a compromise: for him his opponents are evil incarnate,
and they are to be treated as such.... So long as they persist in adhering to what he
considers to be a false religion they must be attacked, but the possibility of conversion is always at the back of his mind. 'He who by word or thought or with his
hands work evil to the follower of the lie or *converts* his comrade to the good,
such a man does the will of Ahura Mazdah and pleases him well' (Yasna 33.2).
His ultimate aim, indeed, is not merely to make war on the followers of the lie, but
rather to convert them and all men to the new religion he proclaimed" (Yasna
31.3).[5] As per *The Cambridge History of Iran*, the Sasanian Zoroastrian "considered all other faiths in error and was persuaded of the wisdom of the ancients and
the superiority of his religious heritage,"[6] which is at variance from the triad's position.

As Dr. S. N. Gajendragadkar observes:[7] "A feature of Zarathushtra's teachings

1    Op. cit., p. 27.
2    "VARUNA THE BAGA," In *Monumentum Georg Morgenstierne*, I (Acta Iranica 21), Leiden: E.
     J. Brill, 1981, p. 73.
3    *The Culture of the Sakas in Ancient Iranian Khotan*, Caravan Books, Delmar, New York, 1982, pp.
     xxii, pp. 48 and 81.
4    Narshakhi, *History of Bukhara*, Translated by R. N. Frye, 1954, pp. 10-11.
5    Op. cit., pp. 83, 40, and 36.
6    Volume 3 (1), p. xlix.
7    "Indo-Iranian-Literature, Life and Ethos." *Journal of the K. R. Cama Oriental Institute*. 1980, pp.

is the regard for equality: Yasna 32.1, 33.3 say whether a man is Airyaman, Verezena, or Xvaetu, or even non-Aryan (Yasna 46.12), he can take part in Mazda-worship."

In a reply to a question: "Do you think then that this enthusiasm was wholly religious like that of the great apostolic reformers?", Dr. Mills observes: "It was mingled of course with vengeful passions, as their opponents were armed forces engaged in active operations. Unless vengeance could have come upon the haters; destruction would have come upon the saints."

In *Zoroaster: The Prophet of Ancient Iran*,[1] Prof. Jackson observes: "The principal facts which the Avesta emphasizes about Vishtaspa are his conversion, his zealous support of the Creed, and his vigorous crusading in behalf of the Faith.... Viewed in its historic light the conversion of Vishtaspa is the main event of the Religion.... Two results followed as a natural sequel to the conversion of the king and his queen; one was, that the religion was at once generally adopted by the court; the other was that it soon began to spread throughout the land.... The Prophet with his own lips asks a question, and in rhetorical style he gives the answer himself. 'Who is it, I Zarathushtra, that is thy righteous friend; or who is it that wishes to be renowned for his great virtue? It is the warrior Vishtaspa, and, with the words of Vohu Manah (Good Thought) I invoke those in his abode whom be has converted by his praising (the Religion)' (Yasna 46.14).... In reviewing the accounts of conversion of Kavi Vishtaspa one can but feel convinced of the reality of the event.... It suffices to say that even if the actual circumstances connected with the momentous event of Vishtaspa's conversion were-not wholly as tradition later represents them, they might at least have been such or similar."[2]

Dr. Boyce observes: "from the *Gathas and the tradition* it appears that it was open to any person of good will and understanding to become magavan, possessed of this gospel: that the prophet preached to women as well as men, to the poor and untaught as well as the wealthy and the learned. 'Zarathustra is not the spokesman of any individual class or group. As the one to whom Ahura Mazda has granted insight in God's design of life, he wants to win his whole ... people for his message, thus leading all of them to salvation, savah, life in its abundant plenitude, as it was in the dawn of creation. When the Zarathustra legend exalts the Prophet as the first priest, the first warrior, and the first herdsman, i.e., the man who united all the functions of the tribe in his person, this is no doubt in good accordance with the central ideas in Zarathustra's religious teaching.'[3] *It may well be that in thus offering hope of salvation to every morally good person who accepted his teachings, Zoroaster broke with old aristocratic and priestly tradition, whereby the humblest members of the community were probably consigned, to an after-life in the kingdom of shadows beneath the earth.* If this is so, it gives force to the prophet's undertaking to bring all those who follow him to Heaven: 'Man or woman ... whomever I shall impel to your invocation, with all these shall I cross the Bridge

---

   70-71.

1   Columbia University Press, New York, 1898, pp. 72. 74, 76 and 83, 67, 68.

2   See also Gherardo Gnoli's article on this subject in the *Encyclopaedia Iranica*, Vol. VI, Fascicle 3, 1993, USA.

3   Kaj Barr, *Studia Orientalia Ioanni Pedersen .. dicata*, Copenhagen 1953, 27.

of the Separator' (Yasna 46.10). *Such equity is likely in itself to have enraged the proud leaders of pagan society,*[1] as it is, I may add, enraging the Parsis now. "While I have power and strength, I shall teach men (not just Mazdayasnis) to seek Asha," says Zoroaster (Yasna 28.4). "For this I was set apart as yours from the beginning" (Yasna 44.11), says Zoroaster, his certainty stemming from beholding God (Yasna 43.5, 31.8, 33.6-7), which leads Boyce to say: "Zoroaster therefore betook himself ... to the daunting task of preaching a new doctrine to his fellow-men" (Boyce, *History*, Vol. I, p. 185). There was potential opposition or danger to the new convert, as Yasna 46.2 clearly suggests, just as it may be today to new converts. Zoroaster tells Mazda: "To do that which you told me was best shall cause me suffering among men" (Yasna 43.11), as the Peterson episode has caused in our own times.

In Yasna 43.3, 53.2, and 45.11, etc., Zoroaster talks about the Messiahs (Saoshyants) who will complete and crown his mission, but there is no reference to limiting their mission to Mazdayasnis alone. Rather, as Darmesteter and Boyce pointed out, it seems probable that each Keshvar had a Saoshyant assigned to it, for "it was very much in the spirit of Mazdeism that, having a Saoshyant in Khvaniratha, one should provide him with representatives in six other Keshvars."[2] (The Indo-Aryans believed that the whole world was divided into seven regions, the central and largest one inhabited by man, being Khvaniratha.) Thus, *Zoroaster seems to have addressed himself to all mankind, from the time of Gayomard to the end of the world when the Saoshyants will come.* The fact that later on a Zurvanite sect also claimed to be the "sect of Gayomart" may suggest a proclivity among the Iranians to claim descent from immemorial antiquity to lend authority to their claims, thus often leading the founders of Moslem dynasties to claim their descent from the Sasanian kings.

*The concept of Savior or Saoshyant* in Zoroastrianism *postulates a universal religion, as indeed attested by the Pahlavi texts* that deal with this subject at length, as already seen in this treatise. Zarathushtra mentions Saoshyants seven times in the Gathas, the Chinvat Bridge four times, and the ordeal of the molten fire at least three times. Zarathushtra refers to them as if the people in his times were familiar about these concepts. *The Cambridge History of Iran, Volume 3 (I)* lends credence to this hypothesis: "It appears that even before Zoroaster a good deal of systematization had taken place, and a coherent world picture had already evolved.... The Pahlavi books, in particular the *Bundahishn*, which is mainly concerned with creation and the nature of the visible world, have preserved a wealth of pertinent tradition and beliefs which must have been inherited chiefly from pre-Zoroastrian times" (pp. 349-350). If this is true, then the Mazdayasni religion itself upheld the belief in the coming of the Saviors or Saoshyants, and therefore it too must have been an open and universal system.

Bulsara's research[3] strongly supports this view. As per Bulsara, "the Iranians appear to have been conscious of their duty to spread their holy faith among other

---

1    Boyce, *History*, Vol. I, pp. 250-1.
2    Boyce, *History*, Vol. I, p. 284.
3    Op. cit., pp. 72-80.

nations of the world, from the most ancient times downwards. The religious litera-
tures of such far-flung nations as the Egyptians and the Chinese supported by the
facts noted in the *Shah Nama*, authorize us to say so in regard to pre-Zarathushtrian epochs."[1] Bulsara is not alone in expressing these views, but he finds that Mr.
M. N. Kuka[2] and Sir J. G. Coyaji[3] are essentially in agreement with him. In his review of Sir Coyaji's book in the *Jame Jamshed* (September 5, 1936), Bulsara has
further corroborated this thesis. Moreover, H. P. Schmidt's research lends credence to the belief that the idea of Chinvat Bridge, Gaeush Urvan ("The Universal
Soul or The Great Vision") as well as various expressions about the cow in the
Gathas, the Vedic Vala myth, etc., pre-date Zarathushtra, and have their counterparts in the Indo-Aryan scriptures. These concepts being universal, as shown by
Schmidt and Insler, it is quite probable that the pre-Zoroastrian Mazdayasni faith
itself might not have been as closed a system as we are often led to believe. This
becomes quite clear from the scriptural references about the spread of the Mazdayasni religion over all the seven Keshwars (continents) then known to mankind.

Bulsara's research contradicts the claim that Zoroastrianism was confined only
to the Mazdayasni people. Since Bulsara's standing as a scholar of Zoroastrian
scriptures is unchallenged, as can be judged from the fact that he was chosen to be
the first Principal of The M. F. Cama Athornan Institute despite being a layman
(Behdin) in an age when priestly scholars did abound, the discerning and independent thinker may learn much from what he has to say on this subject. It is possible
that the later research findings may contradict some of his conclusions, for instance, in the case of Mithraism. However, he has arrayed an impressive mass of
evidence to prove his point. Indeed the very fact that he did so four decades ago
when the orthodox feelings ran so high among the Parsis shows that the contrary
opinion would have been readily untenable then as it has been now.

It may be added that D. F. Karaka also finds historical evidence for Zoroastrian
missionary activities in China: "In the sixth century, Parsi ships used to trade with
China; Parsis were settled in China as *missionaries*, traders and refugees; that in
758 A.D. Parsis were so strong that they had, jointly with the Arabs carried out a
'riot' in Canton ... and later Masudi noticed many fire-temples in China."[4] Also
see my forthcoming paper on this subject.

It should be noted *The Cambridge History of Iran*, Volume 3 (l), published
recently in 1983, echoes Mr. Bulsara's views: "In the wake of the Iranians came
something of their religions ... it is likely that Manichaeism and Zoroastrianism
attracted greater interest in intellectual and official circles; both were recognized
by the Chinese government, and must have seemed particularly deserving of
political support as religions of Central Asians, whom the Chinese were ever at
pains to conciliate. Zoroastrianism, well established on the frontier as near as
Turfan, first appears in China early in the 6th century, when it is spared from a
general persecution of foreign religions. If the term "the Heaven-God of the Hu"

---

1   Op. cit., p. 72.
2   "Prehistoric Relations. Between Iran and Egypt," *Spiegel Memorial Volume*, Bombay, 1908, pp. 31
    ff
3   *Cults and Legends of Ancient Iran and China*, Bombay, 1936.
4   *History of the Parsis*, Volume I, p. 27.

is correctly interpreted to mean the Ahura Mazda of the Zoroastrians, it would appear that the rulers of the northern Chou state in the mid 6th century admitted the Iranian religion to their territory. In the early T'ang period there were five shrines (miao) of the Heaven-God in Ch'ang-an, three in Loyang, and others in the western provinces, and now it is clearer that Zoroastrianism is meant. The Chinese themselves were not allowed to participate in any of the foreign ceremonies. The shrines are said to have contained no image and to have consisted of a small room facing west in which Heaven and Earth, Sun and Moon, Water and Fire were worshipped. Having escaped a persecution by Buddhists in 732, the Zoroastrians succumbed to the xenophobic movement of 845, when their magians were dismissed (p. 554). The remarkable diffusion of Iranians throughout Central Asia and into China was clearly due to two causes: their love of trade, and *their desire to propagate their own religion*" (p. 275). "Among the Iranian nations, the Sogdians took the lead not only in trade with Central Asia and the Far East, but also as transmitters of ideas and the agents of cultural exchange.... *They also introduced Zoroastrianism into China*. The Chinese court recognized Zoroastrianism in the early 6th century, and a number of Zoroastrian temples were built in western China in the early T'ang period. The Chinese were anxious to propitiate the Central Asian peoples at their borders, and Zoroastrianism, as one of the religions of Central Asian people, was spared persecution, until 845, when it fell victim to xenophobic sentiments in China, and its recognition was withdrawn" (p. lxxii).

It is also worth noting that *The Cambridge History of Iran*, Volume 3 (1), which represents the recent most and most extensive research ever done on this subject, also supports Bulsara: "For their coinage, the Hephthalites developed a special kind of writing, derived from the Kushan script, and samples of it found in Turfan show that their written language was Middle Iranian. It must be assumed, then, that the spoken language of at least part of the Hephthalites was also Middle Iranian.... More important for the study of Turkish culture are the Sakas (Scythians) whose language was also Middle Iranian. These Scythians, who were known to the Old Persians and Greeks from as early as 600 B.C., held sway from the Pontic Steppes to the river Jaxartes until around the start of the 5th century A.D. In the 2nd century A.D., they became overlords of north-west India ... One branch of the Sakas who founded a kingdom in Khotan (in the Tarim basin) were zealous Buddhists who may have been converts from Zoroastrianism (but not from Zurvanism or Manichaeism).... *Sogdian Buddhism, however, showed the influence of the former religion of the country, Zoroastrianism*, which appears to have staged a revival in Sassanian times. In 630, Hsuan-tsang came across only ruins of Buddhist temples, while former Buddhist monasteries had been given over to the Zoroastrians.... the basic technical terms and proper names of Old Turkish (Uigur) Buddhism show the influence of Sogdian teachers in that they are predominantly derived, not from Sanskrit, the sacred language of Buddhism, but from Middle Iranian and, in particular, Sogdian. *Some words even betray the Zoroastrian past of the Sogdians*.... From this large number of Middle Iranian elements in fundamental Uigur Buddhism it is clear that it was neither the Indians nor the Chinese but the Sogdians who first brought about the conversion of the Turks to their religion.... *As was the case with the Chinese, the popular Buddhism of the Uigurs was influenced by the ideas and images of Iranian religion*; for instance, the fundamental doctrine of Buddhism is the law of retribution in some future existence for all good and evil deeds, called karma, a doctrine that was perhaps softened, possibly by filial piety, under the influence of Zoroastrianism. ... Many of the symbols and pictures are known from older Iranian prototypes.... The idea of "Light" and "West" also suggest some Iranian origin (pp. 614-619).... *The prevalence of Mazdaism in Georgia is confirmed by the archaeological evidence*, which includes bowls showing the sacrificial figure of a horse standing before the ritual fire-altar. According to the *Life of Saint Nino*, who converted eastern Georgia about A.D. 330, the Georgian national gods were named Armazi (to be identified with Ahuramazda of the Zoroastrian pantheon), Zaden, Gatsi, and Gaim. When Saint Nino offered up prayers to God, the Almighty sent down hail "in lumps as big as two fists" on to the abode of the heathen idols and smashed them into little pieces. Simple folk whom Saint Nino encountered at the town of Urbnisi worshipped the sacred fire of the Zoroastrians, and also images of stone and wood.... The pantheon of ancient Armenia was likewise an international, syncretic one.... Here stood a mighty golden statue of Anahita, patron and protectress of Armenia, and famed all over the Iranian world as goddess of waters and fertility. A bronze head of Aphrodite/Anahit from Satala is in the British Museum (p. 39(a)). Anahit's father was Aramazd, the mighty Ahuramazda of the Iranians, the Olympian Zeus of the Greek pantheon.[1]

"Mithra, god of covenants and of light, was also widely popular; a high priest of that name officiated at the temple of Armavir around 200 B.C. In the form "Meherr," Mithra features later in the Armenian national epic "David of Sassoun" as the Great Meherr ... The popular goddess ... Astghik's lover was the Iranian deity Verethragna, god of war and victory, known in Armenian as Vahagn. Venerated in the guise of Heracles the dragon slayer, Vahagn was the son of Aramazd (Ahuramazda) ... *Armenian and Georgian demonology has many Iranian counterparts*. Thus, the daeva or demon spirit of the Avesta was feared in Armenia as in Georgia. The Armenian word is dev, Georgian devi (pp. 534-535).... Kanishka I is in any event by far the best known and most celebrated member of the Kushan dynasty. Despite the absence of any narrative history of his reign, which is known principally from coins and inscriptions, certain facts emerge from the legends which surround his name. *It is unlikely that as Buddhist sources allege Kanishka*

---

1    *The Cambridge History of Iran* (Vol. 3(1), pp. lxxii-lxxiii) further states: "They (Sogdians) also introduced Zoroastrianism into China. The Chinese court recognized Zoroastrianism in the early 6th Century, and a number of Zoroastrian temples were built in western China in the early T'ang period.... The Sogdians in particular, as already mentioned, played an important role in transmitting elements of Iranian culture to various peoples of Central Asia through trade and religious missionaries." Elsewhere in this volume (p. 621) it is stated: "The Uigar (Turkish) version of the visit of the Magi to the infant Jesus gives evidence of this missionary activity among fire-worshippers, in other words among the Iranian people. There is also evidence in Hsuan-Tsang's report of a fire cult amongst the Turks of the western Qaghanate of the steppe in the 7th Century, while, in the inscription to the memory of prince Kultegin of A.D. 733, ... there is even a mention of Iranian Zurvanism."

*was himself a convert to Buddhism, for his foundation of a dynastic fire temple at Surkh Kotal in Afghanistan suggests that the state religion of the Kushans was a form of Mazdaism.* Yet the appearance of the figure of Buddha on one of Kan-ishka's coins confirms that this emperor was at any rate sympathetic to the Buddhists, as the Buddhist tradition maintains (p. 204).... Transoxiana was the largest country outside the limits of Iran proper that was from early times inhabited by Iranian peoples – either as settled agriculturists (the Sogdians and the Chorasmi-ans) or as nomads (the Sakas). Owing to its geographical situation it came only in particular periods into the field of vision of those peoples who have left us histori-cal chronicles and other forms of written sources (p. 232)....

"In the Achaemenian period there came fresh fusions. That god of enigmatic origin, Tir (seen in Tiridates, etc.) of the Iranians, corresponds to the old god Nebo (Nabium), the glittering planet Mercury. In the Aramaean syncretism of Hatra, Dura-Europos, and Palmyra the ancient oriental gods seem to be clothed in Iranian ideas and interspersed with like figures from the Greek pantheon (p. 498).... In 539 B.C. Cyrus peacefully took possession of Babylon, and the kingdom of Irani-an peoples, taken over by the Achaemenian dynasty from the Medes, expanded to become the first real world-empire of ancient history.... For the Sassanians, too, the lowlands of Iraq constituted the heart of their dominions, and when this heart finally fell a prey to the onslaught of Muslim armies, their rule over the east like-wise was broken. Thus *Iraq, in spite of seeming to lie so far west of the region of Iranian settlement, belongs rather to Iran itself than to "Aniran,"* as Sasanian documents describe non-Iranian areas of the empire. The name al-'Iraq, for all its Arabic appearance, is derived from Middle Persian eragh "lowlands." From the time of the Medes the political centre of gravity of Iran had lain in the west; it was here that all important cultural development had taken place" (p. 481). (Even the name of the Iraqi city, Baghdad, is Iranian, meaning "Gift of God," or "Given by God.") ... "Religious thought and practice in highlands (Iran) and plains (Iraq) in-termingled from early times. Images on seals portray the same motifs" (p. 497).[1]

While Bulsara's research may be rather outdated now, the recent research of Sir Harold Bailey still seems to support his findings about the Hunas. After studying the language of the Hunas with erudition and intense scrutiny so characteristic of him, Sir Bailey observes: "If then the basic language of the Hiung-nu (Huna) people was North Iranian, in effect a Saka dialect, the name in its oldest form Hyonnah will be the plural of the name Hyaona-, later Hyon, in the Zoroastrian tradition. In that tradition the Hyaona- were the enemies of Zoroaster's patron King Vishtaspa.... Here then is a sheer conjectural reconstruction of what happened. At a period about 1000-8000 B.C. the Hyauna-people (named in connexion with the name Huna-, Zoroastrian Pahlavi hyon) of the time of Zoroaster (circa 1000 B.C.), enemies of patron King Vistaspa, ruled by a king with an Iranian name Arjat-aspa-("winner of horses"), emigrated to the

---

1    Professor A. V. W. Jackson of Columbia University challenges Geldner's view that Zoroaster's faith "possessed rather the elements of a national religion" and asserts that "national events and external changes in the world's history have contributed" to such an erroneous impression rather than "any inherent and essential difference" between Zoroastrianism and other universal faiths (*Zoroaster, The Prophet of Ancient Iran*, Columbia University Press, New York, 1898, p. 2).

East. In 771 B.C. the Chinese were defeated by westerners and moved their capital for the next 300 years to near Lo-yang. These Hyauna called in Han times Hyonnah (later Hiung-nu) by the Chinese, were (in the second century A.D.) driven out of the East and passed in the fourth century A.D. through Khotan, where they were called Huna; and they went on into north India at 500 A.D. under the name Hara-huna and Sveta-huna, the Red Huns and White Huns. Others passed on into Iran where they were the Karmir Hyon and Spet Hyon, the Red and White Hyauna).... And this and much more is the material to be set out in full detail in my ninth volume of *Khotanese Studies* now in preparation."[1]

## Conversion and Iranian Kings

When various factors reduced Zoroastrianism to an ethnic faith despite the Prophet's ardent yearnings to the contrary as delineated above, the Iranian kings, unlike Vishtasp and Asphandyar, ceased to engage in active religious crusades to spread Zoroastrianism. The Achaemenians have set a glorious example for their religious tolerance. However, it was not because Zoroastrianism prohibited any proselytizing, since the Sasanians after them practiced it often. "Doctrinally it is impossible to reconcile his (Cyrus') verbal acknowledgments of alien great gods with his own acceptance of Ahura Mazda as the one true God, Creator of all; but in this he was only acting, however illogically, in accordance with the conventions of the civilizations he had subdued.... It would plainly have been impossible for the Persians to impose their own religion on the numerous and diverse peoples of the ancient lands they now ruled. A parallel is furnished in modern times by the British.... Evidence of religious and political propaganda made beforehand on Cyrus' behalf suggests that one of the main causes (of Cyrus' rebellion against the Median King Astyages) may have been that Astyages held to the Old Iranian faith of his forefathers, whereas Cyrus put himself forward as a champion of Zoroastrianism, and so attracted support from ... Medes as well as Persians.... There were skillful Persian propagandists at work among the priests of Babylon who had con-vinced them of the success of Cyrus' planned uprising.... and the fact that he (Sec-ond Isaiah) was evidently ardently and dangerously active in the cause of Cyrus, seems good evidence that the Persian king was not only a believer, but one com-mitted to establishing the faith throughout his realms if he could overthrow Astyages .... (Cyrus') propagandists in Ionia ... were Zoroastrian magi ... The im-print of Zoroastrian doctrines on the works of both Second Isaiah and Anaximan-der shows that these priestly agents were well instructed in the theology of their faith; ... and concerned to sway political events in order to gain recognition for the religion they served.... However sincerely Cyrus may have wished to achieve power in order to establish Zoroastrianism as the religion of state, he was clearly driven also by vast territorial ambitions."[2] As per *The Cambridge History of Iran*, Volume 3 (1), Christensen has contended that Cyrus's lenient religious policy, far from hurting the Zoroastrian believers, facilitated their proselytizing" (p. 439).[3]

---

1    *The Culture of the Sakas in Ancient Iranian Khotan*, Caravan Books, Delmar, New York, 1982, pp. 92 and 97.
2    Boyce, *History*, Vol. II, pp. 65, 43, 47 and 48.
3    In his well-researched book, *Zoroaster: The Prophet of Ancient Iran*, Jackson has written an entire

As pointed out by me elsewhere, the parallels between Yasna 44 and Isaiah are so striking that scholars believe Isaiah must have been aware of the contents of Yasna 44.

In his Behishtan inscriptions Darius complains: "Those Elamites were hostile and they did not worship Ahuramazda," the reason being, some of them had already adopted Zoroastrianism.... "This is a striking example, at their own threshold, of the Achaemanians' tolerance for the beliefs of the 'anarya'" (that is, non-Mazdayasnis).[1] Professor Richard N. Frye of Harvard University, who is one of the most eminent Iranists of our times, goes even further than Boyce, and asserts: "Why should the Elamites worship Ahura Mazda at all unless Darius felt that all inhabitants of Persis should do this?"[2] Xerxes often destroyed the temples of people hostile to him, particularly the Athenian temples. Duchesne-Guillemin, as per Jamasp Asa's translation,[3] writes: "None of the commandments of the Fravarane creed is mentioned (by the Achaemenians). Xerxes is closest to the Avesta doctrine, with his fight against the *DAIVA* cult." Thus, Xerxes seems to have shown missionary zeal enjoined by the Fravarane creed, at least for Iranians who had not yet adopted Zoroastrianism, even though they were Semitics or non-Iranian such as the Elamites.

While the Achaemenians in general tolerated alien faiths, it seems Daeva-worship and idolatry, so vehemently condemned by the Prophet, was often too much for them to tolerate. Thus, Darmesteter reports that "it was to carry out Magian principles that he (Xerxes) destroyed the Greek temples."[4] Boyce posits: "It was to acts such as this, offending their gods, that the Greeks attributed the Persians' defeat at Salamis and Plataea.... In general the religious picture which emerges from Herodotus' account of the war is no more edifying than is usual.... The Persians were ready evidently to entreat local gods on occasion, while at other times risking their displeasure by plundering and destroying their shrines. (However) *With the Daeva-sanctuary, Xerxes's words make it clear, there was a religious motive for the destruction* ... Cyrus and Darius ... would have wished all their Iranian subjects to be their co-religionists; and the evidence of later times suggests that the Zoroastrian magi would have been zealous in urging them to bring this about."[5] As concluded by the illustrious scholar Dr. J. C. Tavadia of the University of Hamburg, "the reference to 'daiva' etc., is taken in the light of the information supplied by Herodotus (I. 183). Xerxes himself speaks of one country that rebelled and where the 'daivas' were worshipped and of one 'daiva' temple which he destroyed. And the one country of which we know anything of the sort through Herodotus is Babylonia. (The other one is Egypt.) And, therefore, there is no

---

chapter entitled "The Holy Wars of Zoroastrianism" (pp. 102-123), which the Pahlavi writings (e.g., *Bundahishn*, 12.33) describe as 'the war of the religion,' based entirely on the evidence gathered from various Zoroastrian writings. He further labors on this subject in his scholarly appendix to this book, e.g., pp. 177, 199, 212, 222.

1   Boyce, *History*, Vol. II, p. 127.
2   "Mithra in Iranian History," in *Mithraic Studies, Proceedings of the First International Congress of Mithraic Studies*, 1975, Manchester University Press, p. 64.
3   Op. cit., p. 120.
4   Op. cit., p. lv.
5   Boyce, *History*, Vol. II, pp. 170-1, 175-6.

ground for supposition of Prof. Herzfeld about Aryan countries and Aryan 'daivas' whom the prophet denounced. It is true that the Akkadian version uses the plural instead of the singular in the above cases, but that alone does not justify his view, and the conclusion based upon it. Thus the doubts we expressed on a former occasion have been justified by the present study."[1] A translation of Xerxes's inscription at Persepolis, "entitled Xerxes's Prohibition of the Daiva Cult," as rendered by Prof. Herzfeld, first published on February 9, 1936 in the *New York Times* is quoted by Dr. Tavadia as follows: "And among these countries there were such where the Daivas were worshipped before. Then with (or after) the will of Ahuramazda, I destroyed the abode of the Daivas, and prohibited: 'The Daivas shall not be worshipped.' Where the Daivas were worshipped before, there I worshipped Ahuramazda along with Brazman-ic `Rta. And there was also something else which was done wrongly (or, made evil); that I did aright (or, made good).... then follow the laws which Ahuramazda has enjoined; worship Ahuramazda along with Brazman-ic `Rta;..." Thus, it is clear that Xerxes enforced or spread the "worship" of "Ahuramazda" "among these countries" "where the Daivas were worshipped before," a practice so prevalent in his days, which may suggest that he may have spread his religion in quite a few countries.

Had the Achaemenian Kings not evinced any tendency to proselyte but held it against their religious grain to proselytize anyone, the world renowned Professor Max Muller would not have made the mistake of asserting so strongly: "If the battle of Marathon and Salamis had been lost, and Greece had succumbed to Persia, the state religion of the empire of Cyrus, which was the worship of Ormazd, might have become the religion of the whole civilized world ... and if, 'by the grace of Ahuramazda' Darius had crushed the liberty of Greece, the purer faith of Zoroaster might easily have superceded the Olympian fables." The fact that even those of the opposite view referred to this quotation quite often, suggests that at least at our unconscious level we tend to agree with Max Muller. Thus, the Achaemenians, despite their excellent record for tolerance, often betrayed their original religious instinct of proselytizing, as did Darius with the Elamites, Xerxes with the Greeks, and the Achaemenians in general with their non-Zoroastrian Iranian subjects.[2]

The record of the Sasanian kings in this regard, however, is not as great as that of the Achaemenians. Jews and Christians were often "victims of Sasanian persecution."[3] The Pahlavi works denounce Judaism in no uncertain terms. The *Denkard* urges that the progress of the Jewish belief should be controlled in order to arrest the spread of its evil among the faithful, as it makes man evil and encour-

---

1    "Some Indo-Iranian Researches," *Journal of the K. R. Cama Oriental Institute*, 1942, 35, p. 22.
2    There are few pundits of the Achaemenian history who can match Prof. J. M. Cook's expertise on this subject. Therefore, what he observes about the religion of the Achaemenians assumes special significance: "This religion had a wide currency among the Iranians, and there is no sign of any feeling that it was the exclusive property of a chosen people to be jealously guarded from outsiders; otherwise the cult of the Persian deities would probably not have been so dominant in parts of Anatolia (Turkey) as it was in post-Achaemenid times. Equally there was no attempt to force Persian religious beliefs and practices on subject peoples who had deities of their own ... the one possible exception occurs in Xerxes daiva inscription" (*The Persian Empire*, Schocken Books, New York, 1983, p. 147).
3    Boyce, *Zoroastrians*, p. 120.

ages vice and immorality, and it brings devastation to the world (Vol. 1, 4, 6, and 5). Many scholars however, believe that the post-Sasanian Pahlavi authors used Judaism as a pretext for criticising another one, they could not with impunity. I have detailed it in another paper (yet unpublished). The following historical facts summarized by Sasanian seem to be poignantly in contrast with the opposite view on this subject: "Zaratusht first preached his new religion to the people of Iran where he was born; but Ormazd has commanded that the excellent religion should be spread among all races of mankind throughout the world. In their commentary on the oft-recurring Avestan formula Fravarane, the Pahlavi versionists add an explanatory gloss that every believer undertakes to proclaim the Zoroastrian religion of Ormazd to the entire world. The *Denkard* sanctions even the use of force for the conversion of the aliens. A Pahlavi treatise devoted mostly to the Zoroastrian rituals attests the practice of admitting outsiders into the Zoroastrian fold. Another Pahlavi tractate treating of the social and legal practices of the Sasanians lays down that if a Christian slave embraces the faith of his Zoroastrian master, he should be given freedom."[1]

Prof. J. R. Russell of Columbia University refers to "Kartir's persecutions" and observes: "the (Sasanian) Zoroastrian high priest Kartir boasts in his inscriptions on the Kaaba-yi Zardusht of having persecuted the Buddhist monks..... There is evidence that the Sasanians destroyed a Buddhist statue in a Kushan Bactrian temple at Kara-tepe and built a Zoroastrian fire-altar in the niche that had held the image, during a campaign *after* the time of Katir."[2]

It seems that conversion in the Sasanian times had got greatly entangled at times with politics, and more often than not the offensive came from other religious groups, often in the wake of their strong proselyting efforts which prompted the Sasanians to counteract their moves with strong efforts at reconverting their Zoroastrian subjects into the fold. The fact that such a devout Zoroastrian as King Khosrow Noshirvan resorted to converting his Turkish subjects even when there seemed to be no overt religious provocation from them, strongly suggests that "there was plainly no reluctance to accept these non-Iranians into the Zoroastrian fold, provided they were instructed and willing converts."[3] This Sasanian attitude also reflects a willingness on their part to resort to Acceptance in order to survive against the life-and-death struggles of their times, an attitude sadly missing today, foreboding nothing but doom for our survival in a rapidly changing world in which we are pitifully entrenched in a fight between a way of life and life itself. Nothing stated here about the Sasanians is meant to be derogatory about them, as they were facing grave dangers from the effervescent missionary zeal of the newly founded Christianity as well as from the Jews who too began to proselytize at that time, as also from other heresies. Rather, it is to their credit that many Sasanian kings still continued to be tolerant of all aliens as long as they were peaceable, loyal, and non-proselytizing. Even though the Sasanians may have lost some of the missionary zeal typical of the earlier Zoroastrians, they were well aware that

---

1   *History of Zoroastrianism*, pp. 325-6.
2   *Iran Nameh*, 1 (4), 1983.
3   Boyce, *Zoroastrians*, p. 134.

the prophet had not proscribed or prohibited proselytization, as otherwise a devout king like Khosrow would not try to convert the Turks or King Behram V convert his Indian bride as per the *Shah-Name* and Boyce.[1] Since most of the evidence for religious struggles in the Sasanian times comes from Christians such as Syrian martyrs or Armenian writers, Elishe Vartabad and Lazarus of Pharb, they are often biased and derogatory towards Zoroastrians in their testimony. Even so Boyce maintains: "Such persecutions continued intermittently through the rest of the Sasanian period," but they "were sometimes provoked by the intransigence of the Christians themselves"[2] and at times by their different beliefs, practices, and assumptions about God and Satan. Christianity posed as much a threat to the Sasanians as modernity is to us today, and if we show the same determination and adaptiveness as the Sasanians, we may be able to beat it.

### Neusner's Findings on the Treatment of Minorities in Sasanian Iran

Professor Jacob Neusner has undoubtedly done the most extensive and authentic research on this subject in the five volumes of his *History of the Jews in Babylonia*. He seems very fair and even sympathetic to Zoroastrians as a rule, and he does not hesitate to refute false allegations of persecution against Sasanians. He once wrote to me: "I revere your religion and wish to see it reborn and prosper. It has much to contribute to our time." What he writes, therefore, deserves our attention: "I do not conceive (the Sasanians) made a concerted effort to Iranize the lands we now know as Iraq. But they did sporadically attempt to impose their religion on the low-lying territories (Iraq), and in Armenia, to the north, these efforts went on for centuries." Under Ardashir, "The Church officials (Mobeds) vigorously persecuted other religions," observes Neusner, "were exceptionally intolerant, and would allegedly imprison and catechize one who sinned against the faith, – the inconvenience of pursuing a repressive policy over many generations, required a revision ... undertaken by Shapur I."[3] The priest Kartir "was able to undertake a vigorous program to eliminate 'foreign' minorities." "His chief interest lay in the propagation of the cult." "Widengren calls Kartir, "the most redoubtable enemy the religious minorities, and hence also the Jews, ever possessed in the Sasanian times.""[4] Neusner basically reasserts the same position in the chapter on Jews in Iran in *The Cambridge History of Iran*, Volume 3 (2), 909-923.

### Evidence from Insler's Gathic Research

Since Boyce laments that "Avestan studies have been neglected of late by trained Parsi scholars, probably because of the daunting philological requirements for their pursuit," and since she finds the translation of the Gathas by Parsi scholars "almost as free and subjective as those of the occultists,"[5] let us examine what a highly-distinguished philologist, S. Insler, has to say about the Gathas. Insler's

---

1  *Zoroastrians*, p. 124.
2  *Zoroastrians*, p. 120.
3  Vol. II, pp. 15, 35-8.
4  Vol. III, pp. 8, 17.
5  *Zoroastrians*, p. 224.

work which Boyce calls "a mine of philological learning,"[1] makes it amply clear that Zoroaster preached to all mankind, a word that appears so frequently in his exposition of the Gathas. Boyce echoes this sentiment as seen above, as also when she says "Zoroaster believed that he had been entrusted by God with a message for all mankind."[2] He renders "HA ZI POURUSH ISHENTO VAURAITE" (Yasna 47.6) as "For it shall *convert* the many who are seeking (to know),"[3] thus presenting us with a clear evidence for conversion in the prophet's own words. Moulton also translated Yasna 31.3 as: "This do Thou tell us, Mazda, that we may know even with the tongue of Thine own mouth, that I may convert all living men."[4] Further evidence for conversion comes from the prophet's own words in Yasna 31.3, which Insler translates: "That commandment which is for Thy adherents – speak, Wise One, with the tongue of Thine own mouth, in order for us to know (all) that, by means of which I might CONVERT ALL THE LIVING – ya jvanto vispeng vaurya."[5]

Zaehner also supports the contention that "the possibility of conversion is always at the back of his (Zoroaster's) mind." "He who by word or thought or with his hands works evil to the follower of the Lie or *converts* his comrade to the good, such a man does the will of Ahura Mazda and pleases him well." "His ultimate aim, indeed, is not merely to make war on the followers of the Lie," he adds, "but rather to *convert* them and all men to the new religion he proclaimed," and he quotes Yasna 31.3 in support of his claim, which is thus in agreement with Insler and Moulton.[6]

As per Dr. Mills' comments on Yasna 31.3, Zarathushtra "declares that this is the doctrine which should be proclaimed for the conversion of mankind. Here we observe that Zarathustrian Mazda-worship was aggressive and missionary in its spirit, and in a proselyting sense by no means indifferent to the final destiny of the Gentile world. (The later and traditional system announced indeed the restoration, and that not as an object proposed to the efforts of charity, but as a necessary result – so by inference.[7]) I can find no trace of this in the Gathas. Here we have only the effort to convert.... So also the general indication of the Pahlavi translator. PAVAN HUZVANO I LAK – ZIVANDAKAN HARUST-GUN HEMMUND. Observe that the religious system contemplated universal proselytism" (SBE, Vol. 31, 37, and 41). As regards Yasna 47.6, Dr. Mills comments that through Armaiti, Piety, God "will convert all those who come to her, seek her light (Yasna 30.1; 45.1). Nay, she will cause all the living to choose and believe in God (Yasna 31.3) – SBE, Vol. 31, 147."[8] Insler comments that "In general, almost all words pertain-

---

1  Vol. II, 2.
2  *Zoroastrians*, p. 17.
3  Op. cit., p. 89.
4  *Early Zoroastrianism*, p. 352.
5  Op. cit., p. 182.
6  Op. cit., p. 40.
7  See *Bundahishn* (West), pp. 126, 129.
8  After discussing this issue at length in *The Gathas of Zarathushtra* (F. A. Brockhaus, Leipzig, 1900), Dr. Mills concludes: "*All the living* could not possibly have been used by such a person (Zarathushtra) with no thought at all of responsible beings outside the Zarathushtrian community, or section of the community" (p. 123). Insler translates Y. 31.18 as: "No one at all who belongs to

ing to the final judgement (such as Kshnutem' in Yasna 31.3) are taken from the legal vocabulary" (p. 182), and as such do not imply generality. The ordeal of the molten fire too has juristical significance as per the Zoroastrian tradition. Indeed the "final judgement" is the main teaching of Zarathushtra, who was the first prophet ever to reveal it to mankind in full though to this day it may not be the re-ligious belief of some people such as the Hindus, the Buddhists, the Shintoists, or the Taoists. Thus, as per Insler at least, Zarathushtra was trying to "convert all the living" to his revelation. The word 'Kshnutem' along with some other words in Yasna 31.3 recur in Yasna 51.9, signifying the explicit message of Zarathushtra in legalistic terms: "The satisfaction ('Kshnutem') which Thou shalt give to both fac-tions through Thy pure fire and the molten iron, Wise One, is to be given as a sign *among living beings* in order to destroy the deceitful and to save the truthful" (In-sler, p. 105). The mention of fire and molten iron provide an expressly Zoroastrian background to this verse which, along with Yasna 31.3, is addressed to all living beings for accepting Zarathushtra's teachings, so unique and unusual in his days. So one could not say that these verses do not refer to winning over "all living be-ings" to his unique gospel, especially as Insler[1] has taken pains to explain how and why he has derived the word 'conversion' "in a technical sense" and why it cannot be translated as 'choose.'

That the Prophet was not talking in generality about the rival factions of the truthful and the deceitful (Ranoibya) in Yasna 31.3, but meant to make it an inte-gral part of his religion, is clear from Yasna 30.9 and 30.11 which just precede Yasna 31.3. In what is generally regarded by scholars as a reference to the contem-porary beliefs of his own Iranian people when he addresses "Wise One and ye oth-er lords," and thus meant to be a specific part of his religion, the Prophet prays that "one shall become convinced even where his understanding shall be false (concerning our ultimate goal)" – Yasna 30.9 (Insler, op. cit., p. 35). In 30.11, he speaks: "(to the adherents): Men, when ye learn those commandments which the Wise One has posed, when ye learn (there is) both a way of easy access and one with no access, as well as long destruction for the deceitful but salvation for the truthful, *then each one (of you) shall abide by (all) the commandments. Wish it so.*"[2] Insler specifies that the Prophet addresses this speech "to the adherents" and is thus not talking about mankind in general, as asserted by the opposite view. Any impartial reader can thus see that in Yasna 31.3 Zarathushtra has nothing but uni-versal conversion in mind.

Prof. K. F. Geldner, who, as an illustrious Parsi scholar, J. C. Tavadia observed long ago in 1931, is well-known for 'his great edition of the Avesta' also translates Yasna 31.3 and 47.6 in the similar vein. Geldner translates Yasna 31.3 as: "The tri-al (examination), which Thou wilt hold with Thy Spirit and Fire and Asha for (as-certaining) vice and virtue which should be a warning to the sensible ones, – tell us that, O Wise One, with the tongue of Thy mouth for the sake of knowledge, so

---

the deceitful (faction) has listened to your precepts and instructions. For such a person has (already) placed house and settlement and district and land in strife and destruction. Therefore cut these down with your weapon" (op. cit., p. 41).

1    Op. cit., p. 127.
2    Insler, op. cit., p. 35.

that I may *convert* thereby all living men." Geldner translates Yasna 47.6 as: "Therefore, O Wise Lord, at the decision through Thy Holy Spirit (and) through Fire shalt Thou make the allotment (of reward and punishment) according to vice and virtue with the assistance of Armaiti and Asha. For this will *convert* many who will experience it."[1] Sohrab J. Bulsara maintains: "The Religion which he (Zarathushtra) brought was, he says, a universal religion intended to be adopted by all mankind. These lines also indicate that Zarathushtra's was a Universal Religion. These lines make it absolutely clear that Zarathushtra had brought to the world quite a new faith which was unheard of before and which he considered his divinely appointed mission to preach to all mankind and propagate universally among them. The incidents of his holy life that we find described in the Spend Nask make this evident to us.[2] The fact that the word Mazdayasni (or any other word even remotely representing it) does not at all appear in the Gathas militates against any contention that the prophet addressed himself only to the Mazdayasnis or Iranians. Rather, the prophet uses the word Nar or Mashya, meaning man, even at such a critical moment as in Yasna 30.2, which clearly indicates that the prophet taught to all mankind. Thus, Insler comments on Yasna 30: "Verse 7 now focuses on the highlight of the prophet's teachings, ... offering protection and *salvation to mankind....* Having spoken of the Wise One's great gift *for the world*, Zarathushtra now turns to his Lord.... Therefore Verse 9 concludes, the Wise Ones and his forces should bring assistance to his prophet, so that he *may ever increase the number of followers convinced by the principle of the good....* This is *the awaited oath of man for his God* if the Almighty likewise intercedes for the cause of the good *in this world*. In the final verse Zarathushtra ... admonishes them ... to heed the commandments of his true God, for *there exists no other possibility to save themselves*" (pp. 160-1). For Yasna 31, Insler strongly reinforces Dr. Mill's contention of the universality of Zoroaster's message: "The theme of this Gatha focuses upon the precepts of the Wise Lord and the benefits which they can bring to this debased earthly existence *if they are brought to realization by mankind in its world*. To justify *the need for mankind to obey these commandments* of the Wise One, Zarathushtra searches into the essence and character of his true Lord and of the moral principles which he created that compelled him to then offer these as a means of salvation for this life (7-13). Again the prophet inquires of his God *how these Lordly values shall be brought to life on earth* (14, 16, 22).... (In Verse 7) The destiny of *the world of man and* the destiny of *the world of God are thus linked* in this cooperative function.... In Verse 19 Zarathushtra solemnly asserts that he has indeed been mindful of these truths in his self-envisioned role *as healer of the world....* The last verse again affirms to the Wise Lord that these teachings are the inspiration for any man who has chosen to serve the good cause of man and God with truth and good thinking" (pp. 178-180). As per Yasna 33.1-8, "The Wise One created this (revelation) and offered it as *a means of salvation to mankind*" (p. 211). Yasna 34.12-15 refer to "salvation from deceit *for all of*

---

1   "Zoroastrian Religion in the Avesta", *The Journal of the K. R. Cama Oriental Institute*, 1933, 24, 11-12.
2   Op. cit., p. 82.

*mankind*" (p. 220). The next Gatha, Yasna 43.5 and 6, indicate that Zarathushtra "has come to save the world with his principles of truth and good thinking." In Yasna 43.14-16, Zarathushtra "entreats" "for his God's support to bring to realization the things which the prophet has come to understand in his spiritual vision (14).... He quotes the fundamental principles which shall *heal this world*" (15-16). He prays: "Let me arise and drive out the opponents of Thy teachings! Let me along with all those who remember Thy precepts!" (43.14), which Insler compares with Yasna 31.1: "Heeding these commandments of yours, we teach those words which have gone unheard" (pp. 229-230). Yasna 44.1-2 "at once sets the prophet as an ally of God and as a person who truly understands in which direction the endeavors of *mankind* should be forcefully enacted.... How might the prophet bring this conception to realization?" (9). "This I ask Thee, tell me truly, Lord. How shall I bring to life that vision of mine!" (9). "Have they truly seen that *vision which is the best for those who exist*" (10). In 44.16, the "point is, ... there must be piety and obedience not only to the Lord ... but also to the worldly representatives of God, the prophet who shall bring the true message to *mankind* and therefore save the *world*" (pp. 70-1, 241, 251).

As per Yasna 45.6-7, "This proper behavior amid men in this *world* shall move the Wise Lord to reveal his intentions (6) and to offer care and attention to his followers" (7). "The whole poem (Yasna 45) is addressed to Zarathushtra's adherents." "Now, I shall speak of what the Most Virtuous One told me, that word which is to be heard as the *best for men*" (5). "Returning to a brief yet important formulation of verse 5 which states that the Wise One assumes his lordship through the awakening of good spirit in *mankind*, verses 8-10 describe such acts ... in the world of men.... Zarathustra urges that 'Those who are alive, (as well as) those who have been, and those who shall be, shall seek after the salvation that comes from Him'" (7), a clear indication that a Peterson can embrace his message any time. "Verse 11 ... concludes with the profound notion that *any man* who acts in this world with good spirit and with such a virtuous conception of the potential good in his own powers does indeed approach the essence of God: 'The person who, in this very way has opposed the guilty gods and mortals, ... such a person, by reason of his virtuous conception, is an ally, a brother, or a father (of Thee)!'" (pp. 79, 254-5)

Yasna 46 opens with the cry: "To what land to flee? Where shall I go to flee? They exclude (me) from my family and from my clan. The community with which I have associated has not satisfied me ... (1). I know that (reason) because of which I am powerless.... I lament to Thee. Take notice of it, Lord, offering the support which a friend should grant to a friend." In Yasna 46, Zarathushtra tried to "search for support and recognition" and is "extremely depressed" because of lack of it.... Verses 5 and 6 are concerned with the principles of hospitality and reception ... in the hope that someone might receive and accept him during his flight." "Verses 7 and 8 then ask for protection from any threat or danger that might be enacted against the prophet ..., all of this, apparently during Zarathushtra's search for a patron." If one meditates properly on these verses, one would never doubt that Zarathushtra *yearned for acceptance from anyone eager to follow him* and was even prepared to flee to another land to fulfill his mission on earth. In verses 9 and 10 *he asks for interested persons, "be it man or woman," who might help him in his mission.* Verse 12 celebrates the *acceptance of his, teachings by Friyana the Turanian.* The Turanians were so hostile to the Iranians of his times and "were identified with the *alien* Turks, who came to replace Iranians in those lands"[1] after the times of King Faridun. Although originally a branch of Iranians, the Turanians later on were regarded as aliens which may have been a main reason for their mutual hatred. Yet Zarathushtra mentions him before mentioning even ardent Iranian followers such as King Vishtaspa and his brothers, a fact that clearly contradicts the theory that one has to be a Mazdayasni or Iranian in order to be a Zoroastrian. [Avan Yasht (para. 54 and 55) provides further evidence that in Zarathushtra's times the Turanians had ceased to be a part of the Iranian people and yet the Turanian Friyana was warmly welcomed into his fold by Zarathushtra. In Avan Yasht (para. 54 and 55) the Pahlavan Tus, the son of King Naodar, "begged a boon" of Ardvi Sura Anahita "that I may smite of the Turanian people their fifties and their hundreds, their hundreds and their thousands, their thousand and their ten thousands, their ten of thousands and their myriads of myriads. Ardvi Sura Anahita granted him that boon."[2]] Verse 13 also contradicts this theory: "Who among men did gratify Zarathushtra with solicitude, that man was deserving of being famed.... We respected him among you as the good companion of truth" (pp. 81-85 and 262-3). In fact all Gathas are so consistently and remarkably eternal, universal, and spiritual in their content that the very theory of restricting its application to a particular people or period will be entirely alien to their precepts.

Thus, in Yasna 47, Zarathushtra "realized that *mankind's only hope* is in the perseverance of its own virtuous spirit.... Zarathushtra thus rightfully concludes this embracing portrait of his Lord's eternal essence of good and virtue" (p. 276). Again, Yasna 48 "deals with basic questions and reaffirmations that concern the beginnings of the foremost existence on earth. Shall the truthful finally defeat the deceitful? ... *His best precepts can then reign in this world....* this good existence shall only arise if mankind is obedient to the commandments of the one true God. Because, by his innate wisdom and benevolence, God has created the way to save the world and has revealed it to his people, but it is only by their adherence to these lordly principles ... that this state of happiness might come to pass. The choice lies with the man therefore, and thus ... the person who does choose the truthful ways and remains steadfast in his decision is of the same nature of the God who created this. The two are indeed unified in their common purpose.... *such men are truly the allies of God on earth*" (pp. 283-4).

What category of people indeed did Zarathushtra try to seek? Yasna 49.5 provides the answer: "The man who has realized that a better world can exist and who has therefore acted only with good thinking, such a man advances the power of the God of truth and his principles on earth.... Zarathushtra implies (in 49.6) that the Wise One should augment his own views if the prophet's description of

---

1    Boyce, *History*, Vol. I, p. 105.
2    SBE, Vol. XXIII, 67.

the true followers in verse 5 has not been embracing enough." In 49.7, Zarathushtra asks: "Which clan, which family, shall abide by Thy laws, thus being one
which shall give good fame to the whole community?" Here he seeks a following
from any quarters that will be true to him and the whole society which included
Mazdayasnis, Daevayasnis, and many more. This sense of totality and universality
is reinforced by 49.3 which says that *his message "has been fated for this world,"*
(Ahmai Varenai Nidatem), as also by Yasna 34.14 which says that his followers
"further the good understanding of (God's) will ... *throughout the whole community.*" Further, in 49.12 Zarathushtra hopes that "all will intercede to help bring the
rule of truth and good thinking to pass *on earth*" (pp. 59, 294-5).

Yasna 50.5 endorses this spirit of all inclusiveness: "Let wisdom come in the
company of truth *across the earth.*" As per 50.3: "She (The Good Vision) shall belong to that person who would strengthen, ... his nearest fellow creature, whom the
deceitful one shall otherwise appropriate," a sentiment which is often echoed in
later Pahlavi texts. 50.8 affirms "The Prophet shall lead those others who are similarly devoted to the ways of truth and good thinking to further the cause of these
high principles on earth.... Such allegiance must compel the Wise One to aid in establishing these very qualities *in the world of man* and thereby to *elevate the life
of man*" (pp. 99, 302-3).

Yasna 51 continues to talk about these eternal verities. 51-2 "describes the
clearest picture of ... the realization on earth of those eternal values which characterize the very nature of the Wise Lord himself. This is the good rule which must
be chosen for the *progress of the world*, and which shall achieve the highest good
and the *most fortunate existence on earth*" (51.1). In 51.20, Zarathushtra addresses
all mankind: "All ye immortals of the same temperament, let that salvation of
yours be granted to us." As per 51.21, "Virtuous is the man of piety. He is so by
reason of his understanding, his words, his action, his conception" and so not his
race (pp. 109, 310).

The last Gatha (Yasna 53) repeats these eternal truths as also the need to teach
(Saskencha) them, a requirement echoed by Yasna 31.1, 55.6, etc., a duty in which
we have sadly failed our Prophet. If one still continues to be deceitful, he damns
not only his own future life, "but he also damns the whole existence" (53.6), a
concept too broad to be explained by limiting Zoroastrianism to a single race.
Moreover, as per 53.6, "These things are exactly true, *(for) men*; exactly, *(for)
women.*" Yasna 53 concludes (Verse 9): "Such is Thy rule, through which Thou
shalt grant what is very good to Thy needy dependent who lives honestly" (pp.
113, 322) irrespective therefore of one's racial affiliations.

Insler has very frankly summed up his views on this subject in his letter dated
December 22, 1982 to the Zoroastrian Association of Quebec, as per its report
(August 1983) entitled "Non-Zoroastrians in Zoroastrian precepts: Do they have a
place?" He writes:

> I am not answering the individual questions separately because my re-
> sponse to all of them is a positive one. Let me tell you why. The funda-
> mental tenet of your religion hinges upon the individual and personal
> choice of each human being to ally himself on the side of good or evil

in the world. Since choice is a primary concept in the religion, it must also be extended in an equally effective manner to the question of acceptance into the faith of those people not born as Zoroastrians. If a person sees the benefits of the religion and chooses, by his own free will to enter it, it is a demonstration in itself of that person's decision to support the forces of good in the world. It was exactly that way when Zarathustra first founded the faith because we see in his great hymns how he urges people to follow the path of righteousness by choosing to follow the principles of Ahura Mazda. Why should it be any different today.

The restrictions concerning initiation into your religion arose at a time when other religions threatened its existence. In the free world such trials do not exist today, and since it is a religion which stresses freedom among its most important principles, the freedom to join the faith should be an option left for every person not born into the faith. Restricting acceptance into the faith only through marriage or adoption or any other type of legal bond is too restrictive. Acceptance into the faith should be left accessible to all who wish to join.

I hope these thoughts will serve your means; I have written them after deep consideration about this matter not only on the occasion of receiving your letter but during past discussions of the questions at other times.

## Renouncing of Baptism

The opposition claims that candidates for Acceptance must renounce their original baptisms, but no such requirement exists among various Christian denominations; most of them strongly upholding that Christianity is an all-or-nothing concept. No formal requirement for renouncing baptism, therefore, every being devised, acceptance of another faith is all that is necessary for one to renounce Christianity, just as there seems to be no formal convention at present for the Parsi girls marrying outside (and thereby presumably ceasing to be Parsi as per the Orthodox contention) or for a Firoze Gandhi marrying an Indira after converting to another faith, to denounce their baptism (Navjote). As a matter of fact, I know of many Parsis who have continued to wear Sudreh-Kusti after converting to another faith and we all know those that do not wear them even as they claim to be Parsis. So what are our own baptism rules before we invent Christian or other requirements for renouncing baptism which do not (or cannot) even exist because of the very nature of Christianity. It should be pointed out, as Jamasp Asa has pointed out in his comments on the *Vaetha Nask*, that conversion and reconversion were allowed in Iran, and that Sasanians converted Christian Armenians to Zoroastrianism on several occasions. In all these cases no formal requirement for denouncing earlier baptism has been noted. There is also evidence that in Sasanian times Sogdian Buddhists were reconverted to Zoroastrianism, "while former Buddhist monasteries had been given over to the Zoroastrians."[1] There is no known reference to their being accepted as Zoroastrians after having converted to Buddhism many generations ago on the basis of a formal requirement of denouncing their Buddhist vows, etc. Few scholarly publications can match the authenticity and assiduity which has become the hallmark of *The Cambridge History of Iran*, which asserts that "it became the aim of the (Sasanian) sovereigns either to convert or reclaim Christians to Mazdaism."[2] It also asserts, as already seen, that the priests played a highly active role in converting or reclaiming Christians to Zoroastrianism. It is therefore difficult to accept these objections because of the clear historical precedence in the past of converting Christians to Zoroastrianism, a precedence which despite its authenticity has left little evidence for any requirement for renouncing baptism.

It becomes apparent from the *Rivāyat-i Ashwahishtān* that there was no requirement or formula for renouncing Islam when a Zoroastrian chose to revert to Zoroastrianism. This was also true even when the convert was a Moslem by birth and not by personal choice. What is particularly relevant for our purpose here is that the only requirement specified in this Rivayat was that the convert followed Zoroastrianism faithfully.[3] Vendidad also does not lay down any requirement or formula for denouncing one's religion before adopting Zoroastrianism but on the contrary asserts that all the sins committed by the converts before becoming Zoroastrian will be obliterated from their record when judged after death, except for homosexuality (*narō-vaēpya*) per Vendidad, purposely "tossing (burying) a corpse" (*nasuspaya*) and "burning a corpse" (*nasuspačya*).[4]

## No Western Scholars Ever Wanted to Convert To Zoroastrianism

The opposition view rejects the Acceptance of those who claim to be scholars on the grounds that no other western scholar of Zoroastrianism has ever wanted to be a Zoroastrian. But not all such aspirants are (or claim to be) scholars, or could be compared to these scholars who specialized in Zoroastrianism as an academic avocation with little or no spiritual interest in it. Moreover, in the earlier days as Christians they were too devout to accept Zoroaster as an equal of Christ and to renounce him was simply unthinkable. Thus, even these western scholars that readily rescued the Parsis of the 19th century from the Christian missionaries 'carping criticism of their dualism,' etc., maintained that Christ came to fulfill Zoroaster's mission, and therefore the Parsis should readily embrace Christianity.

Even Moulton, "whose zeal for the Prophet burned a little too brightly," as per Zaehner,[5] wanted us to turn Christians. Bishop N. Soderblom and Rev. J. H. Moulton "found it difficult, as Christians, to admit a large Iranian influence on their re-

---

1   *Cambridge History of Iran*, Vol. 3 (1), p. 615.
2   Volume 3 (1), p. 499.
3   Hêmît-î Asavahistân and Nezhat Safa-Isfehani, *Rivāyat-I Hēmīt-I Ašawahistān: A Study in Zoroastrian Law: Edition, Transcription, and Translation*, Cambridge, Mass: Harvard University, 1980, pp. 184-8.
4   See Alberto Cantera, "Legal Implications of Conversion in Zoroastrianism" in *Proceedings of the Conference Held in Rome, September 21-24*, 2005, ed. Carlo G. Cereti, Istituto Italiano, per l'Africa e l'Oriente, Rome, 2010, pp. 56, 63, 64.
5   Op. cit., 161.

ligion."[1] Moulton's retort was: "we have not to argue against the perversely ingenious people who write as if there was a complete set of *Sacred Books of the East* on the shelves of a public library in Nazareth."[2] And our contemporary Zaehner "who was also a devout Christian himself" (as per Boyce) holds his breath after trying to give his very best tribute to Zoroaster by comparing him to "Moses or Mohammad" (op. cit., p. 170). Same is true of William Jackson, the guru of Dhalla.[3] Darmesteter and Boyce's criticism of our Purity Laws, noted above, has been echoed by many. This subject could be a very fruitful topic for further research in a Master's thesis or booklet.[4]

Herzfeld spent most of his erudite energy on painting Zoroaster as primarily a "backstair politician," "a cunning and hypocritical intriguer." Nyberg surpassed even Herzfeld in his scholarly attempts at depicting Zoroaster as a shaman and "drunken witch-doctor muttering gibberish." Same could be said of late Rev. Dr. Mills. To quote H. P. Schmidt, one of the greatest Indo-Iranologist of our times: "Mole denied Zoroaster even the title of prophet.... To a mitigated extent this attitude is also present in the work of Boyce, also Schlerath, ... (though) neither neglect the moral and ethical character of Zoroaster's teachings. In Boyce's work it is, on the contrary, quite prominent."[5] Thus, one cannot expect even those Westerners most sympathetic to our cause to turn Zoroastrian. Even the learned proponents of the opposition view have rejected Boyce's allegation of the prophet having three wives.[6] To expect religious allegiance from the western academicians who are primarily interested in purely academic pursuits is therefore not justified. The readiest admission of this reality comes from a noted academician, Dr. James Whitehurst of Illinois Wesleyan University, who, having had an opportunity to review my writings on this subject, responded in a letter dated December 23, 1983: "I think you are dead right in your analysis of this subject, and I wish you success

---

1   Duchesne-Guillemin, *The Western Response to Zoroaster*, 1958, p. 87.

2   *Early Zoroastrianism*, p. 296. Unfortunately Moulton did not take into account the fact that Jerusalem indeed was long under the Persian rule and "the temple of Mars at Jerusalem in the time of Khusrau II, mentioned in the Acta Sanctorum is almost certainly a Varhran fire," as per the *Cambridge History of Iran*, Vol. 3(2), p. 903 and L. H. Gray, "Zoroastrian material in the Acta Sanctorum," *Journal of the Manchester Egyptian and Oriental Society*, 1913-14, p. 44. However, an Achaemenian fire-temple can be located as far as in Southern Cappadocia, not inconceivably with all the literature on Zoroastrianism available then, before Alexander destroyed most of it.

3   "Nor is the Creed circumscribed by the borders of Iran alone," says Jackson. "From the Avesta we know that other lands and climes came in for a share of the good tidings of the Faith." "*No great religion is confined to the bounds of its own country.*" In Yasna 26.9 and Visparad 16.2, Jackson sees "an idea of universal brotherhood" (op. cit., p. 83). Jackson also gives a detailed account of the "averred conversions of Hindus" and "fabled Greek conversions" based on various evidence from Zoroastrian scriptures, and concludes: "The story of the spread of the Faith, so far as we can gather it from tradition, implies that missionary efforts carried the Avesta to foreign lands as well as throughout the territory of Iran. Tales are told of Hindu conversions, and even Greeks are fabled to have accepted the Creed" (*Zoroaster*, pp. 84-92. See also pp. 283-285).

4   The well-known French scholar, the late Dr. Paul Du Breuil, admitted at a World Zoroastrian Organization symposium held in London on June 30th, 1984 that he very much wanted to become a Zoroastrian, but the only reason he shied away from becoming one was he could not bear the idea of making his Parsi friends so unhappy and distressed by his act of conversion. (See the forthcoming report of this symposium by World Zoroastrian Organization for further details.)

5   Op. cit., pp. 88-9.

6   *Journal of K. R. Cama Oriental Institute*, 1980, 48, 193-210; Kotwal, op. cit., pp. 128-9.

in your undertaking. I read with special interest the section on Western Scholars writing on Zoroastrianism. As I believe I told you before, you have hit the nail on the head in regard to motives for scholarship. This, mixed with devotion to our own faith (on the part of many of us) makes the matter even more complicated, as you note. I myself have the highest regard for Zoroaster and for his followers, and regard your faith as probably the closest to my own (including some forms of Judaism also); still I am hardly a candidate for *navjote*, due to life-long commitments in my own community of faith."

At times even well-meaning academicians do little justice (and often injustice) to us by their fabrications. For instance, in 1971 Gnoli tried to view Zoroaster's imagery in the light of lunar symbolism, which led H. P. Schmidt to retort that "There are too many presuppositions made and too little attention is paid to Zarathushtra's own words."[1] Keen academic competition often leads to conflicting or opposing theories, when the best of these scholars build up their own theory and discredit others'. While this is okay for academic purposes, it gives one no justification to deny admission to learned aspirants of Zoroastrianism, who generally happen to be well versed in Zoroastrianism in order to adopt it, on the grounds that these scholars did not want to be Zoroastrian. And if they did want to be Zoroastrian, would the opponents find the such Navjotes valid then? Well, in our times Aga Pour-e Daoud and many other Iranian scholars have earnestly wanted to be Zoroastrian and I know at least one, Dr. Ali Jafarey, who has become one. Jamasp Asa translates Duchesne-Guillemin as saying that "the late Pour-e Daoud, the Iranian scholar of Zoroastrianism, wanted to become a Mazdean."[2]

## The Triad's Theory about Proselytizing and Non-Proselytizing Religions

The opposite view divides religions into two groups, and ascribes proclivity towards proselytizing only to those religions that "believe that whatever a man does here in this life, he will go to heaven if he professed a certain religion" and not to others, but it has little merit, and it does not mean that Zoroastrianism does not enjoin conversion, especially when conversion in Zoroastrianism is of a very different kind and postulates a willing choice on the part of the convert, which led K. R.

---

1   *Indo-Iranian Journal*, 1979, p. 112.
2   Op. cit. p. 251. In a well-researched article, "Iranian Divinities in Sogdian Painting" (*Acta Iranica*, Vol. 4, pp. 19-29), which is based on a more comprehensive treatment of the subject in his forthcoming book on Sogdian paintings, Prof. Guitty Azarpay observes: "It was on the basis of written evidence that the *majority* of the native Sogdian divinities were assumed to be Iranian concepts. This assumption now finds support in the Sogdian representational arts, primarily in the form of wall painting." He adds: "This mixture of pre-Zoroastrian and Zoroastrian practices in Transoxiana is reflected also in religious concepts of this time." He also cites the findings of A. IU. Iakubovskii and other contemporary Russian researchers in support of his claim as this area now belongs to Russia. Further proof of the spread of Zoroastrianism among non-Iranians is given by A. V. Pope and P. Ackerman: "Which class of the population of Central Asia professed Buddhism, Mazdaism, or Manichaeism, we do not exactly know but when the Arabs arrived, and indeed during the first centuries of Islam, Mazdaism was professed not only by the inhabitants of the towns, *but also by the nomads of the steppe, the Turks*. It seems, however, that the Zoroastrian religion lasted longer among the aristocracy, as we see it in the valleys of Chirchik and Angran" (*A Survey of Persian Art*, Vol. II, Oxford University Press, p. 454).

Cama to call it an act of great merit. Even a scholar so sympathetic to the opposite view as Prof. John Hinnells maintains: "In the East there are some Parsis who believe that conversion has never been a part of the Zoroastrian faith. I cannot personally, from the outside, imagine that anyone with the living passion and conviction of the Prophet, could have kept his faith to himself. I do not see or understand how the community could have grown unless he set out to convert people to his faith."[1] This contradicts the theory about the grouping of religions. Homji's own conclusion contradicts the triad's theory: "*it is not our religion, but the much later socio-political oriented custom on which we have based the non-admission of converts into our Faith....* Such puerile arguments can no longer cut any ice and it is time for our women to raise the standard of revolt against such flagrant breach of human rights and of the status of women, by appealing, if necessary, to the United Nations through their own Governments."[2] However, ever since the Ulema Committee's unanimous report supporting conversion was severely suppressed by the community in 1905, it has been as a rule so difficult for the priests ever so dependent on the Punchayats and the orthodox to say what they believe to be true in this matter.

Moreover, Christianity which has the largest following under this proselytizing group of religions, for instance, is rational in some respect and in other respects is it beyond our understanding (Isaiah 1:18 and I Corinthians; Chapter 1) and thus will defy the rather simplistic categorization in this regard. The basic tenet of Christianity is to be Christ-like, and emulate Christ's acts, not in a superficial way but in a characterological manner, so as to effect change in one's life. By following Christ, doing good becomes a part of one's life-style, not just a facade, so that one can "honor God first and honor others before ourselves" (Romans 12:10) and "be perfect (mature) as thy father in Heaven is perfect" (Matthew 5:48). The assumption that Christians begin with the acceptance of a mystery of salvation and love which can be felt but not understood and that actions, in fact, need not be performed at all is not what the Bible preaches (Isaiah 1:18 and the Book of James, verses 22-25). Thus, any deductions made from the incorrect premises about other religions are incorrect and misleading.

## Evidence from *Pursishniha*

In *Pursishniha*, Jamasp Asa and Humbach translate Question No. 48 entitled Demerit For Not Diffusing The Religion as follows (p. 71): *Question*: (If) one is very diligent in duty and meritorious deeds, (and) discriminates an upright thing from that which is wrong: (and if) he is beneficent to the creation of Ohrmazd and its increaser, (but) does not propagate the Religion, then, is it a merit or not? *Answer*: He is not diligent in duty and meritorious deeds, and he is not a discriminator, and he is not beneficent, and he is not an increaser, and he is not good, and he does not (perform) duty and meritorious deeds, who does not propagate the Good Religion. He has not conveyed, O Zarathushtra, he will not convey from now onwards. He is not a diffuser, O Zartuxsht, (i.e., an upright thing has not been propagated by

---

1  As quoted by H. B. M. Homji, "O Whither Parsis," Karachi, 1970, from *Parsiana*, January 1974.
2  Op. cit., p. 127.

him) ... (i.e., he does not propagate Religion, and duty and meritorious deeds, as he ought to propagate).[1]

## Unanimous Approval of the Peterson Navjote by the Council of Mobeds in Iran Vs. the Opposition's Concern for Overseas Reaction

Every argument that possibly could be used to deny Acceptance by its detractors has been employed here or elsewhere, and so their concern about its possible repercussions in some countries is understandable. However, the Council of Mobeds in Iran, the highest authority in Iran on Zoroastrian doctrines, have found little basis for such a concern and have unanimously supported Acceptance on scriptural grounds on May 24, 1983, exhorting that: our Prophet "has never reserved ('the propagation and promotion of the religion') for the Aryans or for a particular caste of people," which differs so radically from the triad's exhortations. These Iranian Mobeds well know the tortures and oppression they had to suffer for nearly 1300 years to keep the flame of Zoroastrianism burning, and yet they have remained faithful to the Prophet's teaching on conversion in their conclusion: "If we Zoroastrians believe that our religion is one of the great living religions of the world, and that it is beneficial to all the peoples of the world, we must persevere to propagate it. We must accept persons who want to· embrace Zoroastrianism. In fact we should follow those who set us an example."[2] The Moslems in Iran have now begun to study our scriptures, and are more aware of what they say on conversion than the Parsis, whose views are tinted by Hindu influences as also by their peculiar socio-economic and psychological factors, if not by community politics. And they know how radically different and benign the Zoroastrian concept of conversion is in view of Zoroaster's insistence that "every man is free to choose between the two parties for himself."[3]

One cannot afford to be complacent just because the Parsis live in a free India as no one can guarantee the tenure of a free India, and there is often criticism of their exclusive ways and practices by others. Living in a democracy has its price too and requires respecting the fundamental rights of others such as those guaranteed under its constitution. Thus, Article 25(1) of the Indian Constitution guarantees freedom of conscience and free profession, practice and propagation of religion. As per Article 13 of the Constitution, even the States cannot take away the fundamental rights guaranteed by the Indian Constitution. As observed by an eminent legal expert, Mr. S. R. Vakil: "The right is conferred not only on Indian citizens, but all persons and this right is enshrined in the Constitution and it cannot be taken away by any alleged negative custom. The opinion therefore expressed by the (opposition view) ... that such Navjotes are illegal or invalid lose their weigh-

---

1   *Pursishniha: A Zoroastrian Catechism*, K. M. Jamasp Asa and Helmut M. Humbach, Part I, Weisbaden: O. Harrassowitz, 1971, pp. 70-71.
2   The opinion of Boyce, who has not only studied Zoroastrian scriptures and history, but has also lived among the Zoroastrians in Iran, tells a lot: *"Irani Zoroastrians have never been opposed to conversion, though, historically, seeking to convert Muslims would have meant death.* There has been much controversy concerning the matter among Parsis." (*Textual Sources for The Study of Zoroastrianism*: edited and translated by Mary Boyce, Manchester University Press, 1984, p. 153).
3   Zaehner, op. cit., p. 40.

tage completely.... On the advent of Independence and coming into force of the Constitution of India two fundamental rights which are guaranteed by the Constitution are the fundamental rights to freedom of religion and conscience – both rights were advocated by our Holy Prophet thousands of years ago. In view of the express language of the Constitution any usage to the contrary has to be considered to be void, inoperative, ineffective and abrogated. Lastly, although it may hurt our High Priests and half-baked scholars, it is not their function to determine *NOW* whether a person who is not a Zoroastrian by birth can profess Zoroastrian religion and wear Sudrah and Kusti."[1]

## Concluding Remarks

A resolution of this life-threatening problem is entirely possible without in any way jeopardizing its rights or existence or religious observations. The religious sentiments of the North American Zoroastrians tend to favor acceptance of non-Zoroastrians amidst them based on their own study and scrutiny of our scriptures.

The appeal of Dasturji Dhalla whose international scholarly stature remains peerless among Parsi scholars, from his Autobiography (pp. 712-715) is still relevant: "*Our press and our communal organizations are continuously waging a bitter controversy over the Jooddin question.* Throughout all these bickerings there runs a major strain of prejudice, conflict and vengeance. The Jooddin question is surveyed on the surface without going into the root of the matter. We never care to study this poignant problem calmly, delving deep down into its intricacies and working on it in a scholarly, scientific, and statistical manner.... *Without the slightest sentimentality it can be said that this Jooddin question has become the thread on which hangs the very existence of this microscopic community....* The time has passed for trying to solve this question through party-politics. Sane and serious thinkers, learned and educated leaders and intellectual social workers of all sections of the community have remained aloof from this intricate problem. I humbly appeal to all these to unite on a common platform and to call a conference to examine with an open mind this difficult and gigantic question on which depends the very existence of the community." For this reason I felt the need to examine gender equality in Zoroastrianism, and present it in Appendix II in this book.

Since most of the Iranian and North American Zoroastrians have already taken initiative in this regard, a non-resolution of this problem by others may become plague us as a constant cause of conflict with them. A resolution of this problem will unite them, just as its non-resolution will ultimately divide them. Everyone must concede them the right to exist and continue its traditions and cultus. However, inaction in this regard may jeopardize its very existence more than any encroachment on its right to exist. In view of their peculiar socio-economic conditions others may not want to go in this respect as far as the North Americans tend to go by their circumstances and destiny. Moreover, a clear distinction needs to be drawn between a Parsi and a Neo-Zoroastrian. New converts will not be entitled to any benefits of the Parsi trusts, etc., in view of various legal verdicts.

This ancient community is going schizophrenic because in the unconscious

---

1   *Parsis and Conversion – An Objective Study*, pp. 23-27.

mind of its remote, ancient past lies vague memories of universal acceptance which, though severely repressed by its recent past, are slowly but steadily re-emerging into its consciousness, forced by the dictates of its helpless present and bleak future. One can either completely block out these memories and refuse to accept reality, or continue to rediscover the past, until the past and present conditions are reconciled in a harmonious whole, and thus cease to be schizophrenic any more. There is such confusion and disparity of views on this topic that even the educated person who is so eager to know the truth feels completely lost. This does not always mean that no one is telling the truth, but rather that everyone is telling the truth as he or she perceives it from their own cognitive conditioning, even becoming oblivious of one's own past writings if not in consonance with the present views on this issue, and such cognitive selectivity on each one's part eludes our grasp of the truth on such a highly emotive issue, the most illustrious example being that of one of the most illustrious Parsis, Sir J. J. Modi, as pointed out by Justice Beaman. May Ahura Mazda therefore ultimately guide them to the truth and grant them the wisdom and strength to live accordingly. "May we be such as move the world towards Renovation, O Wise One!" (Yasna 30.9), and not be its casualty. Amen!

## PART II: Rebuttal of the Trio's Response

It is very frustrating to respond to the trio's rejoinder to my *Argument for Acceptance* as it is so circuitous and synechdochal, and misses most of the evidence presented by me. Unfortunately in their rejoinder *Antia's Acceptance: A Zoroastrian 'Armogih' (Heresy)* from the beginning to their concluding remarks a very flagrant, unscholarly and ubiquitous tendency towards deriding Antia as a person, starkly stands out as their strategy, instead of addressing the real issues raised by Antia, and it is so unbecoming of their status. It begins so ostensibly by quoting Alexander Pope "A little knowledge is a dangerous thing. Drink deep, or taste of the Pierian Spring...." However they leave us with no taste of the Pierian Spring but only with an acrid taste of epistolary yammerings and mordent vilifications, even though they ostensibly set out to show the fallacy and illusiveness of Antia's arguments. Although they concede that Antia does not claim to be a scholar, they scorn his "long-winded attempt" instead of addressing all the points raised by him. It is very frustrating to deal with the Trio's response to *The Argument for Acceptance* as it is so circuitous and obfuscation radiates from the very first paragraph. One may wonder on what basis they can state Antia "implies that only in the North American milieu will Zoroastrians be able to study the actual teachings of Zoroaster ---- (p. 2)." No page reference is offered to support it. Certainly, this is a distortion of his views, and it is not even central to his thesis or acceptance. They resort to such divergence too often to convince any truth seeker.

The trio warns the community that acceptance "would inevitably toll its death knell" but the reverse is rapidly emerging as the sad truth. They denounce Antia as a "modern self-seeker who claims to be expert," "half-baked self-proclaimed interpreter," consequently having "opinion (that) are crude, ill-considered, often at times puerile – ridiculous," and " not tempered by the study of original texts," etc. I would gladly admit to be "half-baked" if they showed me the way to be "fully-baked" and show me even one such original text they accuse me of being ignorant of. Regrettably, however, their rejoinder is so diffuse, so off-the-mark, so irrelevant to the actual issues raised, so sophistical, so bereft of textual evidence, that for years I saw little sense in responding to them, and left it to the readers to judge both responses. Many enlightened souls shared the same feeling with me. However as I finally set out to publish my book on this subject, I realized the book won't be complete without a rejoinder once and for all, especially as the seasoned reviewers such as those of *Parsiana* failed to realize its sophistry, and the triad's own irrational and comically irrelevant reliance on Boyce, rather than on actual textual evidence.

### "It is God's Will That We Are Born Into a Particular Religion"

Those who oppose Acceptance rely often on Mary Boyce. All the same, they overlook many of Boyce's contentions, such as that the Parsis had become "as a caste within Hindu society" and the Rivayats advised the Parsis to allow their Hindu servants to enter the religion if they wished so. They maintain that "people are born into a particular religion according to God's will and plan" and quote Yasna

43.1 as their basis. However according to Yasna 43.1 God "rules at will," and so one speaks of Asha, Armaiti, and Vohu Mana *which only Zarathushtra taught for the first time in human history.* He has also emphasized free will as per Yasna 30.2 and 31.9. They finds the Rivayat of 1778 as recommending the Hindu servants' acceptance in the faith as fraudulent, but there are many other Rivayats recommending it too. Yasna 43.1 does not at all have the implication they claim just because Ahura "rules at will" and grants wishes, since one prays therein for seeking Asha, Armaiti, Asha, and Vohu Mana, which are the very basis of Zoroastrianism, and not of any other religion. They contend that Boyce's remarks do not support conversion as she indicates "the difficulties a new convert would face and (it) is another reason why there has been no conversion." (p. 4). But, at its very outset, Boyce describes Zoroastrianism as the world's first proselytizing religion. She offers us many other instances of conversion, as already shown.

They base their claim that people are ordained by God to follow the religion they are born into on the basis of Yasna 43.1, a claim which is not only *not* supported by it, but is also proven so very false by all the other Gathic verses I have quoted.

This dictum for adhering to the religion one is born into clearly reflects a Hindu or theosophist or Ilme-Khshnoomist belief, which is not in consonance with Zoroastrian teachings. One may well find an echo of their views in Dr. F. S. Chiniwala's book *Essential Origins of Zoroastrianism*, 1942, Bombay, pp. 190, 191, 202, 204, 205, and 295. The reader is warned in the Introduction that "Khshnoom line being most abstruse and relating to the unseen realms and the spiritual facts of nature will be found most difficult as it were Greek and Latin by the usual groomed student of Avesta". (p. 12). I find it to be so true despite my avidly reading up on it from my early teen years, inspired by the saintly personality of this author himself as well as by the fact that the founder, B. Shroff, was the next door neighbor of my mother and Guru Dasturji Dabu, and my both parents knew the Chiniwala family rather well and Jehangir Chiniwala and my father also studied together in the Wilson College in Bombay. My mother corresponded with Ustad Shroff's daughter for long. (It is, however, worth noting that Ilme Khshnoom also declares that in the end all mankind will become Zoroastrian). Boyce, following Dr. Haug, regards Ilme Khshnoom "as a thorough-going adaptation of theosophy with belief in one impersonal God, planes of being and reincarnation, much planetary lore and a complete disregard for textual or historical accuracy,"[1] which is so very antithetical to what Zoroaster taught. The staunchly conservative philologist, Dr. J. M. Unwala also derided the Ilme Khshnoom in "Interpretation of the Avesta scriptures", 'as decidedly not scientific', at the XII All India Oriental Conference in 1944, (p. 9). Dr. James Moulton, who was a contemporary of the founder of Ilme Knshnoom, describes it as "a thorough going adaptation of Theosophy, naked and unashamed, Mahatmas and all." He notes with some sarcasm: "The doctrine of the esoteric meaning of ancient scriptures is conveniently applicable all around. Every 'prophecy of scripture is of private interpretation', belonging to the adepts

---

1    *Zoroastrians*, p. 205.

alone.[1]

In the Ratanbai Katrak lectures, University of Oxford, 1985, pp. 20-21, John Hinnells seems to explain why the Parsis, unlike the Iranis, do not tend to favor conversion: "In ancient Iranian religion there was the idea that Zoroastrianism is not simply 'the Good Religion' but *the 'best religion'* and it is one for which over many centuries Zoroastrians have suffered and died. But most modern Zoroastrians" (i.e. Parsis) "believe that there is truth in all religions; hence there is not the same necessity for conversion. Further, they argue that religion is intimately related to personality. Parsis commonly believe that people are born into the religion that God thought appropriate for them. In India many Parsis, under Hindu influence, accept the idea of rebirth (it is not part of Historical Zoroastrianism); they therefore generally argue that one is born into the religion appropriate for that stage of the soul's development." Even so, they maintain "that it was only during the heretical (Zurvanite) phase of imperial Iranian history, the Sasanian times, that there was evidence for Iranians seeking to convert people to Zoroastrianism." Hinnells wisely comments that the terms 'race' and 'ethnicity' "remain ambiguous," and are "fluid concepts determined not by any objectively defined essence but as a result of social processes." (p. 46) As a close associate of Boyce, Hinnells's views are helpful in properly understanding Boyce's observations.

If one must stick to the religion we are born in, then why do our scriptures so virulently condemn the Bible as compilation of "lies" and "falsehoods" (*Dadestani Dini* 37.89 ff), "faulty in every way, senseless, ignorant and foolish", "full delusion" (S 14), "feeble story about the inconsistency, unbounded statements, and incoherent disputations of Christian believers all wickedness has been known to arise through the devilish faith" (*Denkard 3*)[2] and "its false knowledge and weakness injures the world." Such remarks could be seen mistaken now, but even so how could the scriptures ever dare to say so if God left us no choice about religion. See also *Shikand Gumanik Vichar* 15. *Cambridge History of Iran*, Vol. 3(2), pp. 560-63 even states that "this last great treatise of the later period of Mazdaism," was intent on "establishing its superiority over the other religions – Judaism, Christianity, Manichaeism, and Islam, all of which he refutes in great detail."

And then why does the *Denkard* uphold Zoroastrianism and denounces Judaism for believing that evil comes from God (*Denkard* 3.150[3]). Madan's *Denkard* 251-2 proclaims the same: "The original world of false religion is that evil comes from the Creator: in this is contained all the evil that creatures suffer from the original creation till the final Rehabilitation. Thus from being beguiled by this original word of false religion proceeds the corruption of character -----." The same sentiment is more or less expressed in Zaehner, *Teachings of the Magi*, pp. 84, 94.

All major religions allow converts in some way or the other for the most part as otherwise they would not be major religions today. While Judaism has re-

---

1    *The Treasure of the Magi*, Oxford University Press, 1917, pp. 184-6.
2    Sanjana's translation, volume IV, p. 456.
3    Sanjana IV, p. 211.

mained primarily an ethnic religion throughout history, it too has often welcomed willing converts. The book of Ruth gives a favorable example of a non-Israelite adopting Judaism, even making her a close ancestor of David. One of Jonah's messages was that non-Israelites can have access to the God of Israel. As the learned author, Lester L. Grabbe notes: "This does not mean that Gentiles would be accepted just as they are because conversion to Yahwism is presupposed, but it goes against the narrow genealogical and exclusivist view of some circles. Some scholars interpret it as 'direct opposition' to the views of Ezra-Nehemiah."[1] Grabbe reports that the Idumeans (Edomites) belonging to Arab tribes, were "assimilated to Judaism voluntarily. Not all Idumeans may have accepted willingly the decision made on their behalf by the leadership and therefore conversion may have been forced on some. Nevertheless, that the Indumeans retained their Judaism, is strong evidence that the conversion was more or less voluntary (p. 330)." Another Arabian tribe living in Galilee, the Itreans, underwent similar conversion (p. 331). There were many converts to Judaism among the Roman upper class, "possibly even through active proselytizing (as is stated by Dio)," p. 398. Moreover, Helena, the queen mother of Adiabene was "a convert to Judaism" (p. 439). Grabbe further observes: "The idea of someone renouncing paganism and joining the Jewish community is an old one, with its root in the Old Testament tradition. Ruth is a prime example. We also have various references to proselytizing in the literature showing that converts were made and – in some cases – actively sought (p. 534)." Considering the fact that Grabbe reviews a rather relatively short period of Jewish history, that is, roughly from 539 B.C. to 138 A.D., sufficient evidence of conversion among the Jews during this brief period is quite glaring. I have so much more data on this subject that perforce I have to present it a separate treatise due to constriction of space. However, one wonders if all major religions allow or encourage converts, why God made rules different for Zoroastrians?

## The Argument for following the Religion We Are Born Into

If one has to follow the religion in which God gives us birth, it leads to innumerable logical problems as we have already noted. Moreover, how true and logical this could be when certain religions like Christianity, Islam, Bahá'í, and Buddhism actively seek to convert others in their faith as part of their mission on earth? And Zoroastrianism itself began as a missionary religion as suggested by the ample evidence quoted for it in this text. What religion does the trio think one belongs to when one is converted, forcefully or persuasively, to the other religion? And what about atheists, aborigines, and those who do not belong to any of the major religions? As Plato (ca 400 B.C.) commented long ago:

> "A certain portion of mankind do not believe at all in the existence of the gods."

Thus, this reasoning not only defies the Zoroastrian beliefs, but also the laws of logic and rationality, and apparently may be embracing the beliefs of Hinduism. However, even under Hinduism one is expected to follow everything else that

---

1    *Judaism From Cyrus to Hadrian*, Fortress Press, Minneapolis, 1993, pp. 46-7, 52.

comes with one's birth – one's occupational status, however low or unskilled it may be, caste status, location, etc., which is contrary to what Zoroastrianism teaches. Visperad 15.1 even exhorts us to transform the unskilled persons into skilled ones.

## Myths About the Purity of Races.

Any attempt at nullifying the validity of conversion on the grounds that God fittingly placed us in the race or religion we are born into, is fraught with serious problems. "Scientists are generally agreed that all men living today belong to a single species, HOMO SAPIENS, and are derived from a common stock, even though there is some dispute as to when and how different human groups diverged from the common stock.

"Because of the complexity of human history, there are also many populations which cannot easily be fitted into a racial classification. - - - - National, religious, geographical, linguistic, and cultural groups do not necessarily coincide with racial groups; and the cultural traits of such groups have no demonstrated connection with racial traits. - - - - There is no evidence for the existence of so-called 'pure' races. - - - - In regard to race mixture, the evidence points to the fact that human hybridization has been going on for an indefinite but considerable time. Indeed, one of the processes of race formation and race extinction on absorption is by means of hybridization between races. – There is no evidence that race mixture produces disadvantageous results from a biological point of views. The social results of race mixture, whether for good or ill, can generally be traced to social factors."[1]

The Jewish people are often regarded as a pure race but "at a very early date, (they) interbred with such neighboring peoples of Western Asia as Canaanites, Philistines, Arabs, Hittites, etc., and thus, even if the Hebrews were originally a pure race, there had been extensive crossing with several other races even in antiquity. – Thus despite the view usually held, the Jewish people are racially heterogeneous; its constant migrations and its relations – voluntary or otherwise – with the widest variety of nations and peoples have brought about such a degree of crossbreeding that the *so-called people of Israel can produce examples of traits typical of every people.* – Hence, so far as our knowledge now goes, we can assert that Jews as a whole display as great a degree of morphological disparity among themselves as could be found between members of two or more different races. – The Bible itself contains numerous references to inter-marriage, both during this early phase of Israel's history and later. – One plausible explanation for the large number of Jews outside Palestine is based on the active proselytism that existed at the time. It was known, for example, that conversion to Judaism was common enough to lead many communities of Jews to create a special class of adherents with full recognition being reserved for their children. – One wonders what might have been the course of Christianity if this settlement pattern of the Jews had not exist-

---

1   *Race and Science: A collection of essays presenting current scientific knowledge on race differences and racial prejudices*, UNESCO, Columbia University Press, New York, 1961, pp. 502-6.

ed. – One final point about race that needs clarification concerns the common error that pure races exist. – But even if racial entities could have been completely isolated from their very inception and kept immolate thereafter from genetic contamination with any other group, genetic theory requires that variation within the group inevitably be present. – In other words, uniformity of race never existed in the past and is an impossible conception except under a kind of artificial and rigorous control that has never prevailed in the affairs of men."[1] These views are not my concoctions but are the findings of the experts on this subject. The literature refuting the racial purity of Jews is so vast I cannot include them all here. However, the above findings should suffice to make one realize the fallacy of rejecting conversion on the grounds that one has to stay in the race or religion one is born into.

There are so many divisions within all religions. So what group one must be born into? Even as I was writing this I read the following in the Wall Street Journal (dated April 4, 2008), which well illustrates this dilemma:

"In 1953, a group of Muslim leaders in the Punjab agitated to have a rival group declassified as Muslims by the still young state of Pakistan. The government's response came in the Munir Report, an eloquent expression of the state's position on religion:

"If we attempt our own definition as each learned divine has done, and that definition differs from that given by all others," the report declared, "we unanimously go out of the fold of Islam. And if we adopt the definition given by any one of the ulama, we remain Muslims according to the view of that alim (scholar) but kafirs (infidels) according to the definition of everyone else." With no agreement on what it meant to be a Muslim, how on earth could Pakistan legislate as if it were an Islamic state? Such debates form the core of Ayesha Jalal's subtle "Partisans of Allah."

Christianity's insistence on accepting Christ as one's Savior as the only way for attaining salvation also causes logical impasse for this theory. How could God give us birth in the religion that supposedly matches our Keshas, Varana, Jiram, etc. and yet He "chooses" only one faith through which salvation could be possible: "I am the way, the truth, and the Life: no man cometh unto the Father, but by me." (John 14:6) and "For by grace are ye saved through faith: and that not of yourselves: it is the gift of God; not of works, lest any man should boast." (Ephesius 2:8,9). Some faiths firmly believe in converting the whole humanity and so won't rest until then as they believe theirs is the only true faith while some other faiths do not subscribe to such beliefs. Why would God create such inequities and inequalities among the religions He Himself "creates"? One can argue ad infinitum against this theory, but contradictions delineated above should suffice for a rational person, our Prophet being a rational thinker par excellence.

The same is true for the Hindu race, as pointed out in a very scholarly way by Benjamin Walker.[2] Here I can only quote his salient comments due to the constraint of space, though it does not do justice to his well-documented and elaborate

---

1   Ibid, pp. 35, 37, 38, 125, 148, and 162.
2   *The Hindu World*, Volume II, Frederick A. Praeger, New York, 1968, pp. 74-81.

thesis.

"The still widely held notions that the Indian castes and peoples have as a result of the social system of the varnas, preserved their original strains; that the Brahmin is of 'pure blood', a descendant of the highest class of the Aryan immigrants; that the Kshattriya is a scion of the knightly families of yore; that vaisyas are the generations of simple peasants of the Aryan highlands; all these are among the fondest illusions of students of Indian sociology. The truth is far removed from these conceptions, and the so-called historical tradition that insists on these features of India's caste origins is a myth which was long regarded as authentic, and provided for the most regressive pattern of thinking in India."

"Anyone who attempted to sort out the pedigrees of the great dynastic families of Ancient India will have discovered that, apart from the difficulty of reconciling the conflicting versions given the available sources, all tribes, both Aryan and non-Aryan, are related from an early stage in their history by ties of blood through a steady process of intermarriage. This development is reflected in their pantheons, for the Aryan deities began to contract matrimonial alliance with the goddesses of the native people soon after their arrival in the Indian plains."

"The early priests, like the early kings, sprang from the union of aboriginal rishi and royal families with the priestly and princely families of the Aryan settlers. Nishada and other non-Aryan rulers of the lowest caste thus rose to become kshattriya kings. The whole fabric of Indian genealogies is shot through with the most variegated alliances of the Aryans and other invaders with indigenous and aboriginal tribes."

"There are numerous recorded instances of native rulers and chieftains of local tribes being accepted as Aryans, like the Dasa chief Balbutha, who is mentioned in the *Rig-veda* as having adopted the Aryan culture and patronized Brahmins; and evidence is available in ancient Sanskrit literature of gypsy bands and wandering tribes straying into Vedic encampments and being admitted into the Aryan fold after performance of purifactory rites. Says A. D. Pusalker, 'The Brahmin missionaries who accompanied the kshattriya conquerors paved the way for social and cultural contact by allowing high-born Aryans to marry non-Aryans.'"

"Many prominent Rig-vedic Aryans were the sons of slave mothers. K. M. Sen observes, 'It is significant to note that many of the best known and most admired characters in Hindu literature were half-caste.' Honored Vedic personages like Ausija, Kavasha and Vatsa were the sons of dasa (slaves) or sudra (low-caste) women. S. K. Chatterji believes that 'Krishna was at least a half-caste.' Suta and Vidura were sudras; and Vasishtha and Agastya were born of a prostitute. There is a verse in the Mahabharata which says Vyasa was born of a fisherwoman. Many others who were originally not twice born, became Brahmins."

"The *Rig-veda* laments the prevalence of marriages between 'black' and 'white' and the fact that Aryans have been made out of Dasas; and there is one anguished cry, almost moving in its utter futility, 'O Indra, find out who is an Aryan and who is a Dasa and separate them.' The Aryans were at length obliged to bow to the inevitable. Old racial prejudices lingered awhile, but after the first antipathy and xenophobia were overcome, the indigenous inhabitants were slowly accepted as Aryans if they fulfilled certain basic religious requirements. Speaking of this period Havell says, 'It is probable that the Aryans were always numerically a very minute fraction of the people of India; and even among those who called them-selves Aryans there were many of mixed blood.'"

"The convention of tracing a person's decent and preserving genealogical trees showing his pure lineage from Vedic and Epic heroes, is a medieval expedient, first propagated by the Brahmins after the miscegenation of Aryan with non-Aryan had become universal and complete. The ancestors of the great Hindu dy-nasties do not shine as exemplars of racial purity or religious orthodoxy. All the great families of ancient India were of mixed origin, Brahmin as well as Kshat-triya, whatever they might have been before the Aryan advent. This needs reitera-tion since there are large numbers of educated Hindus who are carried away by sentimental attachment to the heroic names of the legendary past, and like to think of them as 'pure kshattriyas in shining armour', of uncontaminated lineage and mighty prowess, united with pure virgins of like unimpeachable descent. But it must be emphasized: pure families and pure castes are pure fiction."

"Even by the Vedic period the Aryans were already tainted by low caste mar-riages and their pedigrees confused by ties with families of low birth, alliance with dynastic houses that were aboriginal, or union with maidens who bore every trace of indigenousness. Non-Aryan women were frequently mentioned as the brides of Aryan heroes.... The process of miscegenation received a further impetus during the Greek and barbarian periods.... Tarn thinks that the Euthydemids actually put into practice the dream of Alexander of uniting East and West, and their success can be measured by the remarkable assimilation of the Greeks with Indians. The Bactrian Greeks as a whole were so completely intermixed that they have been called 'the Goanese of antiquity.' The complete absorption of the Greeks was merely a matter of time; they became first Eurasians, and finally Indians." What I have left out of this evidence is equally important, but this should suffice. One may also refer to S. V. Viswanatha's *Racial Synthesis in Hindu Culture*, London, 1928. We have already quoted *Denkard* 268.3-8 as advising us: "Since Creator Ohrmazd created creation from one substance, he caused man(kind) to be born of one father, .. and so ... being born of one father should esteem each other as their own selves."[1]

Even before the Aryans entered the Indian and Iranian subcontinents, "the essence of their shared parental Indo-Iranian identity was linguistic and ritual, not racial," according to David W. Anthony, who is the foremost researcher on this subject. "If a person sacrificed to the right gods in the right way using the correct forms of the traditional hymns and poems, that person was an Aryan. Otherwise the individual was a Dasyu, again not a racial or ethnic label but a ritual and lin-guistic one – a person who interrupted the cycle of giving between gods and hu-mans, and therefore a person who threatened cosmic order, *r'ta* (RV) or *Asha* (AV). Rituals performed *in the right words* were the core of being an Aryan. Simi-larities between the rituals excavated at Sintashta and Arkaim and those described

---

1    Translation by Zaehner, *The Dawn and Twilight of Zoroastrianism*, 1961, p. 280.

later in the RV have solved, for many, the problem of Indo-Iranian origins."[1] "Common Indo-Iranian was most likely spoken during the Sintashta period, circa 2100-1800 BCE." Old Indic language may have separated from the oldest Avestan tongue about 1800-1600 BCE. (p. 408).

Anthony repeatedly emphasizes that the Rig Veda defines "Aryan-ness" as a *religious-linguistic* category and some Sanskrit-speaking Aryan chiefs, and even some Rig-Vedic poets were not of Aryan origin. "So even the Aryans of the Rig Veda were not generally 'pure' – whatever that means. The Rig Veda was a ritual canon, not a racial manifesto. If you sacrificed the right way to the right gods, which required performing the great traditional prayers in the traditional language, you were an Aryan; otherwise you were not. The Rig Veda made the *ritual* and *linguistic* (italics original) barrier clear, but *it did not require or even contemplate* (italics mine) racial purity.... Race really cannot be linked in and predictable way with language, so we cannot work from language to race or from race to language.... Anyone who *assumes* (italics original) a simple connection between language and genes, without citing geographical isolation or other special circumstances, is wrong at the outset."[2]

The Ilme Khshnumist theory which no one had heard of until 1906 when its founder, Behramshah Shroff, first propounded it in a lecture in Navsari after waiting many years since he claimed to have first encountered it, talks about Varana, Jirum, Keshash, vegetarianism, reincarnation, hidden souls on the mount Demavand, ritualism as an end in itself, and Bateni (inner secrets) which only the select elite can understand and interpret, even as others have no clue where they are coming from, etc., stand in total and inexorable contrast to the rational, logical, universal, and non-mystical teachings of Zarathushtra. Mysticism in Zoroastrianism, if it can be called so, is of a very different kind and it comes from conscientiously observing and imbibing all the seven attributes of Ahura Mazda in oneself in order to be God-like (Y.34.1, etc.). Although Shaked finds some trace of mysticism in Zoroastrianism, Rev. Jean de Menasce has extensively studied this subject and has denied the existence of any form of occult or esoteric teachings in Zoroastrianism, as have many others. "There is nothing in the Mazdean tradition of revelation to suggest a selective and occult initiation."[3]

Its Varana theory does not hold up to Yasna 12.7. This theory asserts that each one of us is born into the religion God finds us best suited for, which leads to more questions than it could possibly answer. For example, the search for a historical Jesus in our times has led historians to conclude that Jesus as a Jew had no intention even to start a new faith – it could have been the work of Paul and others later on. As James O'Donnell maintains in his book, *Augustine: A New Biography* (2005), Christianity was not essentially formed in 33 A.D. as claimed by St. Augustine. He claims it is not even "strongly grounded in the New Testament itself."

1   David W. Anthony, *The Horse, the Wheel, and Language: How Bronze-Age Riders from the Eurasian Steppes Shaped the Modern World*. Princeton, N.J.: Princeton University Press, 2007, pp. 408-9.

2   Op. cit. p. 11.

3   In Baum and Campbell, *The Mysteries – Papers from the Eranos Yearbooks*, New York, 1955, p. 148.

There were many different versions of Christianity from its very start. Even in Islam, there were Sunnis and Shiias at first and now Ismailis, Voras, Memons, Ahmedias, etc. In Buddhism too there are various sects, though nothing to beat those in Hinduism. If God has preordained our birth in a particular religion, how can He do so as there are so many sects and how does He determine which sect of a particular religion we are to be born into and on what basis, if they are really all God-made and not man made? If Christianity and Islam believe in converting everyone they can in their fold, how does it logically support the theory that everyone should adhere to the religion that God has placed them in?

This dilemma leads to more questions than we could possibly discuss here, including the dilemma faced by persons converting to other faiths by choice and/or by force, as well as by intermarried persons, as also by persons converting to the relatively new faiths such as Bahá'í. Almost every religion has factions, often at war with each other, as is evident from the clashes between Sunnis and Shias in Iraq at present as well as in the past. As Dr. Vali Nasr of Tufts University observes: "Many of the forces that draw on hard-line Sunni rejection of Shiism also aim harsh opposition at Suffism.... Shias whose mother tongue is Arabic are not by that fact equal members of the Arab nation.... Wahhabis condemned the veneration of saints and their shrines as polytheism and viewed Muslims who engaged in this action as heretics ... (and) invaded Karbala and desecrated the shrine of Imam Husayn." Nasr documents such instances at length, e.g., the Wahhabis invaded and conquered the Shia region of Al-Hasa in 1913 and even called for a jihad against the Shia and tried to convert them or kill them. Taliban declared Afghan shias to be infidels and massacred at least two thousand of them in 1977-1978. Wahhabi fatwas "denounced the Shias as apostates and even sanctioned the flailing of Shias" as late as 2002.[1]

Christianity too has at present many sects, each claiming to be authentic, but the recent discovery of the Judas Gospel suggests that "Christianity" in the ancient world was even more diverse than at present. Some Christians believed in two Gods – one good, one bad, and some even believed in many Gods. Modern historians have started studying the historical Jesus and claim that Jesus never intended to start a new faith, etc. Judaism, Hinduism, and Buddhism too have many divisions. Which one will the opposite view hold as an authentic one? We would be better off listening to the age-old advice of Parmenides: "Heed not the blind eye, the echoing ear, nor yet the tongue, but bring to this great debate the test of reason." But alas! As Winston Churchill warned of fanatics: "They won't change their mind and they can't change the subject."

Regarding the spread of Zoroastrianism in Persia, Richard Frye wonders: "Given the mixed population of Persepolis, we are uncertain whether the transition to an Iranian "Zoroastrian" predominance proceeded gradually or whether at certain times, as for example during the reign of Xerxes, attempts were not made to impose Mazda worship on the population. – When we remember that *much, if not most, of the population of Pars was Elamite*, (Italics mine), it would have been

---

1    *The Shia Revival: How conflicts within Islam Will Shape the Future*, W. W. Norton & Co., New York, 2006, pp. 60, 92, 97, 158, 236, etc.

impolitic to ban burial there." "Possibly," Frye observes "the Magi in Fars did expose the dead bodies as Herodotus tells us, but no Dakhmas or carved stones for exposure of bodies can be clearly dated to Achaemenid times. If it was practiced, one may speculate that it was exceptional, but this does not mean that those who buried the dead in coffins or stone receptacles were not Mazda worshippers, or even followers of Zoroaster in particular, since reference to exposure of the dead is not found in the old parts of the Avesta. – To explain how over the centuries the Avesta, as we have it, was compiled is hardly possible, – but Fars would have been a good area in which Zoroaster's special doctrines were mixed with autochthonous and Indo-Iranian rites and beliefs to eventually produce the religion as we know it from Sasanian times. – Gradually, but more definitely under Xerxes, the Iranicization of the Elamite population of Fars proceeded."[1] Thus, in the very center of the Zoroastrian stronghold in ancient Iran, the indigenous non-Iranian Elamite population was integrated into the Iranian race, surprisingly so if Frye is right that Elamites formed the majority of the population in Pars.

Amélie Kuhrt[2] echoes Frye: In the 11th and 10th centuries Iranians "moved into Fars and intermingled with the local Elamites. As they had been living for several hundred years in close symbiosis with the Elamites of Fars, it is possible that they no longer considered themselves as markedly distinct (Amiet 1992).... The Assyrians list Medes as just one of many populations groups (in Fars).... *The region was clearly an ethnic hotch-potch.*" (Italics mine.)

After centuries of neglect, Elam started getting some publicity after the 1960's as reflected in the work of Edith Porada, *Alt-Iran: die Kunst in vorislamischer Zeit*, Baden-Baden: Holle, 1962, and translated into French and English in 1963 and 1965 respectively, *Elam* by Pierre Amiet in 1966, and in Walter Hinz's *The Lost World of Elam: Recreation of a Vanquished Civilization*. Since then, quite a few discoveries about Elam have come to light, as listed in *Elam and Persia*[3] but it includes publications up to 2003 only. It concludes that Persia is not the heir of Media, but of Elam, and Darius devalues the Anshanite/Elamite heritage as "echoed in the treatment of Elamites in the reliefs on the Apadana as articulated (in this book) by M. C. Root," which I think may be due to the Elamites rebelling against him thrice. This book proffers multiple evidence, hitherto unknown, to demonstrate various Elamite influences on Persia, and concludes: "We stand on the cusp of a major shift in perception about the cultural legacy of Elam," and "this shift may have an impact on perceptions of (Persia's) modern national identity" (pp. 491-2).

Thus the Parsis being a pure race is an idealistic illusion contradicted by historical facts, which are so many I have no space to cramp them all here, as I have detailed them elsewhere. But this should be enough.

---

1   "Religion in Fars under the Achaemenids", from *Orientalia: Duchesne-Guillemin Oblata*, 1984, pp. 171-177.

2   *The Ancient Near East c. 3000-330 B.C.* Vol. II Routledge, London, 1995, p. 653.

3   Edited by Javier Álvarez-Mon and Mark B. Garrison, Winona Lake, Indiana, Eisenbrauns, 2011, 493 pages.

## Mazdayasni Hypothesis Not Corroborated by What Zarathushtra Himself Says in the Gathas

Zarathushtra's own spirited pronouncements in the Gathas do not support the Mazdayasni hypothesis. For example, in Yasna 31.1 he talks about words that have gone unheard. In 31.5 he was destined "to discern that very good thing which has been created for me by Asha, in order *for me* to bear in mind with Vohu Mana (that thing) *of which I am to be the seer*: Even those things, Ahura Mazda, which either shall not be or shall be." This verse rules out anyone else having precedence over him in knowing about the religion, as he clearly ascribes it all to himself – even about foreseeing the future, that is, about the Final Judgment.

In Y.32.1-5 Zarathushtra castigates the old gods worshipped by his contemporaries as well as their worshippers as "the offspring stemming from evil thinking, deceit, and disrespect. Hateful, too, are your actions, by reason of which ye have become renowned" in the area inhabited by the Aryans. "They continue to retreat from good thinking and disappear from the will of Ahura Mazda and Asha." "In this way ye have deceived mankind out of the good way of life and immortality, much as ye have deceived yourselves, the gods, (of it) by such evil thinking, and the evil spirit himself." It is inconceivable that such gods were any good at any time before Zarathushtra and if they were, it will be hard to explain Zarathushtra will approve of them as Zarathushtra thus was destined to be the first one to establish Mazda-worship (Mazdayasni religion) as explicitly claimed by himself in Y.31.1.

In Y.32.8, Zarathushtra says that "Even Yima (King Jamshed, "a Mazdayasni") was tried for these (capital) sins."

In Y.32.12, Zarathushtra laments that the teaching of the deceitful ones deflected men from the best action and ruined the life on the earth.

In Y.32.14, he complains that kindling the Haoma, a rite very prevalent among his so called "Mazdayasni" ancestors was ruining the good vision (religion) brought by him.

In Y.33.3 Zarathushtra welcomes "whoever who continues to serve the good vision" (religion) he taught after welcoming members of his family, community or clan and thus he does not close the door on others not his own.

In Y.49.1, Zarathushtra laments that "he has been falsely judged to be a great spoiler, apparently a heretic bent on undermining the traditional social and religious establishment."[1]

In Y49.2, Zarathushtra accuses his detractors to be true spoilers or heretics.

In Y33.4 he is determined to crusade against his own people: "Mazda, (it is) I who, through worship, shall turn away disobedience and bad thinking from Thee and opposition from the family, and the nearest deceit of the community, and scorners from the clan, and the worst counselor from the pasture of the cow (good vision)." He does not thus cast himself in the role of a reformer for the "Mazdayasnism" but a prophet with an entirely new vision that his own folks found it so much at odds with their ancestral beliefs.

In Y.43.11, Zarathushtra exclaims: "When I was first instructed by your words,

---

1    Insler, p. 294.

painful seemed to me my faith in men to bring to realization that which ye told me is the best (for them)." This initial hesitation on his part indicates the mission entrusted to him by Mazda was not reforming the hypothetical Mazdayasni religion but propagating an entirely new religion which was best for men, the best that mankind had not known yet, and therefore people were hesitant to accept it.

In Y.44.10, Zarathushtra again asks Mazda: "Have they truly seen that Daena (religion, spiritual vision) which is the best *for those who exist*?" and so not just for the so-called Mazdayasnis, and if it is the best, it could not have existed before him. What he says in the next verse (Y.44.11) fully supports this surmise: "I have been accepted by them as Thy foremost (follower). Do Thou look upon *all others* with enmity of spirit," "All others" implied all those who competed with him to be followers of Mazda. If Zarathushtra's main mission was to establish that no one besides him was to merit that honor, and not merely to reform the prevailing faith and beliefs, why would he urge Mazda to look down upon all others "with enmity of spirit?" And in Y.45.8 and elsewhere Zarathushtra professes to have a vision of Mazda. How many so-called Mazdayasnis before him did claim such a vision of God? And if he merely tried to reform the "Mazdayasni" religion, how do we explain Geush Urvan (soul of the universe) begging Mazda to send a savior to which Mazda responds: "I only know of one, Zarathushtra." (Y.29.8)

Zarathushtra's doctrines are so original and so ahead of his time, that it is quite improbable the "Mazdayasnis" could have been even conversant with them for Zarathushtra to reform them. And why would Zarathushtra so bitterly complain to Mazda: "To what land to flee? Where shall I go to flee? They exclude (me) from my family and from my clan. The community with which I have associated has not satisfied me, nor those who are the deceitful rulers of the land. How, then, shall I satisfy Thee Wise Lord?" (Yasna 46.1).

In Y.46.11, Zarathushtra complains: "During their regimes, the Karpans and Kavis yoked (us) with evil actions in order to destroy the world and mankind". Does it not suggest the need for something more than a reformer and does not it unambiguously refer to the need of saving "the world and mankind from destruction" and not just reform the "Mazdayasnis?" And in Y.46.12, does not Zarathushtra single out Friyona, a Turanian, as his ardent supporter, even though the Turanians were the bitter enemies of Iranians? Clearly Friyona cannot be called a "Mazdayasni." Indeed, "Who(ever) among men did gratify Zarathushtra Spitama with solicitude, that man was deserving of being famed." "If Zarathushtra's mission was limited only to the "Mazdayasnis", he would have certainly said so here. (Y.46.13). There is not even an indirect or remote reference to the "Mazdayasnis" in the Gathas. It seems the word Mazdayasni came into being only as a result of his revelation and only after he himself had envisioned Mazda (Y.43.5, 7, 8, 9, 11, 13, 15, etc.), no Iranian before him ever claiming it, including King Jamshed whom he condemns in Y.32. Zarathushtra himself asks Mazda: "Tell me truly, Ahura. Have they truly seen that vision which is the best for those who exist?" (Y.44.10), and "How shall I bring to life that visions of *Mine?*" (Y.44.9), implying thereby he was the first one decreed by Mazda for the revelation. Much has been made of the phrase "Mazdayasno Ahmi, Mazdayasno Zarathushtrish" but here

Zarathushtra the prophet places Mazda before him just as one finds in the Kalma prayer of the Moslems. Otherwise, how can one explain the paradox created by being a follower of the old "Mazdayasni" religion which Zarathushtra finds so wanting in the Gathas, and at the same time being the founder of the Mazda-Worship as the result of a divine revelation unprecedented in the entire Iranian history.

Also, how can one explain what soon follows: "I praise the Good Religion (which is) Mazdayasni" when the title "Good Religion" has only been used for the religion preached by Zoroaster for centuries. And, how can one also explain what follows next "Ahuirish Zarathushtrish" (Ahurian Zarathustra's religion") which is often referred to as Mazdayasni only? Thus, the "Mazdayasni" hypothesis is too far fetched, and runs counter to the Gathic theology. Otherwise, how can we explain what Yasna 12.7 claims: "Of whichever faith (Varna) are the waters, of whichever faith (are) the trees, of whichever faith (is) the beneficent cow (or earth) who confers on us all good things, of whichever faith (is) Ahura Mazda who provides sustenance to the righteous man, of whichever faith (is) Zarathushtra, of whichever faith (is) the King Vishtaspa, of whichever faith (is) Frashaoshtra and Jamaspa, of whichever faith is the holy Saoshyant, of true actions, to that very faith and of that very (divine) Law (indeed, I belong), A Mazdayasni (indeed) (Mazda Worshipper) I am." Yasna 12.7 thus knows of and endorses only one faith, that of Zarathushtra and his disciples, leaving no space at all for his predecessors. And this divine law is so universal that it comprises the total universe – not just mankind, but also the waters and the plants and the earth and the animal kingdom and even the Saoshyant who will bring about Frasho-kereti, final renovation of the world. Ilme-Khshnumist interpretation of Varana, Jirum, etc., as leading to each person being born into a particular religion is thus not substantiated by Yasna 12.7. The thirteenth chapter (verse 44) of Tir Yasht compares Tishtrya (Tir) Yazad, residing among the stars as lord with Zarathushtra who plays a similar role among men, that is among all mankind.

Fravardin Yasht tells us that even the waters and the plants increased in growth and rejoiced at the birth of Zarathushtra, making his religion universal in a very unique sense by making it a part of the universe itself. Such references are not rare in the Avesta.

From the Gathas to the later Avesta we find references to Zarathushtra's religion being the only true one. Even before Zarathushtra's advent on this earth, Vohu-Mana tells Mazda: "This one, Zarathushtra Spitama, has been found by me here to be THE ONLY ONE who has given ear to our commandments," (Yasna 29.8), which tellingly rules out the Mazdayasni theory. And Yasna ends with a clear statement: "There is only one path which (is) of (following) Asha – all the other ones are no paths." (Yasna 72.11).

## Elam and the Mazdayasni Theory

Iran was not a vacant land when the Persians went there, but had been occupied by Elamites, a Semitic race, since at least the middle of the third millennium B.C. There are clear historical records suggesting that they were invaded by Mesopotamians, and in turn they invaded Mesopotamia themselves. They were

powerful enough to attack Babylonia during the last millennium B.C. The existence of the Elamite language is attested in medieval history, and the name Elam is
recorded in the records of the Nestorian church as late as the thirteenth century
A.D.

The history of the Middle Elamite period is richly documented by D. T. Potts
in *The Archaeology of Elam: Formation and Transformation of an Ancient
Iranian State*, Cambridge: Cambridge University Press, 1999. Potts gives his
rationale for asserting that "the Achaemenid empire, however 'Persian' it may
have been, in one sense evolved from the Neo-Elamite social, cultural, linguistic,
and perhaps even political milieu, or at least made the claim of Anshanite
ancestry. Without denying the ethnic and linguistic identity of the early Persians,
Amiet has nevertheless suggested that the Elamites *became* Persian by a process
of acculturation, a process which he refers to as the ethnogenesis of the Persians
via Elamite acculturation, ... while Steve suggests that centuries of symbiosis in
highland Fars effected a fusion of Elamite and Persian ethnic elements." Potts
adds that "the rise of the Achaemenids began in Anshan at a time when ...
numerous petty kings held sway in ... western Iran." He cautions against
overestimating the power of those kingdoms: "Certainly we read of no 'conquest'
of Elam, Susa ... by the Persians in the same sense as we hear of the conquest of
Media and the removal of gold and silver from Ecbatana and Anshan *c.* 550 BC....
Perhaps this indicates that the Elamites and Persians were much more closely
bound than otherwise thought and should not be treated as opponents.... The
symbiotic existence of Persians and Elamites, whether in Susiana or in the
highlands, had acculturated the Persians to Elamite and, via the Elamites,
Babylonian and Assyrian culture as much as an acculturation of Elamites was
effected by their contact with the Persians.... In this sense, the rise of the
Achaemenids was more comparable to the change in political leadership via an
*ethno-classe dominante* ... in an area long accustomed to the institutions of
kingship and statehood, than it was to the ascendancy of a 'new' tribal group over
an 'exhausted' civilization. As de Miroschedji has rightly observed, the arrival of
Cyrus the Great in Susiana ... may have appeared to a lowland Elamite as nothing
more than the restoration of the old kingdom of Anshan and Susa." (pp. 306-307).

For confirmation of Potts's thesis, see Walther Hinz and Jennifer Barnes, *The
Lost World of Elam; Re-Creation of a Vanished Civilization*, Sidgwick & Jackson,
London, 1972. Thus, Elamites and Persians ultimately became merged into one
entity, which ultimately came to be known as Persian, which challenges the
Mazdayasni theory and any claim of racial purity of Persians and their later-day
descendants.

"That the Iranian tribes, upon their arrival in south-western Iran, encountered
both the vestiges as well as the living representatives of the age-old Elamite
culture is hardly a novel observation," as already noted by Wouter Henkelman.[1]
He has also written a comprehensive history of the Iranians and Elamites in order

1   *History of the Ancient Near East/Monographs – V*: in Lanfranchi, Giovanni B., Michael Roaf, and
    Robert Rollinger, *Continuity of empire: Assyria, Media, Persia*, Padova, Italy: S.a.r.g.o.n. editrice
    e libreria, 2003, pp. 181-231.

to "illuminate the role of the Achaemenid Empire as heir to Elam.[1] Nevertheless, in the first chapter of this book he notes that a comprehensive history of the Iranians and Elamites "still remains to be written," as observed by him in his 2003 publication. "By the time the Persian Empire emerged," observes Henkelman, "Elamites and Iranians had been living side-by-side for five hundred to one thousand years. This is an observation of tremendous consequence, for it is unthinkable that it did *NOT* result in a profound mutual influence." For instance, Cyrus (Kurash) is an Elamite name which per Henkelman was "prompted by the status of that culture, not by the linguistic milieu of Cyrus's parents as suggested by D.T. Potts, and it supports well his thesis of ethnogenesis and acculturation. He also notes that of the three Elamite rebels mentioned by Darius in his Behistun inscription, only one has an Elamite name. However, the very fact of these three Elamites rebelling against Darius, despite Henkelman seeing in the Persepolis Fortification (P.F.) tablets "one of the most powerful attestations of Elamite-Iranian religious acculturation" (p. 62), nevertheless does not fully support his thesis, especially as many authors, including myself, have noted Darius's proclivity towards Gathic beliefs and his regret that Elamites did not worship Ahuramazda. Moreover, Henkelman's sole reliance on the P.F. Tablets for comparing the Iranian and Elamite religious beliefs and practices is not quite justifiable, especially as he himself concludes "they do not yield anything as to the beliefs that shaped Persian religious life" and "they only document" the sacrifices sponsored by the Achaemenid state in Fars. Apart from these reservations, Henkelman has made a significant contribution to the portrayal of ethnogenesis of Elamite and Iranian cultures, which paradoxically, however, led to the ultimate disappearance of the Elamite cult and beliefs in Zoroastrian Persia, as if sadly predicting what was to happen to the beliefs of the Zoroastrian Persia under the not-so-benign nor tolerant rules of the invading Arabs. (See my review of his book.)

The acceptance and freedom granted to the Elamite cultus by the Achaemenids, per Henkelman and other notable scholars, were never witnessed again in Iran or even elsewhere for the most part: P.F. tablets reveal that "Elamite and Iranian gods are being worshipped side by side and the individuals carrying out the sacrifices may have Elamite or Iranian names," which "reflects processes of religious acculturation that must have started at least a century earlier." (p. 188) As *Encyclopaedia Iranica*[2] notes: "The majority of royal inscriptions were written in Old Persian, Akkadian, and Elamite versions, but Elamite had by then absorbed Iranian influences in both structure and vocabulary," which tends to support Henkelman's thesis, and what he states next: "The Elamite gods, after having benefited from a final revival of the cult under Darius and Xerxes, disappeared forever from the documents. Elam was absorbed into the new empire, which changed the face of the civilized world at that time." (p. 311). Thus, the Semitic Elamites came to be completely absorbed into the Zoroastrian Iranian populace.

---

1    *The other gods who are: studies in Elamite-Iranian acculturation based on the Persepolis fortification texts*, Leiden: Nederlands Instituut voor het Nabije Oosten, 2008.
2    Vol. VIII, Mazda Publishers, Cost Mesa, California, 1998, p. 311.

See also Hinz 1972; *The Cambridge Ancient History*, Volume II, Part 2, Cambridge, Cambridge University Press, 1975, pp. 379-416 and 482-506; *The Cambridge Ancient History*, Third Edition, Volume II, Part 1, Cambridge, At the University Press, 1973, chapter VII, Persia c. 1800 1550 B.C., pp. 256-288; *The Cambridge Ancient History*, Vol. I, Part 2, 1971, pp. 644-680; *The Cambridge History of Iran*, Vol. 2, edited by Ilya Gershevitch, Cambridge University Press, Cambridge, 1985, pp. 1-109. Even a brief perusal of these publications suffices to reveal how different Elam was racially, culturally, linguistically, and above all in religious beliefs and practices from the later Persia it eventually got transformed into, thus shattering the roots of the Mazdayasni theory. While there is some evidence that some Elamites survived beyond the Achaemenid rule, all the surviving evidence suggests they were ultimately absorbed in the ensuing Iranian culture.

### King Vishtasp's Conversion Derided.

Even the universally acknowledged notion that King Vishtasp was converted by Asho Zarathushtra is challenged because he had not discarded his ancestral religion while supporting the religion of Zarathushtra, and because of the existence of pre-Zoroastrian beliefs – embodied in the scriptures, which most scholars, except however for Boyce and her adherents, believe were rejected by the Prophet and were re-introduced into Zarathushtrianism only later on by the clergy. Moreover, Zarathushtra holds his message as "unheard before" his times (Yasna 32.1) and perceives himself (Yasna 46.1 etc.) at odds with his clansmen and relatives. The high level of complexity and novelty of Zoroaster's philosophies as evident in the Gathas as well as his constant and vehement denunciation of his contemporaries and their rejection of him for years clearly contradict their contention that Zarathushtra accepted the religion into which he was born, and removed the extraneous and corrupt elements. Most of all, they have hardly touched upon the opinion of other scholars on this subject. They even reject the opinion of their own hero, Erachji Meherjirana on the flimsy ground that his translation of Yasna 28.8, 46.14, 45.11 which he cites in reference are not correct, though they know well that literal translations were not feasible before modern philology took roots among our priests. This was unnecessary, as I made it explicitly clear that "the question is not whether they (these stories) are true or not. The question is, how could such devout souls, so conversant with Zoroastrianism as to write its sacred texts, blaspheme their Prophet by saying Greeks and Hindus adopted his religion when only a Mazdayasni could become a Zoroastrian? - - -" It should also be noted that Erachji cites "the Denkard and the Zardusht Namag", etc., also to support his thesis. He also cites "the 5th Book of the *Denkard*" to state "that God had sent this religion for all the people of the world".

But they ignore it all. Kotwal in his commentary on the propagation of religion tries to distance himself from his hero but in the process admits: "In the Avesta there is evidence that Zoroastrians of old used to do 'missionary work' in India and even in China", which apparently contradicts the Mazdayasni theory. J. H. Moulton is more forthcoming: "If He (Zarathushtra) revealed the true religion for the first time, his parents must have followed a false one."[1] It is surprising that they ignore all other evidence negating their Mazdayasni theory, including those that maintain that the very word 'Mazda' and the intricate and hitherto novel theology behind it, could only be of Zarathushtra's own coinage and vintage, and hence negating any notion that the Mazdayasni religion existed prior to Zarathushtrianism. So I am submitting some more observations that contradict their Mazdayasni hypothesis.

If King Vishtasp was not converted by Zarathushtra, per trio, how come he waged battles to convert other peoples per *Shah Nameh*, and why does the *Shikand Gumanik Vichar*,[2] declare that Kai-Spendat and Zargar and royal sons (Zatak) spread the religion and "even wandered to Arum (Asia Minor) and Hind, (which were) outside the realm, in propagating the religion." Also, why would *Din-i-Virjikart* 11[3] state on the basis of the eleventh Nask that "Zaratusht the Spitaman, having brought the religion from Auharmazd, King Gushtasp accepted it, and made it current in the world; and such-like as these." And so not just for re-forming his ancestral religion and beliefs. Bahman Yasht[4] says Ahuramazda and Zarathushtra "conversed about religion, and Vishtasp shall accept that religion" and Bahman "made the religion current in the whole world." *Denkard*[5] refers to Zarathushtra preaching his religion "for the preservation of mankind from hell" and often refers to mankind, but not to the supposed Mazdayasnis only. It also declares that at the end "every one shall practice the religion of Mazda-worship with eagerness."

*Denkard*[6] describes Ahuramazda trying to convince Vishtasp of "the true prophesying of Zaratusht" and his "desire for the acceptance of the religion of Mazda-worship by Vishtasp and for its propagation in the world." How could Vishtasp propagate the religion in the world if it was meant for "Mazdayasnis" only and why is "the prophesying of Zaratusht" mentioned here if his mission was just to reform the old religion? Why he is called "the first Athravan (priest)," etc; in the Farvardin Yasht, if Athravans existed before him? And why if Vishtasp is said to have propogated the religion in the world, can his crusades be logically limited only to his defensive efforts against the offensives of his enemy Arejatas-pa? How about the crusades of his son and grandson?

The non-conversion policy of the Parsis is also supported on the grounds that no Zoroastrian King, forced the conquered people to submit to their religious beliefs, despite the scholarly evidence to the contrary already furnished in this text. As pointed out by me, the Sasanians also tried to convert Turks, Buddhists, Hindus, Jews, and Christians.

M. H. Dodgeon and S. N. Lieu refer to Kirder's effort to spread Zoroastrianism "also in non-Iranian land" under the heading: "Attempt by Kirder the Mobed

---

1    *The Treasure of the Magi*, Oxford Union Press, 1917, p. 117.
2    Chapter 10, 64-68, SBE XXIV, pp. 170-71.
3    SBE XXXVII, p. 442.
4    Chapter 2, 15-17; SBE V, p. 198-9.
5    Book 9, chapter 51, 5-8: SBE XXXVII p. 285.
6    Chapter 4, 74: SBE XLVI, p. 671.

to introduce Zoroastrianism to Conquered Roman Territory."[1] Martin Sprengling also bears this out by saying that Kartir (Kirder) returned loot in captured non-Iranian lands to its (Iranian) owners, in which he wanted to spread Mazdean religion. "A return of at least some Iranian loot to non Iranian lands in which a new kind of Iranian church was to be introduced would very probably contain some measure of Capataio Benevolentiae," (p. 43). "He finishes off his story, his achievements outside of Persia being enumerated, in detail, on the Kaabah" inscriptions (in Persia)."[2]

Historically there is no validity to the assertion that no question of conversion arose for Zarathushtra, as there were no other religions in existence then, because the Hindus, Chinese, Egyptians, Assyrians, Greeks, Elamites (the evidence for which lie right inside Persepolis itself up to our own times), to name only a few, did have their own beliefs, just as the pre-Zoroastrians said to have their own belief systems which Boyce reveals "can be reconstructed partly from comparison with closely declared Vedic texts and the Brahmanic tradition of India, partly through what clearly seems to be pre-Zoroastrian elements surviving in Zarathushtra's own revelation revived subsequently by his followers."[3] See also Schmidt's research quoted by me. An Assyriologist has recently claimed in scholarly journals that Zarathushtra had essentially copied the Assyrian religion; see my rebuttal of him for more information.

However, it is not feasible even for a religious genius such as Zarathushtra to devise a religious system without utilizing the prevailing concepts, customs, common beliefs, archetypes, language, etc., even as he assigns them new or higher meaning. That does not detract anything from his status as a founder or Prophet of a new faith. But as Zaehner complains, Zarathushtra is the least served of all Prophets.

No prophet or faith before Zarathushtra has integrated free-will so vehemently and intricately in his theology, as I have detailed at length in my paper on free will, that conversion in Zoroastrianism can only be based on one's free and fully-thought-out choice, and therefore Acceptance is not likely to lead to strife and conflict among nations or races.

According to Touraj Daryaee everybody *before the advent of Islam*, all other sects falling outside the state religion authenticated by Adurbad Mahraspand "are called a false religion (ag-denih)", thus negating the interpretation or misinterpretation of this word as applying to a Zoroastrian convert to Islam.[4] I have elsewhere detailed pre-Islamic Sasanian attempts at Zoroastrianising Georgia and Armenia in my essay on Sasanians and Romans. Albert de Jong even advises that "the practice of translating Ag-dēn by 'Muslem' should be avoided, because many of the passages 'on those of the evil religion' are clearly traditional and derive from pre-Islamic religious rulings on conversion and apostasy, probably formulated in the

---

1   In the *Roman Eastern Frontier and the Persian Wars (A.D. 226-363), A Documentary History*, London: Routledge, 1991, p. 65.
2   *Third Century Iran – Sapor and Kartir*, Oriental Institute, University of Chicago, Chicago, 1953, p. 64.
3   *Textual sources*, 1984, p. 8.
4   *Sasanian Persia*, I. B. Tauris, New York, 2009 p. 85.

time of massive conversion to Christianity,"[1] which Daryaee's above observation fully validates. De Jong further observes that Ag-dēn included three types of "others" – believers of other religions, inner-Zoroastrian heretics and sorcerers, and devil-worshippers."[2] Shaul Shaked tries to delineate the notion *ag-dēn* at length, and holds that "this is a term that encompasses any deviation from our notion of good religion." He quotes *Herbedestan* 11.7 which contains the word *ag-dēn*, and suggests "that the possibility of conversion to Zoroastrianism was open during the Sasanian period."[3] Kotwal and Kreyenbroek translate *ag-dēn* as "infidel," which does not agree with the trio's version.[4]

## PIETY AND POLITICS.

### Gathic Spirit Mauled.

It is often contended by Parsis that no perfect translation of the Gathas exists, and Insler's translations are too academic to understand the Gathic spirit, and instead provide their own for Yasna 28.6, 31.3, and 47.6. Even if we can accept them regardless of Boyce's finding, quoted by me earlier, that Gathic translations by Parsi Scholars are "almost as free and subjective as those of the occultists", their own translation "convincing all living ones" or "many desiring ones" do not in fact rule out Acceptance. They maintain that the Pahlavi translation also do not suggest conversion, but they know it well that the Pahlavi translation of the Gathas, though of enormous importance in many ways, is not always reliable because of the greater antiquity of the Gathic language. All the same, Dr. Mills, as already quoted by me, perceives the Pahlavi translator indicating conversion in Yasna 31.3 and the Pahlavi texts quoted by me at length, readily embrace it. Despite my delineating the fact that "Insler has taken pains to explain how and why he has derived the word 'conversion'," they fault him "for jumping to the idea 'to convert'" (in translating the word 'Var') instead of 'to turn' without countering Insler's rationale. Even Insler is not spared here.

Moreover, they fault Insler's translation of Yasna 44.10 as grammatically incorrect, and substitute Insler's "That vision which is the best FOR those who exist" with "That religion which is best AMONG the existing ones", which to most people may sound tautological and to Asho Zarathushtra who preached the first proselytizing religion in human history, it may sound as a play on words, even if one finds Insler wrong here. But those like me who have known Insler and studied his works well, will, to say the least, be amazed by the trio's remark. Such sophistry is surprising in view of the common understanding that scholars differ in translating Gathas, and as Insler stands out in Boyce's estimation, whereas they do not. *If they have the real scriptures at hand to quote, how necessary it is to put one translation against another and one scholar against another.* If they fail to provide scriptural basis for their stand against Acceptance, other scholars do pro-

---

1    *Irano-Judaica V*, Jerusalem, 2003, p. 24.
2    Op. cit. p. 21.
3    *The Sasanian Era*: The Idea of Iran, Vol. III, I. B. Tauris, London, 2008, pp. 106-117.
4    *The Herbedestan and Nērangestan*, Vol. I, Paris, 1992.

vide evidence for it as I have outlined already. And I keep finding even more such evidence:

Shaul Shaked concedes that "it is perfectly true that in that (Sasanian) period it (Zoroastrianism) did address itself to all mankind" and quotes passages from *Denkard* such as Madan's *Denkard*, II 8-18, p. 40 to "stress its universal character:"

"The Creator Ohrmazd sends this religion not only to the Kingdom of Iran but the whole world and to every variety (of human beings)."[1] This passage, observes Shaked, "reflects good Sasanian doctrines: an active proselytizing effort appears to have prevailed in Sasanian Iran, being perhaps mainly provoked as a competition against the zealous propaganda carried on by the numerous religious movements which tried to win adherents from each other and from the official State religion." This can be seen from the inscriptions of the Sasanian kings, and especially from those of Karder, as well as from other Pahlavi texts, e.g. *Pahlavi Rivayat Accompanying The Dadistan-i-Dinik:* "This is the greatest virtuous deed of a follower of evil religion (Ag-den): when he comes from evil religion to the Good Religion."[2]

Shaked also quotes Rev. Father Jean de Menasce as saying: "There is nothing in the Mazdean tradition of revelation to suggest a selective and occult initiation. So open is the Mazdean preaching that it provides an appropriate basis for the holy war waged in the name of the faith by defenders well-armed with the temporal sword (p. 176)."

## DISTORTIONS AND MISREPRESENTATIONS.

Those who endorse Acceptance are often accused of not having the capacity to find out for themselves what is laid down in the original texts. But then where are these so-called original texts? Do they really exist? If so, why not quote them? How does one develop this so-called capacity? Does a Ph.D. degree entitle one to claim it? Does it enable one to translate and interpret ALL our scriptures and at the same time attain spirituality and spiritual insight they demand so as to be able to always lead right? Where one can go to attain it? What about even learned priests disagreeing among themselves? Those who justify Acceptance in Zoroastrianism are accused of not having a fairly accurate grasp of the teachings of Zarathushtra, and are denounced per Yasna 32.9: "The false teacher distorts the scriptures, he indeed through (his) teaching (distorts) the scheme of life- - -." (Insler's version of Yasna 32.9 is "The one of evil doctrine (the evil spirit) has ruined the (true) words. He has ruined the intention of life by his own teachings. He has robbed the esteemed power which really belongs to good thinking.)" I leave it to the reader to ultimately decide who really distorts Mazda's words enshrined in the Gathas.

## Conclusion

In "The Continuity of the Zoroastrian Quest" Dr. Boyce observes that Zoroastrian-

---

1   *From Zoroastrian Iran to Islam*, Variorum, Ashgate Publishing Ltd. Great Britian, 1995, pp. 176-7.
2   Ed. B. N. Dhabhar, Bombay, 1913, p. 9, pp. 177-178.

ism survived because it always allowed room for "whatever changes and develop-ments may now be desirable" and for "very positive teachings which went with, not against, the normal bent of human nature". In addition to making it clear that Zoroastrianism is a creedal religion, Boyce in her *History of Zoroastrianism* (Vol. I, p. 251) makes it again very explicit that Zoroastrianism "was open to any person of good will and understanding to become *magavan*, possessed of this gospel: that the prophet preached to women as well as men, to the poor and untaught as well as the wealthy and learned." Boyce even quotes Kaj Barr in order to emphasize it: "Zarathustra is not the spokesman of any individual class or group. As the one to whom Ahura Mazdā has granted insight in God's design of life, he wants to win his whole ... people for his message, thus leading all of them to salvation, *savah*, life in its abundant plenitude, as it was in the dawn of creation."

*If the opposition does not share the truth in this matter with the community*, ul-timately the truth will prevail and *the community will surprise them by sharing it with them*. One can see this happening already from the articles and letters one reads in the Parsi media *which are too numerous to be quoted here*. But an article in *Parsiana* (Aug. 7, 2006, pp. 19-20) raises the same issues I raised more than a quarter of a century ago. Written by a former Bombay Parsi Punchayat trustee, J. Kanga, it well depicts the frustration with the trio, felt by all levels of our society. Regarding the book, *Conversion Caucus* (written by one condemning conversion), Kanga ruefully remarks: "*It is more like a professor correcting a student's essay, criticizing his interpretation but not quoting the exact scriptural directive against conversion - - - I consider it very unscholarly to totally ignore any evidence which does not fit his thesis*", an echo of my own comments. His reference to Boyce gave me a deja vu feeling. "It should be stretching our credibility to the extreme," he complains, "to think that our high Priests are unaware of what is stated in our vari-ous scriptures. (They)--- have indulged in 'suppresio veri and suggestio falsi'. *I hereby openly challenge any of our high priests to produce the evidence or admit that there is none*". "The truth about conversion is revealed and openly discussed even at the risk of being abused by the fundamentalists. *I have seen with my own eyes the misery that many Parsi children suffer – in the name of religion*," (which is the same reason that guided me, but by now it seems to have been resolved here except for a few die-hard orthodox. See Appendix II.) *This issue has given an op-portunity to unscrupulous preachers to divide our small community by scaring the orthodox into believing that our religion is in danger*.... They have thus been able to form cults, projecting themselves as messiahs and encouraging their lumpen followers to *indulge in disrupting meetings* (to which I too was subjected), — *What would be left of their (orthodox's) agenda if this issue of conversion were not there?*

"Hence their fanatical efforts to keep this issue alive by not allowing open de-bate and preventing the truth from coming out. Hence the deafening silence! – *If they ('average decent Parsis') express any opinion contrary to these views they are subjected to abuse---*. Otherwise why are intelligent and highly educated and capable professionals - - - not speak out?" He urges the Bombay Parsi Punchayat (BPP) to ask "*all the high priests to justify their stand with evidence from our scriptures*". "How long can an intelligent and progressive community" be silent on such a vital issue?, he concludes. While the reliance on BPP which is not in essence a religious institution seems rather misplaced, his emphasis on "vigorous public opinion" is validated by our own experience in North America where many enlightened souls have enlightened others by their own studied views. As Dasturji Bode's wife wrote to me on June 13, 1983, Bombay Samachar's response to "Ms. Dolly Dastoor Seeks Answers to Religious Problems" was "They were given by our servants 80 years ago". This is so true as we may never again be fortunate enough to have such giant and forthright savants.

In the last few years this issue has become so pronounced that *Parsiana* (April 2003, p. 2) came out with an editorial, "Dialog, not Diktats" : "Most High Priests and their fundamentalist supporters not only want to keep spouse and children out, they don't even want the Parsi Zoroastrians to continue in their fold. They offer no explanation for their beliefs ... over the years priests have given contradictory views and the community has been subject to their erraticism. Circumstances and events appear to dictate what the priests will state at a particular time and place. But they cannot change facts as easily. Zoroastrianism not only permits but enjoins conversion ... the Priests are contradicting the original tenets of the religion which enjoin conversion. They can be thereby charged of selectively citing scriptures to suit their convenience," which, however cannot really be true as *there exists no such scriptures one can cite.* There is no space here to quote innumerable *Parsiana* editorials and letters to *Parsiana* since 2003. They are in fact resorting to even worse, misrepresenting the Prophet himself.

Such an awareness, however, has come rather late after I espoused this cause long ago but I am glad it has finally arrived. May it thrive! "Are they the High Priests of Zoroastrianism or of Parsi Zoroastrianism? And who is their Prophet then?" wondered Kanga. Ultimately the truth should prevail thanks to such blessed efforts. While the articles and letters to the editor on conversion themselves will provide ample material for a book, space does not allow us to quote them all here.

As noted by Soli Sorabjee, a legal luminary, the previous judgments on this issue would appear to conflict with the equality provision of the Constitution "and Parsis have little to worry as judicial pronouncements have unequivocally laid down that converts ... cannot avail of the benefits" of Parsi Charities. However, he notes: "An absolute inflexible prohibition upon admittance "of persons who are not born of Parsi fathers ... smacks of arbitrariness."[1]

I ran into similar criticism of one of the trio from the most orthodox sources: **"In both these instances cited by Dasturji there is an attempt to misguide the readers. What's infinitely worse and deplorable is (his) distorted translation and his convenient interpretation thereof. All of which reminds us of the predictions of 'Zand-i-Vohuman Yasht', etc., that in bad times, it will be the white-turbaned gentry that will sink the ... Zoroastrian ship"**. (All bold letters in the original). Strong words from an unexpected source. (*Deen Parast*, Vols. 3.11 and 3.12, March April 1994, p. 7). As I was cleaning up the materials I had

---

1    *The Times of India*, July 15, 1984. P. I.

collected on this subject, I also ran into a comment in *Jame-Jamshed Weekly* (Oct. 9, 1994, p. 15) by N. H. Dadrawala: "One does not have to be a scholar to question the obvious double standards and acrobats of our High Priests.... Our scholar's 'arrogance, conceit and 'holier-than-thou' attitude is only natural. Those who really 'know' never make any show or ostentations of their knowledge." "We look at our High Priests and pray for the community."

There seems to be a pattern for "an outright verdict of falsification and fabrication" as complained by Pallan Ichaporia when one of the trio challenged the endorsement of conversion by the Vaetha Nask, translated by another member of the trio itself. His scholarly response, too long to quote here, leaves no doubt about his claim.[1] I am unfortunately used to all sorts of allegations. One misguided soul from Bombay even urged the North American Mobeds Council in 1983: "Unless this blasphemous and sacrilegious man is nipped in the bud by the orthodox American Parsis right now, they will have a tough time pinning him down later. The Mobed's Conference ... is a good forum to take him on and demolish him for good." The Council instead decided to respect each priest's views. He was bothered by "brazen-faced outbursts from this arch-heretic" because Antia said "Even the Sudreh may have to be revived so that our children will find it easier to have and wear them.... Ashmog would be a more appropriate appellation" for Antia.

In my lifetime, however, I have seen the length and size of Sudreh shrinking among men and women. He accuses Antia of wanting to change, modernize and shorten our prayers and rituals. This again is a distortion and a misrepresentation. Antia sees Zoroastrians here undergoing such a drastic change that he endeavors to retain whatever could be retained, in the true spirit of *Shayast Ne Shayast*, preserve what is possible, as we have no control over what is not possible when the ship is sinking fast. Even Dasturji H. Mirza states in his booklet, "Sassanian Zoroastrianism" (p. 16), that "even in religious matters changes due to circumstances have become inevitable. Generally it is believed or propagated that all ceremonies, customs, and practices have come down to us in original form straight from the Avesta and teachings of the Prophet. This is not correct. Whether we like it or not, changes have taken place perceptibly or imperceptibly in all ages." Even the most orthodox Parsi of today does not observe all the piety and purity that even the most liberal Parsis did a century ago.

When Parsis first went to England they took Parsi cooks with them, as did Sir J. J. Modi, in keeping with the purity laws, and even he was debarred from performing higher ceremonies for breaking the rule of not traveling by sea, as it would pollute water. Even the orthodox priests resented the publication of *Dastur Darab Hamzyar's Rivayat* in the nineteenth century, as even then they already could not observe all the pieties and rituals mentioned therein. Nowhere in my *Argument For Acceptance* have I downplayed the role of rituals, but only lamented "the full force of modernity's disruptive power" affecting us more than anywhere else in the world" and "as deeply into the community" (pp. 4, 6).

Instead of understanding the North American milieu, the orthodox critics brand the author as an anti-ritualist. *But a fair minded reader would not find a single*

---

1    *Bombay Samachar*, Nov. 15, 1992.

*sentence to support it.* Keeping the religion alive, although all the rituals cannot be performed here by us, is not tantamount to rejecting rituals. Even as we go to press, we find comments from a "learned Parsi scholar": "The current crop of arch-Dhongis (arch-fakers/pretenders) have deviously managed to fudge every issue strictly pertaining to our unique religion – from calendar to conversion, from dualism to Dakhmenashini – using denial and procrastination tactics. - - - Should this continued fakery be allowed through the disruptive hands of control freaks, then we must bid good-bye to the Dhongis (fakes) with their pretend Zoroastrianism, and break away."[1] It will be a sad day for the minuscule community if it ever happens.

Tanya Luhrmann who devotes seven pages to Peterson's conversion in her book, *The Good Parsi*, (pp. 179-185), rightly comments that "it may be too painful for its (Bombay's) Parsi residents to acknowledge the reality of the new circumstances against those embedded memories.... Denial only goes so far", (p. 184) – I, for one, see here, not necessarily a deliberate denial, but some form of a cognitive dissonance which leads them to reject those beliefs which are not in consonance with their long-held values and cultural conditioning, as pointed out by me in my concluding paragraph. I am here reminded of what Professor Thomas Kuhn, commented in connection with Galileo's refutation of Aristotle: "We like to forget that many of the concepts in which we believe were painfully drummed into us in our youth. We too easily take them as natural and indubitable products of our own unaided perceptions, dismissing concepts different from our own as errors.... Our own education stands between us and the past,"[2] and the future, I may add.

As Luhrmann astutely observes "The very existence of the debate forces the community to become aware of the inadequacies of its options in the contemporary context. The hysterical tone of the debates may reflect not only passion about possible outcomes, but also the fear that the community cannot agree on a solution, cannot resolve this central problem, because no resolution is possible". "Zarathushtra's teachings are forgotten", she concludes by quoting someone, "rational thinking leaves them, and the Parsis rush to fight an enemy that does not exist" (p. 185). While I have written critically about the problem I have with Luhrmann interpreting the present-day Parsis' problems very negatively and selectively in terms of colonialism, I find these remarks apt and true-to-life.

Uproar against the views on the subject can be found in many columns of the readers' views in the Parsi press, but the views of the learned Zoroastrian scholars such as Prof. K. D. Irani and Farrokh Vajifdar reflect their expertise on this subject and substantiate my findings: "We have been acquainted with the suspect methodology by which attempts to assert the reverse of our religion's injunctions regarding conversion have been made. They are in the nature of factoid claims achieved by careful contrivance and are simply not probative. We encounter rather weak efforts at glossing our texts at the same time as claiming to 'correctly' interpret them. Being groundless, they do not stand up to its scrutiny, and, yet it appears that the fictionalizing process is energetically and deliberately pursued. Among the

---

1   *Parsiana*, October 7, 2011, p. 6.
2   *The Copernican Revolution*, New York, 1959, pp. 95-96.

minor but blatant fictions is the entirely false invocation of the *Qisseh-ye Sanjan*'s five conditions as proof that Jaydev Rana granted asylum to our forefathers provided that no conversion of his Hindu subjects was attempted. There is NO SUCH CONDITION among the five to which we supposedly agreed - - - - That these texts may be distorted to suppress or yield entirely alien or out-of-context (evidence) is a willful exercise against which we must take issues - - - No less unpleasant is the tendency of our own Bombay prelates – to, whom we once used to entrust our religious and spiritual guidance – to manipulate texts to suit their predilections - - - -, (such as ) just one Parsi scholar had translated the root VAR, thrice located in the Gathas, as "convert". Kanga, Punegar and Taraporewala have proved them wrong. We, ourselves having no personal or vested interest and certainly no hidden agenda."[1] Hopefully the truth will prevail in the matter.

Recent findings that King Darius, in a manner resembling the tradition of Jadirana, conferred full Iranian citizenship on his Greek enemies who defected to the Persians, and conferred vast land grants on them, and even allowed them to marry Iranians, betray even Mary Boyce's thesis that the Achaemenids in their pride distanced themselves from the *anaryas* (non-Iranians), especially as the Greeks were their uttermost enemies, who ultimately led to their downfall.

Even though I have many more questions in my mind about the *Qisseh-ye-Sanjan* written so many centuries after our arrival in India and far away from Sanjan, and even though it does not seem feasible to me that we migrated only to Sanjan first and then migrated outwards, I always wonder even if we take it for granted that Jaydev Rana or Jadirana (although historians have failed to confirm his name or dynasty) extracted a promise from the Parsi Pilgrims not to convert others, if he were so to say, alive today he will so readily favor Acceptance by the Parsis seeing the pathetic need for it even more than the die-hard, self-destructive opponents do today. His apparent purpose, in keeping with the noble Hindu spirit of Dayaa (mercy) and sympathy for the suffering, was to save the Parsis from harm by not sending them back home by a stormy sea to their oppressors.

The idea of converting did not and could not psychologically exist in the Hindu psyche then until the advent of Islam in India, which did follow, but much later until the Muslims invaded Sanjan and conquered it. It seems to me that the very idea for not converting others could consciously or unconsciously have been invented or inspired in India only after the Muslim conquest as historically, psychologically, ideologically, theoretically, and logically it has no place at all in any polytheistic system, if one is at all conversant with the vast literature on this subject. Thus it is not at all far-fetched to conceive that Jaydev Rana (if one ever existed and belonged to the noble and universal religion of Hinduism which regards the whole universe as one big, united family, etc.), if alive today, would encourage us to survive and thrive by accepting at least the children of inter-marriages, if not other willing ones. And that is what indeed many Hindus are advising us to do. My forthcoming essay on the *Qisseh-ye-Sanjan* further corroborates my stand.

That indeed is the noble and tolerant spirit of the Hindus who simply fail to understand our opposition to acceptance and some even rebuke us for this self-de-

---

1    *Parsiana* Oct 2001, p. 30-41.

structive attitude, even in public media, because they too want us to survive, and they tell me so. Let's face it: no Hindus, no Parsis. If you have any doubts whatso-ever about it, just realize what happened to the millions of Zoroastrians that still survived in Iran at the time when we migrated to India. Our ancestors surely must have known about the noble and tolerant spirit of the Hindus and Hinduism. We cannot repay our debt to them for their acceptance of us. The concept of conver-sion was rather foreign to Hinduism which tends towards Acceptance, ultimately making others one of their own, assimilating them completely in its fold as they did Meher-worshipping Zoroastrians and their Mobeds in north India long ago as well documented by Helmut Humbach. I have detailed elsewhere at length the trade relations between ancient Iran and India, and its clear implications for the Parsis migrating to India, of all places.

Even though, due to denial and/or (euphemistically speaking) cognitive disso-nance prevailing in the community on this subject, no amount of new facts are go-ing to change the minds that are so firmly set in their opinions and cognitive rigid-ity, the efforts made here to present facts on this subject hopefully would enable open-minded readers to see the light on the subject. I therefore do not see any sense or meaning in pursuing this controversy further as I have exhaustedly writ-ten all that I possibly could on this subject, and sincerely but humbly I hope my labor would be of some use to fellow journeymen and future Zoroastrian genera-tions seeking the truth on the subject. Amen!

## PART III. Review of Zoroastrian Studies' The facts as versus Dr. Kersey Antia's Argument for Acceptance

Whenever somebody in recent times has tried to reveal the truth on the matter of acceptance in Zoroastrianism, rejections of such claims come rushing forth, e.g. Firoze Masani's rejection of Dastur Dhalla's views and Dastur Mirza's rejection of Mr. H. E Eduljee's views. Thus it is not surprising that many attempts have been made to vehemently denounce the author's views on the subject. Usually such rebuttals, written in an adversary style, hardly deserve any response, as they are long in innuendos and diatribes against the author, and are short in substance. However, as noted in AFA: "There is such confusion and disparity of views on this topic that even the educated layman who is so eager to know the truth feels completely lost.... Such a phenomenon is called cognitive dissonance in psychology, a subject on which the author has written many papers as a psychologist, and the reader is therefore urged to be aware of its presence in his or her journey to the truth." There is hardly any research on cognitive dissonance, practiced en masse, as by the Parsis in this regard. This author's interest in cognitive dissonance is yet another reason for writing exhaustively on Acceptance, as it affords an opportunity to him to publish further research on the subject of cognitive dissonance by masses. However, most of this review was written in January, 1986, when I was recuperating from a cornea transplant and was off work, and therefore it mostly contains the data available to me at that time, though I have tried to catch up with the later evidence as much as I can as a non-academician, and on my own spare time and meagre resources.

AFA was written not to advocate indiscriminate conversions to Zoroastrianism, as Z.S. willfully implies, but to justify the acceptance of a very unique, self-inspired, self-taught American, Mr. Joseph Peterson, on the basis of Zoroastrian scriptures and history, in face of intense opposition by some Parsis. *Since Z.S. admits the existence of "the few documented cases" which "are notable only for their very rarity," in the very third sentence of its rebuttal (page 1) and several times since, it only serves to strengthen the AFA*. Nothing, however, can be so insulting and demeaning to the greatness of our Holy Prophet, as to resort to such assumptions that "all mankind" most likely meant to Zarathushtra, a small group of Iranian people he knew, *Yasna Ha 32.3 (which describes the Aryan land as only the seventh part of the world)*, being a clear proof of it. The constant references to the spread of Zoroastrianism all over Hafta Keshwar, all the seven regions known to the Indo-Aryans, in all Nyaeshes, Yashts and other prayers, and later in Kalme-i Din to 'bar khalque', literally all over the world, testify to the fact that it meant to spread his religion all over the world, *a tradition derived directly from the Gathas*. There is ample evidence of Elam (ancient Iran) and Mesopotamia carrying on regular trade and cultural relations with the people of Indus Valley even before the Aryans invaded India, that is, even before the time of Asho Zarathushtra.

The observance of religious rituals in the entire North American continent depends solely on part-time mobeds, as the community cannot maintain full-time mobeds for various reasons. And yet the Z.S. derides them. The launching of "a

Z.S. project" for mobeds forced two high priests of the trio to attack it severely: 'To put it mildly, Z.S. has taken the community at large and the Athravans in particular for a ride."[1] See also Dasturji H. K. Mirza's article, "On Some Private and Public Activities of AET," in *Bombay Samachar*.[2] As lamented by Mirza, "religion is becoming a mere source of income, a means of exploitation."[3] What *Bombay Samachar*[4] observes under the heading of "5th North American Zoroastrian Congress" should enable the reader to judge for himself/herself how Z.S. is perceived by the progressive Parsis in India itself. To quote this article "What right" does Z.S. then have "to sermonize about preserving our ancient rites, rituals, customs, etc. After all there are numerous Zoroastrians in North America, some of whom have been Navar-Martabs from Udvada, Nausari, and Bombay. Their study of our scriptures is in-depth, and much better than the persons who are merely parroting one view."

Z.S. asserts: "After 1000 years in India, the Parsis still pray in Avestan," (and the Zoroastrians of North America also invariably devoutly do), and yet Z.S. Alleges: "the same reformist lobby that calls for conversion has brought with it demands for prayers to be altered, shortened or recited in vernacular tongues...." (p. 3). Rather, it was maintained that Mr. Joseph Peterson's example in learning and praying in Avestan was the best reason why the Zoroastrian children in North America should pray in Avestan. If there was any need felt for praying in English, it was not at all related to the Peterson Navjote. Z.S. maintains that since only the Iranian Zoroastrians and Parsis have kept up the faith, one cannot afford to tamper with their integrity, (p. 3), an appeal already made by the AFA. However, the Iranis have so warmly welcomed Mr. Peterson along with an overriding majority of North American Zoroastrians. *It is time therefore for the self-proclaimed Z.S. leader to stop making political capital and gaining publicity by meddling in their affairs when they are doing their best to manage them half the world away from Z.S.*

As regards Z.S.'s contention: "Where is the authority universally accepted and recognized by an accredited world Zoroastrian Body, which could authoritatively pass on to the prospective converts the knowledge and practice of the faith?" (p. 3), it may suffice to note that there will perhaps be no Zoroastrianism today had the early adherents of Zarathushtra waited for such a body. "Will these new Zoroastrians be ... reduced at best to second-class status should they visit India or Iran, unable to enter fire-temples," asks Z.S. (pp. 3 & 4). If so, it won't be the fault of these new Zoroastrians and they will definitely be allowed to enter and worship in fire-temples in Iran where the religion originated. Moreover, they will have no connection with India and so will see no need to visit India. *And so this argument seems to be a ploy to play to the orthodox gallery*, as also the allegation that "the proponents of conversion are so intent upon reducing rituals to a mere skeleton" (p. 4), and is fraught with misrepresentation of the North American milieu, which makes it impossible for even the most ardent orthodox among them to follow all

1    *Parsiana*, August, 1985, pp. 80a-80c.
2    November 17,1985.
3    *Atash Adaran*, Bombay, 1983, p.ii.
4    Dec. 1, 1986, p. 15.

religious practices, and yet they do better in this regard than many Parsis in India. Rather, it is to their credit they try to maintain whatever they can in the spirit of *Shayast ne Shayast*. "Then what is the necessity of the Navjote ritual of the convert in the first place," concludes Z.S. in the same breath (p. 4), an incorrect deduction derived from an incorrect premise. "And why do they insist on his, the convert's acceptance by those who do still practice these rituals?" asks Z.S. Mr. Peterson has not asked for such an acceptance by the Parsis. Z.S. ought to know this but cannot wait to exploit it. What he so ardently wants is following Zarathushtra and Zoroastrian rituals on his own. *And even Z.S. concedes that "no sensible Zoroastrian has the slightest objection to anyone following Zarathushtra's philosophy, reciting the Avesta, or practicing rituals of his own. These are indeed meritorious acts."* (p. 4) *This is, however, a shade different from the triad's views on the subject.* However, the logic behind Z.S.'s assertion that "there is no elitism or selfishness on a spiritual level, no denial that Zarathushtra's teachings can be followed by all in their personal lives" but "should not be confused with the integrity of a community and its culture" seems to be true for the Parsis (though not for the Iranis). But it presents inherent logical contradictions as well as seriously undermines the universal teachings of the prophet, which of course are explained away by asserting that "*to Zarathushtra . . . . the universe meant Iran and mankind meant the Iranians*." (p. 2), (the italics are not our own).

Z.S.'s charge that "Antia relies largely on secondary material, often of dubious scholarly value" (p. 4) is not only misleading but highly insulting to the deceased great scholars he quotes. Arguing in a highly unscholarly manner, *Z.S. finds it convenient not to provide any substantial material*. The opening sentence in AFA (p. 1) underlines the author's interest in contrasting "the views of many eminent Dasturjis and scholars, both past and present". "1 have tried to provide as much evidence as was possible in my circumstances (which refers to being preoccupied as a psychologist with a full-time job and a private practice as well as the duties of a volunteer high priest as opposed to the Z.S. leader's known preference for a full-time involvement in religious affairs with adequate remuneration for the same) in order to inspire readers to decide on the whole of this manuscript rather than any portion of it with which he may not agree." (p. 1) From the very first page onwards, the author quotes views in contrast with the triads'. Z.S. finds it hard to counter them, but keeps picking on and harping on S. J. Bulsara, whose views are quoted for his courage in voicing them over 80 years ago when feelings ran high on this subject, as also for his being an Avesta-Pahlavi professor in various universities and for his being the lay Principal of M.F. Cama Athornan Institute which has severely condemned the Peterson Navjote.

As stated at the onset in AFA, the author does not expect the reader to agree with him on all the counts, and if one feels Bulsara, Dhalla, Meherjirana, Zaehner, etc, are wrong or *Desatir, Dabistan,* and *Ithotar Rivayat* are forgeries, Antia's arguments do not break down at all just because of that. *If the learned S. D. Bharucha did not find the* Ithotar Rivayat *spurious, it must have some merit.* Moreover, the author quotes it only after ensuring that the conclusions from other Rivayats basically support it, and Boyce and even Dasturji Jamasp Asa's own translation of Duchesne-Guillemin's book confirm it. *Rivayat-e Dastur Darab Hamziar* published in Gujarati by R.J. Dastur Meherji Rana in 1896 in Navsari says that it is appropriate to accept a Durwand (non-Zoroastrian) in the fold if he professes faith in the Good Religion (p. 425). It does not at all limit such acceptances to children only. If the author based his opinion solely on allegedly forged Pahlavi books, or a weak source, which rather Z.S. itself has done in alleging that Zarathushtra had three wives, then he perhaps could be guilty of a "voluminous display of intellectual sloth." (p. 5).

*At least three Rivayats address this matter.* The Rivayat of Nariman Hoshang, for instance, declared that "slave boys and girls who have faith in the good religion" should be converted by having the navjote performed, and later, when they show themselves steadfast, should undergo the bareshnum. These rituals would render them clean and enable their masters to eat out of their hands without fear of pollution. The question of the conversion of slaves was again raised in the Rivayat of Kamdin Shapur, dated 966 H./1558 A.D. The Irani priest detailed the procedures necessary to make slave girls ritually pure for marriage.[1]

The Rivayat of Kaus Mahyar, written in 970 A.Y. (c. 1600 A.D.), dilates on this subject forcefully by asking the Iranian priests whether those non-Zoroastrians who had engaged in the most polluting occupations could be converted: Can a grave-digger, a corpse-burner and a "darvand" become Behdin? Their answer: If they observe the rules of religion steadfastly and (keep) connection with the religion, and if no harm comes on the Behdins (thereby), it is proper and allowable.

Z.S. finds Prof. Whitehurst's views of no relevance (p. 5). Rather, Whitehurst's views, as explained later, are totally lost on Z.S. which it should re-study.

Z.S. objects to the author "invoking the authority of Avestan and Pahlavi texts," (p. 5). The author studied all the three texts since his early life, and regards them all with great respect when the three are in harmony with each other, failing which he follows the convention of accepting what is said in the Gathas first, then later Avesta, Pahlavi, Persian, and Gujarati in that order. The emphasis on universality is so very integral to Zarathushtra's message that the Avestan and Pahlavi literature faithfully represents it. Z.S., unable to refute it, resorts to personal attacks instead. So Z.S. cannot hold it against one if one finds ready reference to proselytization in Avestan and Pahlavi literature, *what is not acceptable is Z.S.'s own insistence on branding Zoroastrianism as dualistic and henotheistic primarily on the basis of Pahlavi literature, and arbitrarily seeing it reflected in the Gathas, instead of seeing it the other way around.* Moreover, using such words as "*idiosyncratic versions of the Gathas*" (p. 5) which are the Prophet's very words, is most unfortunate, and it implies bias against them in favor of later literature simply because of the Gathas' structural peculiarity as divine songs.

Z.S. claims that as per the Pahlavi texts "the people being converted" were those who "renounced demon-worship" or who were "non-Zoroastrian pagan Iranians," (p. 5) and alleges "Antia has not, it seems, verified his references" (p. 5). While the former is often true, the data presented in this regard are simply so massive that it is surprising how Z.S. can confine conversions only to the former. Such

---

1    Dhabhar, *The Persian Rivayats*, p. 276.

a synechdocal treatment is quite evident throughout the Z.S. response.

Z.S. complains: "His essay does not adequately answer the question as to why conversion was so rare." A reader only needs to compare this allegation with what an independent lay reviewer says: "On the contrary, he (Antia) imparts to the study his own original contribution. He informs the reader as to why conversion, which was a way of life in ancient Iran, was later rejected by the community...."[1]

Z.S. also complains that "the texts he cites do not prove anything like the scale he favors. In almost every case, his 'example' proves to be dubious or curious or simply wrong." (pp. 5-6). But Z.S. conveniently stops short of substantiating such a serious allegation by not giving actual 'examples' from the text. As regards the scale of conversion, one should realize how the whole of Media, Elam (Pars) and non-Aryan Armenia on Z.S.'s own admission became Zoroastrian. Moreover, the Zoroastrian's prayer to spread his religion over all the seven regions (haft kesh-war) still adorns our literature. More evidence can be found later on in this text.

Following is the point-by-point rebuttal of issues raised by Z.S. under the heading of 'Critical Analysis':

1. Vaetha — Z.S. states: "Clearly, Antia must not have known about this forgery ...." Clearly Z.S. has not read my text properly, which clearly states (p. 2) that Humbach and Jamasp Asa have well countered the contention of the ardent Z.S. supporter Kotwal that Vaetha is a forgery. So the truth is quite the opposite. Pallan Ichaporia, Humbach's colleague, has also supported its validity.[2]

2. Z.S. invalidates Dasturji Dabu's opinion because he "did not implement his belief." So did Dasturji Dhalla, because the community vehemently opposed it. For a Dastur to speak his mind against the popular opinion on this subject is more than one could expect in their times. Moreover, it is rare to find an ardent convert in absence of any missionary activities.

3. The "opinion of illustrious Parsis" are "just opinions" and not facts. Well, they were presented expressly as opinions of community leaders and not facts which are derived exclusively from scholarly research.

4. This is a comment on Mr. Nani Palkhiwala's opinion, which Z.S. disregards as facts but contradicts itself by commenting on it nevertheless. Even so, it misses the mark of Mr. Palkhiwala's learned remarks.

5. How can one "carelessly and deliberately omit" Boyce's mention of Zoroastrianism as "virtually an ethnic faith" and perpetrate "a distortion of scholarship at the expense of innocent readers" when Antia is actively addressing the very issue and trying to show how and why Zoroastrianism became "virtually an ethnic faith" *under a sub-heading that clearly spells out this point*, as well as when one prefaces more than once on the same page (p. 3) Boyce's remarks with the words: *"She also provides us a clue as to why and how we ceased to convert others;" "Boyce gives yet another reason why Zoroastrianism later became confined to Iran.... Boyce provides yet another clue to this problem."* Moreover,

---

1    *Parsiana*, August 1985, p. 75.
2    *Bombay Samachar*, November 15, 1992.

*Boyce is also quoted saying almost the same thing on p. 3* "As numerous Iranian peoples were brought gradually to accept Zoroaster's teachings, they came accordingly to regard these as a part of their own racial heritage, to be treasured accordingly, rather than as a universal message of salvation for all mankind." *The ethnicity of the faith is spelled out far more cogently and clearly in this quote than even in the statement which Z.S. accuses the author of deliberately omitting.* This should help the reader to figure out who is deliberately misguiding whom. Such rather Machiavellian manipulations unfortunately run throughout the Z.S. Text, which regretfully impede honest communication on the subject, and avoids factual presentation of material.

Boyce herself gives examples of Iranians in western Asia Minor permitting non-Zoroastrians in their shrines and "even to draw in others, such as the Macedonians of Philadelphia", even though it "carried the danger of diluting its own traditions," thus allowing Acceptance to triumph over ethnicity which did not ever constitute the real teachings of Zarathushtra. The fifth book of the *Denkard* makes it explicitly clear that the religion was not sent to Iran only but was sent to the whole world, and "everyone can benefit from it." In fact, the high priest (Adurfarnbag I Farroxzadan) states that the religion is currently spreading throughout the world, and will continue to grow and grow until the end of time. De Jong believes this comment may belong to the pre-Islamic times. (op. cit. p. 25). Boyce explicitly and unequivocally clarifies this issue further by emphasizing that Greeks characterized Zoroastrianism as the "Persian religion", "as if it was an ethnic faith like the others which they encountered; *but (however true this had become in part) it was in fact a creedal religion, the oldest known in history. A person was not born a Zoroastrian, nor did he enter the religious community through a physical rite (such as the Jewish one of circumcision); but he became a Zoroastrian on attaining maturity by choosing to profess the doctrines taught by Zoroaster*".[1] Boyce thus leaves no room at all for the Z.S.'s (and even the trio's) exuberant but unwarranted reliance on her opinion for justifying their claim that Zoroastrianism is an ethnic religion – quite the contrary. According to Almut Hintze, who now occupies Boyce's "chair" in Zoroastrianism, in Yasna 39.1-2 the worshipers venerate the souls of all human beings "wherever they may have been born" (kudo-Zatanamchit) and they "are explicitly described not as coming from worshippers' own local community or land, but as possibly having been born elsewhere. Their birthplace being irrelevant, what matters is that they are committed to truth" (Asha).[2] Hintze states that the *Avestan* Herbedestan chapter 5 specifies that any family members could engage in the activity of Athauruna – disseminating the religion.[3] Boyce regards it as missionary work, and K. Hoffmann explains it as working as an "itinerant priest." The only requirements were "the greatest esteem for truth, and one who was less needed for running the household." They would teach the religion … and perform rituals." In the very same *festschrift* (pp. 251-277), Maria Macuch translates the Pahlavi version of

---

1    *A History of Zoroastrianism*, Vol. III, E.J. Brill, Leiden 1991, pp. 219 & 363.

2    Hintze 2007, pp. 269-270.

3    *Exegisti monumenta: festschrift in honour of Nicholas Sims-Williams*, pp. 171-190.

Herbedestan, which explains Athauruna as Asroih (priesthood) and Herbedestan as a religious school (Madresa): "Although the Avestan text was adapted to the changed legal conditions of the Sasanian age with its different laws regarding men and women," she concludes, "it seems as though its main goal, that of spreading the Mazdayasni religion, was still understood perfectly by the Pahlavi exegetes of the Avestan text."

6. Z.S. complains "Antia seems not to ponder sufficiently on the material he quotes at great length." The materials quoted are in fact much shorter than were the original ones for various reasons. Rather, what Z.S. says right after accusing Antia of "not pondering sufficiently" seems so enigmatic: "He (Antia) does not answer the contention that the prescriptions, ritual-ethical and hygienic, of the religion are indeed of such rigor that they best and perhaps only, be fully observed within the context of a refined, national culture". It is Z.S. that "is not pondering sufficiently" as through Boyce, Antia had addresses this development very vividly. However, is this what our prophet really intended to happen? Z.S. turns a blind eye to the prophet and short changes him in its zeal for ethnicity which has its valid place, but not at the expense of the prophet's universal message.

7. Z.S. makes the accusation that "Antia and his colleagues provide living proof of Boyce's contention, as they seek to weaken those ritual and communal observances ... rather than a confused and fragmentary system based upon a diet of 'strained Gathas' and fresh air." Zoroastrians in North America attend more rituals and communal observances and learn more about religion than any of their contemporaries elsewhere, and John Hinnells has borne it out in his Ratanbai Katrak lecture series. Their efforts are clearly visible not only in establishing Dar-e Mehrs all over the continent in a span of only a few years, but also in successfully maintaining them, when so many fire-temples fall into disuse so often in India. What is more important, they try to understand the meaning behind rituals, prayers, and customs. Their priests and preachers are devoted volunteers unlike the Z.S. leader. The use of the phrase "*strained Gathas*" is unfortunately so outrageous and so offensive to our prophet. On page 5 Z.S. complains that Antia "does not adequately answer ... why conversion was so rare," but on page 8, Z.S. quotes Antia's reasons for the same, and even applies them to the North American scene, thus contradicting itself just at the turn of the page.

8. Z.S. again accuses the author of preferring to pad his essay with quotations than do the hard work of thinking about the content of the latter. Or is it quite the opposite as explained later?

9. As regards "the steel mills of Jamshedpur constituting a great big cosmopolitan fire-temple," Z.S. laments "one must figure out what it all means and in what way it is relevant to his argument." Or, is it disinclination to put religion into actual practice?

10. Here Z.S. could not figure out what Antia says while others have easily done so. Moreover, Z.S. here glosses over the fact that Kotwal supports Whitehurst's thesis that Parsis question ritualism today, and so there is no "abrupt transition" here as Z.S. alleges.

11. Z.S. is confused about the connecting point in this author's arguments. Nevertheless, he concludes Antia "scoffs at rituals and purity laws and yet arbitrarily performs certain rituals which suit his convenience. On what authority should one dispense with rituals or shorten them willy-nilly?" To realize the apparent truth that all rituals and purity laws are hard if not impossible to be maintained in a North American milieu (as albeit everywhere else) is not at all tantamount to saying one scoffs at them. And yet I maintain Diva 24 hours a day and pray every day. My wife prays every day for hours. I remember when I was in Bareshnum for my Navar, other priests prevailed over me not to get up in the Ushahin Geh too to pray as I insisted on praying in all five Gehs. Rather, it shows one's tenacity to adhere to one's religion against all odds. Just because we are simply not able to perform higher rituals here because our ritual rules themselves do not permit them, why drum up utterly false charges and that too against priests who go to great length to volunteer their services? It does not mean we perform rituals that suit our needs. We the priests do not dictate to the laymen in North America but serve their needs and perform whatever ceremonies we possibly could. There is no question of disposing with rituals when one does not refuse to perform what one is able to, or when one does not shorten them. Rather, the practice of shortening them is rather rampant in India and often advocated by the Indian high priest visiting here. Even in India drastic cuts have been made in priestly traditions, for example, Boiwalas in Atashbehrams do not undergo the same restrictions that were strictly required only a decade or two ago; Muktad for 18 days are not in vogue, mobeds are not available for inner ceremonies, etc. If Z.S. could understand our helplessness against the Zeitgeist, the spirit of the times, as highlighted by Prof. Whitehurst's analysis, which it has missed entirely, it will not accuse this author in this vein. A Zoroastrian has to try a lot harder for various reasons to remain a practicing Zoroastrian in North America than in India or elsewhere and the hard times predicted for the preservation of our faith in our scriptures have already arrived here. We do not ask for sympathy for our predicament because we have brought it on ourselves, wittingly or unwittingly, by choosing to migrate here, but since Z.S. advises us constantly to help migrate more Zoroastrians for a better life here, we do not expect Z.S. to add insult to injury.

Z.S.: Antia "is on record as having stated that the wearing of the Sudreh-Kushti, for example, is optional." *Antia has never ever stated so.* However, when the Z.S. leader visited Chicago in 1982, certain Zoroastrians urged Antia to counteract Z.S.'s controversial teachings. When unjustly harangued by Z.S. supporters about those not wearing Sudreh-Kusti, Antia actually opined: "I do not condone those not wearing Sudreh-Kusti." However, the Z.S. supporters deliberately or indeliberately misconstrued the word 'condone' as 'condemn', though they later apologized as the whole event was fortunately recorded on a tape. Antia had even protested against this insinuation in a letter dated February 12, 1983, to the then-President of the Zoroastrian Association of Chicago.

However, what is most distressing about this event as recorded on the tape is the blatant assertion by the Z.S. leader that Zoroastrianism is not monotheistic, not even dualistic but is henotheistic, a view completely antithetical to the very teachings of Zarathushtra in the Gathas. What Antia actually exhorted the listeners then, as always, was wearing Sudreh-Kushti is like making a fire-temple out of one's body and carrying it all along with one. I may add that it keeps our inner fire ever burning, ever ready to fight the evil. It inspires us to keep ourselves pure in mind, speech and action, improve the world we live in, and bring it nearer to Frashokereti, the final renovation. It may be added that it also helps us pray for God's protection, thank the Lord for all the good things in life, maintain the delicate balance between the Geti and Minoi world, between the earthly and spiritual worlds, follow the divine order of Asha and the will of God, develop Good Mind, help the poor, and restore the Kingdom of God on earth, etc. All these concepts are woven into the Sudreh-Kushti prayers. Every time the author performs Navjote of a child, he explains them to the child. Sudreh-Kushti is Zoroastrianism in miniature. It is so deeply rooted in antiquity that along with the Hindu's Janoi, it is the most ancient religious symbol known to mankind and yet it is so much in harmony with the needs of the modern times. Rather, the modern man desperately needs such an inspiring symbol to guide him constantly on the path of true spirituality in these difficult times, especially when he cannot depend on so-called preachers who may be simply after his gold.

When the modern man is desperately searching his roots, he can ill afford to throw away such a perfect emblem of his roots. Gone are the times when a Zoroastrian in India and Iran prayed five times a day and did Kushti as required, a practice this author maintained for a long time, but it is still comforting to know that in the spirit of *Shayast ne Shayast* we can serve the same purpose by wearing and performing the Sudreh-Kushti regularly, and let it guide us consciously as well as unconsciously. In our times, we are getting increasingly aware of the effect of the Unconscious Mind and Archetypes, as well as conditioning on our behavior. Since Zoroastrians have been wearing Sudreh-Kushti for so many thousands of years, it has by now become an unconscious element of their being – a 24-hour automatic switch-on to their spiritual roots, a constant reminder of their divine destiny, an unparalleled Minoi inheritance, a constant reminder of divinity within us, and a symbolic spiritual conditioning unparalleled in the religious history of mankind. In the North American milieu we are forced to deal only with logical rather than metaphysical explanations for wearing Sudreh-Kushti. Whitehurst's thesis suggests that this will eventually be so, if not already so, even in our strongholds in India. We are therefore left with this option and have to use it as best as we can. If we do not, it bodes ill for our survival. It is here that Whitehurst's views can be useful: since the Gathas unmistakenly regard Man as the co-worker of Mazda, and implore Man to assist God in fulfilling His divine plans by making right choices, we can use our Kushti prayers to inspire ourselves and our children to make right choices and use the earth's resources for Frashokereti or, in other words, as Whitehurst puts it, our "concerns should be directed toward the production and distribution of the earth's resources so that the material potential of this planet might be used for the benefit of as much of mankind as possible".

Our Kusti prayers represent these ideals very well, and can become the foundation on which will rest the rational faith of the future Zoroastrian as well as converts. As many Zoroastrian children unfortunately do not learn much more than Kushti prayers, it is all the more important that we concentrate on these prayers. One of the reasons that led the priests to perform Mr. Peterson's Navjote was the fact that he made his own Sudreh-Kushti, and he was so completely convinced of the absolute essentialness of having his Navjote done for becoming a true Zoroastrian. As Antia observed at his Navjote: *"Peterson is the best reason why a Zoroastrian should wear Sudreh-Kushti."* Not only has Antia worn Sudreh-Kushti ever since his Navjote, but his children, all born in U.S.A., also find wearing it very meaningful. It was for this reason that the suburban issue of *Chicago Tribune*, one of the world's leading papers (Sept. 28, 1977) carried a 2-page article on this author, entitled "Clothes, Job Lead to Ancient Faith" and explained at length the significance of wearing Sudreh-Kushti. Such outstanding is the influence of the Navjote ceremonies done by Antia on the Irani Zoroastrians in Chicago that they too have started doing the Navjote of their children at an early age, instead of waiting until adulthood as is their tradition. Thus, the Z.S.'s allegation is highly mischievous and misleading in this regard, *to say the least.*

Z.S. also asks, as seen above, "on what authority...?" Rather one should ask Z.S. *what authority does it have to criticize priests, and constantly criticize the part-time nature of the North American priests*? Priests have their own organizations, whether in North America or elsewhere, to decide on priestly matters, and they would not tolerate any interference by self-proclaimed lay preachers, who have hardly any record of volunteering for any cause but their own. The community has had the good fortune of having several learned Dasturjis as well as lay scholars who served the community as preachers, in their part-time. Many Dasturjis, such as Dabu, Kotwal, Kaikhushru Dastur of Udvada, and Minocher-Homji were full-time teachers before they became Dasturjis. Dasturji Mirza taught Avesta-Pahlavi in order to survive as a Dastur. Without part-time priests it will not be possible to run even Bombay fire-temples. Volunteer part-timers, as priests or laymen scholars are only continuing a glorious tradition, while Z.S. leaders seem to lack miserably on this noble tradition of selfless service, and seem to mislead the public by running down volunteer part-time priests. The issue of Z.S.'s own authority has been recently brought to the forefront as seen above. Z.S. founder is the *only* self-proclaimed preacher in our long history who has charged fees for his lectures, services, etc.

12. Since Z.S. concedes that the Rivayat question about conversion "surely implies that they were ... at least an extreme rarity". The Peterson case being "an extreme rarity," if not the only one of its kind known to history, logically Z.S. should accept it as such. However, as the triad did not concede even such a rarity, it does not matter to them whether the converts were children or adults, as long as it can be said that they were converted, and for this reason the issue of converts being children or adults was not raised in AFA. Any omission of sentences from Boyce or others' works here or elsewhere does not in any way alter the real thrust of the argument. As I call myself Zoroastrian and try to live as one, I would not

deceive or deviate from the truth (Asha) in any way, and most of the time I do not even know how to, as I am not even inclined to try it. That's the real meaning of sud-reh and following Tarikat in modern times.

13. & 14. Dr. Undevia had to consider all the facts mentioned by Z.S. and many more. It is therefore improper for Z.S. to challenge a highly acclaimed scientific researcher such as Dr. Undevia and his conclusions without providing a fact-filled rejoinder he deserves.

15. The main reason however for mentioning these sources is made so perfectly clear in the booklet (p. 10, lines 12-16) that it does not befit one to even drum up such a charge. Z.S. here avoids the answer to the question: How could our sacred texts blaspheme our prophet by depicting Hindus and others becoming Zoroastrian when only Mazdayasnis could become Zoroastrian. Even if the Pahlavi word Hindugan means India, and even if only the Persian settlers there and in Asia Minor practiced Zoroastrianism, per Z.S., they settled there a millennium after the times of King Vishtasp and Zarir. Moreover, Kotwal's admission that "In the Avesta there is evidence that Zoroastrians of old used to do 'missionary' work in India and even China," already noted in the text (p. 10), (as well as many other notations, noticeably the ultimate absorption of the Elamites into the Persian fold and the adoption of Zoroastrianism by the Armenians), contradicts the Z.S. stand.

16. & 17. Same rejoinder as 15.

18. E. Meherjirana's understanding of religious traditions was uncanny given the state of the arts then, and so it is not right to say: "The references seem to have thrown in (by Meherjirana) for lack of anything better." Z.S. notes: "Antia quotes all this from Kotwal/Boyd but does not trouble to verify their references; it is strange that in quoting the Gathas themselves, he is content to rely on tertiary matters." If one understands the medieval milieu under which Meherjirana worked, and faithfully served the community before the advent of modern savants, one would not even raise such an issue. Nor do Kotwal and Boyd concern themselves about verifying these references and justifiably so. Even the Pahlavi text does not always translate the Gathas correctly. *What is, however, more important here is: even the hero of Dasturji Kotwal does not share Kotwal and Z.S.'s views.* As Mary Boyce told a group of Chicagoans in November 1985, the Parsis did not regard conversion as wrong until the 19th century, and Meherjirana's views prove it. Recently J. K. Choksy's research also has pointed to the same conclusions. What is most obvious, is not that Antia's references or texts are invalid, but that the triad's opinion was not the one that a study of our history and religion would lead to, because many other Dasturjis besides Dhalla and Bode have had drastically divergent opinions on this subject. Since Z.S. emphasizes traditions so much, and since Kotwal and Boyd prove that Erachji best represents Parsi traditions and learning faithfully for his times, it is not appropriate for Z.S. to belittle him and his views, and much less to distort the truth.

19. The challenge North American Zoroastrians are facing is: Could they remain Zoroastrian if they cannot follow higher rituals as they are not brooked by our purity laws, etc., even if they want to? "One who practices rituals is guilty, on

Antia's views of ritualism," says Z.S., a typical Z.S. canard, *but this allegation is not legitimately derived from any of Antia's statements* which rather suggest a healthy respect for rituals, and a plain wish to return to the medieval days when our very existence was not threatened by modernity. He has observed strictest ritualistic and ethical requirements possible in his life, and is not impressed by mere lip-service to rituals. As Z.S. maintains that a "deritualized man" loses "divine connection to guard him," one hopes Z.S. will find it for itself, because Antia has found it since he was nine when his religious awakening and journey began after joining the Cama Athornan Institute in 1945. "Antia might be well advised to renounce the priesthood," notes Z.S. and rests its case on unwarranted accusations, even as it claims to be so devoted to the welfare of priests. In a lengthy article in *Bombay Samachar* in 1985 (as also above) this author has already exploded the myth Z.S. and its kind have spread about Zoroastrians in North America "abandoning ritual for motives which appear to be a mixture of laziness, ignorance, and conformism".

20. Even Prof. Zaehner is not spared the wrath. Z.S. faults him for predicting the extinction of Zoroastrianism as a cult (not as a race or religion), though its leader predicted the extinction of the race itself in a *Wall Street Journal* article (May 27, 1982, p. 18) "It is a great tragedy, this wonderful religion may soon die out," which seems to have even prompted the heading of the article as: "After 3400 years, India's Parsis Fear that They Are Dying Out". To call Zaehner "an embittered misanthrope," "a troubled man with a chequered past," etc. is not Zoroastrian in spirit to say the very least. This author has known about Zaehner's views ever since as a teenager when he read Sir R. P. Masani's angry letter in the Reader's Column of *The Times of India* criticizing them. But as W. B. Henning observed during the third series of Ratanbai Katrak Lectures "There is scarcely a point on which there is unanimity. Each scholar will dissent from his fellows on one point or the other.... A controversy between these two scholars (Herzfeld and Nyberg) was natural and inevitable; for their disagreement on everything that concerns Zoroaster is complete." (*Zoroaster*, Oxford University Press, 1951, pp. 35 & 4). If there is such a diversity of opinions on scholarly grounds, how much more will surface if we start judging scholars on the basis of their personality and lifestyle, *including that of the Z.S.'s leader.* Boyce has spoken highly of Zaehner as being one of the first scholars who, despite being a devout Christian himself, maintained that Christianity was as much rooted in Zoroastrianism as in Judaism, perhaps even more, a fact already recorded in the text (p. 15, lines 3 & 4), but missed by Z.S.

21. Dasturji Dhalla had the courage to express his liberal views even though it adversely affected his livelihood as a high priest. Z.S. has yet to show such moral courage. Dhalla was a living embodiment of Zoroastrian virtues. Therefore, what Z.S. alleges is most regrettable: "There seems to be an undercurrent of hypocrisy, not only in Antia, but in the source he cites as authorities on ritual," which in this case is Dhalla, though Dhalla is quoted as an authority on our religion and not on rituals. To call Dhalla a hypocrite on the basis of rumors that he "insisted on the meticulous performance of his funerary rites," which even if true, could very well

have been inspired by factors consistent with his amiable personality when alive. After all, he performed all religious ceremonies he could as a Dastur. While Z.S. charges others of using "unprofessional methods", "scholarly dubious" material, "spurious sources", "scholarly fantasies", and what not, how can Z.S. justify its allegations against Dhalla purely on the basis of rumors? Such allegations are typical of the orthodox who said the same thing about S. D. Bharucha. My inquiries about its veracity with those who knew Dhalla have negated the Z.S. rumor. Z.S. inquires why Antia had his child's Navjote done in India? As a matter of fact, he really did not want it done in India, because of the Z.S. leader "threatening that Peterson and the priests who had performed the ceremony would be "bashed up" if they attempted to come to Bombay and enter the fire-temples." (*Mid-day*, August 4, 1983). However, his aged mother wanted it done in India, and he decided to respect her wish, though such Talibani maneuvers are not without risks to their targets.

22. Z.S.: *Mazda means 'Wisdom", not One God*. Nothing better can be expected of an organization which does not regard Zoroastrianism as monotheistic, even as it professes to follow traditions which clearly support the meaning of Mazda as God or (Lord) Wisdom. Yasna 41.2 declares Mazda to be "the most beneficent of those who exist". However, such evidence abounds in the AFA which Z.S. passes over. It seems Z.S. does not even spare Mazda if the meaning of the word does not conform to the Z.S's, even though the whole world knows it as the word for God or Wise (Lord).

23. No need at all for those that charge Antia of "intellectual sloth", etc., to ask why Yasna 33.3 and 4 reflect 'the universal claim' of Zarathushtra, as the explanation follows immediately in the text and is provided by Schmidt, one of the most learned scholars of our times.

24. Z.S.: "Antia's remark of winning 'treatise-prizes' at the age of 19 is utterly irrelevant." This remark relates to Antia's study of Zoroastrianism convincing him at an early age that Zoroastrianism was not meant only for the Mazdayasnis. Various research articles in *Mysteria Mithrae*,[1] for example, reconfirm the Iranian origin of Mithraism. "In its broader aspects Mithraism needs also to be reviewed," it maintains, "in a wider setting which extends from Egypt to ancient Bactria." Even Michael P. Speidel who sees "only a few Iranian elements" in Mithraism, admits that "there is indeed much tangible Iranian in the cult." (*Mithras-Orion*, E.J. Brill, Leiden, 1980, p. 2). While Mithraism was basically different from Zoroastrianism, how would some of the Zoroastrian elements infiltrate into non-Zoroastrian hands if they were strictly supposed to be the prerogative of the Mazdayasnis only as claimed by the triad. Moreover, despite having expressly stated in the text (p. 15) that "these influences seem to be an unfolding of the divine plan to make Zarathushtra's precepts reach mankind," Z.S. finds Antia's remarks "utterly irrelevant."

25. Z.S. gives its own undocumented opinion on the subject of Xerxes' Daiva inscription, conversion and Turanians whereas AFA is based on many research

---

1    Ugo Bianchi, Ed., E.J Brill, Leiden, 1979.

findings that contradict it. King Noshirwan (Khosrow I)'s conversion of Turks as noted in AFA rules out any possibility of their being anything other than non-Iranians. While the early Turanians were Iranians, later Iranians addressed all their tormentors as the Turks, or Turanians. This is also explained by Boyce.[1] *CHI* (Vol. II, p. 691) finds Xerxes' violation of the sanctuaries of non-Iranians "understandable in view of the negligible role such edifices played in Iranian worship."

Z.S. hurls yet another insult at the prophet: *"the mythical 'Seven Climes' of the world, does not presuppose acquaintance with other peoples, only an extension of the world he (Zarathushtra) already knew"* as if his knowledge was limited only by that, the Avestan and Pahlavi works clearly testifying to the contrary. AFA specifies on p. 17 that it refers not to the Zoroastrian settlers, but to the spread of Zoroastrianism among the *local* population of Cappadocia" per Boyce and even underlines the word local. See also #5 for Boyce. Boyce even reports that the Sakas there converted to Zoroastrianism at the time.[2] I have elsewhere detailed at length the contacts between the Elamites and the Harappans, etc. in India in ancient times. Further, as R. Ghirshman observes, Anahita "enjoyed most popularity beyond the western frontiers of Iran, and her cult spread to Lydia, where she was called 'the lady of Bactria,' to Pontus, Cappadocia and Armenia. It was probably even more popular than that of Mithra.... Artaxerxes introduced to the cult of this religion the worship of Anahita in the form of an image, in imitation of the Babylonian and Greek religions, in both of which worship of images was found. *His intention was apparently to introduce a religion that would be common to all the peoples of his Empire".*[3] Ghirshman's views are reinforced by *CHI* (Vol. 2, pp. 670-671): "There is testimony that the cult of Anahita was spread throughout the Iranian empire by Artaxerxes II, who introduced statues of the goddess." It is interesting to note that Zohak (Azhi Dahaka), a non-Iranian, sacrificed to Anahita in Babylon according to Avan Yasht (5.29). *The Mazdean King Kanishka* who later wooed Buddhism may have been guided by the same instinct that Artaxerxes II showed for the preservation of the empire. Zoroastrian settlers in Asia Minor must have had little use for such religious syncretism which was apparently practiced by the local inhabitants. The satrap of Sardis, it seems, was worried not because non-Zoroastrians began following the religion of Iran, but that they did not do it right.

This seems to be an effort on the part of the King to win over the Greeks and others to an acceptable religious formula based on Iranianism: Strabo considered Cappadocia "almost a living part of Persia". Even though Strabo lived when the Persian influence had waned and there was no need for Persian settlements in Asia Minor, "he speaks of Cappadocia as having many temples of Persian gods and many fire-temples and many fire priests". (op. cit., p. 107), and Pausanias reported Iranian fire ceremonies as late as the second century A.D. How is this possible unless the *local* population had joined the Persian faith in large numbers?

---

1    *A History of Zoroastrianism*, Vol. I, p. 105.
2    *History II*, p. 275.
3    *Iran*, Penguin Books, 1978, pp. 270, 314, and 316.

26 to 36. Z.S. unjustly lumps these under Antia's instead of under S. J. Bulsara's views. Why? The reason for quoting Bulsara's views is made very explicit on p. 20 in AFA. Z.S. asks: "Why rely on an article from an obscure Persian magazine of the 1930's?" *The Journal of the K.R. Cama Oriental Institute*, in which Bulsara's article was published, is by no stretch of imagination 'an obscure Persian magazine'. Moreover, it is the best journal one can find in India for research on Iranian topics, and in the 1930's and 1940's its standards were quite high because of the abundance of reputable scholars then, which makes it the best source for locating earlier scholarly Parsi views on the subject, the latter being an explicit reason for writing AFA.

26. Z.S. "There is more padding and less content." Every argument in AFA is supported by a reference. It is Z.S. however who fails to do the same. What *CHI* says in this regard is already noted in AFA. Prof Richard Frye of Harvard also confirms: "Some Arabs were Zoroastrian".[1] Many Babylonians adopted Iranian names, but as Iranians also adopted Babylonian names, it is difficult to prove the former adopted Zoroastrianism.

Z.S.: "Bulsara and Antia seem to be unaware of the serious methodological problem of using Firdausi's poem,, (*Shahnameh*) as a straightforward early historical resource." Bulsara knew far better and followed here the scholarly convention of quoting *Shahnameh* only when the evidence from other sources supports it. Z.S. is no match for Bulsara.

Z.S.: Antia "treats all this material on much the same level, whether it is the work of a reputed scholar or the emotive musings of an amateur (as for instance the ridiculous suggestion that the ancient Semitic names of the months are really distorted forms of the names of the Yazatas, a completely unscholarly fantasy that Antia solemnly repeats without a word of analysis." (p. 2). Z.S. again ignores the reason for quoting Bulsara. To deride Bulsara's views as "emotive musings of an amateur" is not only un-Zoroastrian, but it also backfires on Z.S. as Z.S. itself seems ignorant of the fact that Bulsara's views on the similarity of Egyptian and Zoroastrian names of the months is well recognized now (*CHI*, Vol. 2, pp. 714-785), which shows at great length that the analogy between the Egyptian and the Later Avestan calendars is not purely accidental. Moreover, it is even possible to establish the date when the two became linked together. The fact that in 632 the first month of Farvardin coincided completely with the fourth Egyptian month, Khoyak, seems indicative "of the analogous structure of the two calendars." (p. 766). This now will enable historians to compare a Zoroastrian date with an Egyptian one and "verify some Later Avestan dates with the aid of the tables available for the Egyptian calendar". Moreover, as *CHI* observes, of all the calendars in ancient times, only the Egyptian and Iranian calendars had "special religious names" of divinities instead of numbers. (p. 774).

Z.S. is so unaware of the fact that any scholarly discussion of Zoroastrian calendar is not possible without discussing Egyptian calendar, and yet it does not hesitate to indulge in undue criticism based on pure fantasy. Thus in what seems to be the most illuminating treatise on the Zoroastrian calendar ever published, Prof.

---

1    Op. cit. p. 26.

Willy Hartner finds it necessary to discuss the old Egyptian calendar (*CHI*, Vol. 2, pp. 764-772) and concludes: "The main, though not the only purpose of the preceding demonstration was to prove that, despite differences of five days occurring on a great many occasions between the two calendars, the Later Avestan Farvardin coincided at times with the Egyptian Khoyak. This was true thus also at the time when the Later Avestan calendar came into being, and thereby the two calendars' close connection appears to be firmly established." (p. 768). "At all times and places we find that calendar and religion form an inseparable unity" says Hartner (p. 714) and these similarities between the two calendars must have led Bulsara to assume similarities in religion and indeed he found Kuka in agreement with him as mentioned in AFA (p. 20). Even if his interpretation of the data were not correct in view of later research, they were based on facts known at the time, and not fantasy, and many other scholars in his times interpreted them same way as Bulsara did. But Bulsara was too great a scholar in his time, and a truly great and pious soul, to deserve to be treated as cavalierly and haughtily by Z.S., which lacks his noble qualities egregiously. One characteristic of an Ashavan is not to forsake Asha as a person or a scholar. Hope Z.S. can claim it for itself.

Z.S.: "In any case, what Parsi would dare to tread on the soil of scholarship in Hungarian or Finnic or Scythian Hun?" (p. 26). On the contrary it seems "the very important role that Scyths played in the history of eastern Europe has commonly been recognized. This is not the case with their role in the history of Central and Western Europe, or rather with their interference in this history. The large group of Scythian antiquities in Central Europe, and in particular in Bessarabia, Transylvania, Hungary and Slovakia, have been dealt by many scholars. Most of them agree that the Scyths must have invaded Transylvania and the Hungarian Plain at the turn of the 6th and 5th centuries B.C., and that soon all contacts ceased between those Scyths and their kin in the Pontic lands. On the other hand, Scythian antiquities of Bessarabia and Bulgaria suggest that a new influx of Scythian elements took place around 600 B.C. Scythian antiquities were also found in many countries beyond the Hungarian Plain. The advance of the Scyths may be followed, via Southern Germany, as far as France." (*CHI* II, p. 19). *CHI* devotes an entire chapter on the Scythians (Vol.II, pp.149-199) to emphasize their role in Iranianizing Western Europe. "The Scyths may even have reached Bulgaria". "Similar masterpieces of the same period found in several sites in Romania and Bulgaria illustrate the impact on Thracian art of the Scythian decorative art, the roots of which go back to Iran". "Some Iranian tribes seem to have lived in the Ukraine before the arrival of the genuine Scyths". "The legend (of four objects falling from the sky) may nevertheless belong to the ancient Iranian tradition. In Avestan tradition the beginning of Yima's (Jamshed's) millennium was marked by divine intervention comparable to the dropping from the sky, in the Scythian legend, of the four golden objects"."According to these (archaeological) data, there were at least two or perhaps three, westward expansion of the scrub culture from beyond the Volga, the bearers of which were presumably Iranians. Only the last of these migrations which is believed to have taken place in the 10th or 9th century B.C. may be connected with the migration of the "Royal Scyths." ... In the 7th century B.C. the Scythians invaded Iran and subdued Media ... where they had ample opportunity to acquaint themselves with Oriental culture and art (and I may add Zoroastrianism). Eventually, however, in around 600 B.C., the Scyths were overthrown by the Medes and expelled from Asia".

"Scythian art spread into Romania, and ultimately some elements of the ancient Oriental heritage, Western Asiatic or Iranian, reached even Western Europe and affected Celtic art." Thus, Bulsara was not "entering the realm of historical fantasy and leaving scholarship part far behind" as Z.S. alleges (p. 24) in a rather unscholarly fashion. *CHI* also supports Zajti's claim that the ancestors of the Bulgarians too were of Hun origin. Since Zoroastrianism tended to become diluted and syncretistic as it moved further away from the center of Iran, the Scythians, who are originally an Iranian people who ruled over Iran for two centuries, may not have been orthodox Zoroastrians, though even in their art they bore clear evidence of their Iranian ancestry. However, if the *Journal of the K.R. Cama Oriental Institute* deemed it fit to publish Zajti's views on this subject twice (Nos. 10 & 13), his views, at least in his time, must have had some validity. The very fact that *CHI* devotes a 50-page chapter on the Scyths underlines their importance as an Iranian people. "About 3000 to 2500 years ago, the southern part of Eastern Europe was occupied mainly by peoples of Iranian stock; nowadays their only traces are archaeological remains and topographic names of Iranian derivation scattered over that area. The main Iranian-speaking peoples of the region at that period were the Scyths and the Sarmatians". (*CHI*, II, p.149). The ancient Persians called Scyths 'Saka' and the Indians called them "Shaka". "Scythian remains have been found in various regions west of Scythia in West Podolia, Central Transylvania, Hungary, Slovakia, etc; they mostly form distinct groups of Scythian culture. But also appear scattered in parts of Romania and Bessarabia". (*CHI* II, pp.183-184).

Antia too has extensively studied these Scyths and presented a paper on them at a scholarly seminar, but the bulk of his writings await a publication offer.

From "Herodotus' account of the Scythians' own religion" Boyce surmises: "it appears that their faith was essentially the general old Iranian one, with, cultically, veneration paid 'in especial' to the hearth fire (Hestia), and carried out without images, altars or temples". She interprets some of the unusual Scythian rites in terms of pre-Zoroastrian beliefs.[1]

Zeuss & G. Nagy, as quoted by Ellis H. Minns, also maintain that the names of Scythian deities have "a distinctly Iranian look". Minns also quotes Theophyloctus (VII.8) as saying of the Scythians: "They excessively reverence and honor fire, also the air and the water: they sing hymns to the earth but they adore and call God only Him who created the heaven and the earth", the latter suggesting a Zoroastrian rather than a pre-Zoroastrian belief. Further, Minns observes, "they disposed of their dead on platforms instead of burying them". A large gold plate from the Oxus Treasure shows a man carrying a bundle of rods in his right hand and covering his mouth with bands, which reminds Minns of "the regulations of

---

1    *A History of Zoroastrianism*, Vol. II, E.J. Brill, Leiden, 1982, pp. 11, 40-41.

the Avesta for preventing the breath from defiling the sacred flame and the BARSOM carried by the Mage".[1]

As Henry Field asserts on the basis of an extensive research on this subject: "....Thus, the Scythio-Sarmatian tribes were linguistically, philologically and culturally closely related to the Iranian peoples".[2]

Shaul Shaked maintains, "It is perfectly true that in (Sasanian) period it (Zoroastrianism) did address itself to all mankind" and presents passages that "stress its universal character." "The Creator Ohrmazd sends his religion not only to the Kingdom of Iran but to the whole world and to every variety (of human beings)." (Madan's *Denkard*, p. 460, II 8-18). "This is the greatest virtuous deed of evil religion: when he comes from evil religion over to the Good Religion".[3]

According to Richard Frye, "Iran was not just the land where Iranian speakers lived, but something more abstract which we should examine.... Iraq with its capital Ctesiphon was called by the Sasanian kings the "heart of Iranshahr".... The ruler spent most of the year in this capital, only moving to cities of the highlands of Iran for the summer."[4] While "Armenia and Georgia were separate kingdoms allied to Sasanian times", yet, as Frye asserts, they were "*not* part of Iranshahr". There were Iranians who lived *outside* the boundaries of the Sasanian state such as Sogdians in Central Asia and the Alans in the North Caucasus. There were, of course, non-Iranians within Iranshahr, primarily the Semitic-speaking people of Iraq. Yet they were considered as part of Iran; other peoples were in non-Iran (Aneran)."[5] If Armenia had been a predominantly Zoroastrian land before the advent of Christianity as admitted by Z.S., even though it was neither Iranian, nor part of Iranshahr, it is quite plausible that Iraq where the Sasanian capital and the 'heart of Iran' lay, adopted Zoroastrianism to some extent. Not surprisingly Frye asserts that "*some Arabs were Zoroastrians.*"[6] Compare this comment from a world-famous Iranist with Z.S.'s comment, "We do not have the name of a single Babylonian (Arab) converted to Zoroastrianism." Compare it also with Taziyane Baste Kustiyan (Kusti-wearing Tazic Arabs) in our prayers – Nirang-e Sarosh Yasht Vadi.

The fact that Armenia was not considered a part of Iranshahr is further evident from the inscription of the Sasanian King Narseh at Paikuli in Iraq, in which he twice refers to his "departing from Armenia to the side of Iranshahr".[7]

27-36 & 39. Z.S. repeatedly contrives to misrepresent Bulsara's views as Antia's, though Antia has repeatedly explained the reasons for quoting them – not as much for "his research which is outdated" as for his bold views which may have even cost him his job, it seems, as the Principal of M.F. Cama Athornan Institute, as an old alumnus informed me that Bulsara was summarily removed from this post to

---

1    *Scythians and Greeks*, Part One, Biblo & Tannen, New York, 1965, pp. 85, 93 & 58.
2    "Contributions to the Anthropology of the Soviet Union", *Smithsonian Miscellaneous Collections*, Vol. 110, 13, 168. See also 169-174.
3    *From Zoroastrian Iran to Islam*, Aldershot, Great Britain: Variorum, 1995, pp. 176-178, 192.
4    *The Golden Age of Persia: The Arabs in the East*, Harper & Row, 1975, p. 8.
5    Op. cit., pp. 12 & 15.
6    Op. cit., p. 26.
7    Frye, op.cit., p. 375-6.

his utter surprise. It required immense moral courage and scholarship to take the stand he did at the time he did, a stand that is conspicuous by its timid avoidance today for political gains.

It should be apparent to the reader by now that Z.S.'s intent is not to search for the truth, but to attack Antia unfairly and deviously by presenting Bulsara's views as Antia's. However, I would like to refer the reader to an article in Gujarati, in the *Jame-Jamshed Weekly*, (July 13, 2003, p. 4) that states "recently a unique discovery has come to light. Today's historians and archeologists opine that a Zoroastrian group went to Europe from Yazd city in Iran. This relates to the 13th century. After facing all the difficulties on their way, they settled in a place called *Jczberny* in a country called Hungary in Europe. There were two or three other groups with them too. These journalists have only a little while ago made a surprise visit with some journalists from Iran (to inquire) about their ancestors that continued to live (in Yazd). They report that their ancestors came from a place called Yazd in Iran. These people have evidence of their ancestors hailing from Yazd. Their houses are very much like the ones in Yazd. Even today, their facial features resemble Iranian (features).... They are surviving there as an ethnic group by farming".

On the basis of life-long research, the well-known Professor M. Rostovtzeff describes "the Scythian kingdom" as "a formation completely Iranian, a northern counterpart of the kingdom of Darius and Xerxes.... We find in South Russia a whole group of products partly manufactured by the Iranians (Scythians) themselves, partly for the Iranians by the Greeks. This Iranian world is the pre-Zoroastrian one which disseminated the cults of Mithra and Anaitis (Anahita)".[1] He adds: *"We have conclusive evidence that in the sixth century (B.C.) there were compact bodies of Scythian dwelling in Hungary: this is proved by well-established archaeological finds which have often been studied.* (Italics are mine). The dates of these finds is certain, the sixth century B.C. This may be compared with the celebrated Vettersfelde find, published by Furtwangler and belonging to the sixth or fifth century B.C. Vettersfelde, as is well known, is in Northern Germany. The question arises, whether the Hungarian and Prussian finds bear witness to Scythian ascendancy, or only to Scythian expansion, in regions so remote from the center of their power.... The finds hitherto made point to Scythian ascendancy in Southern Bulgaria and in Dobruzha (near the mouth of the Danube) from the fourth century (B.C.) onwards". (p. 42). He provides ample references to support his thesis, which is also supported by Ellis H. Minns.[2] In his opinion, "the Scythians' close affinity with the Sarmatians, whose Iranian nationality is not disputed, and the evidence of Herodotus, confirmed by archaeology, as to the *religion of the Pontic Scythian tribes of South Russia was Iranian, nearly akin to the Medes and Persians*, but belonging to another branch of the stock. It is well known that the linguistic evidence ... is in no way opposed to this hypothesis. But sufficient emphasis has not been laid on the archaeological evidence, which seems to me almost decisive. We have seen that very ancient monuments, which we have

1   *Iranians and Greeks in South Russia*, Russell & Russell, New York, 1922 & 1969, pp. 9, 11.
2   *Scythians & Greeks*, Cambridge, 1913, pp. 150 & 236.

every reason for assigning to the Scythians, can only be explained by Iranian parallels; and that it is impossible to define the general character of Scythian art, except by connecting it with Persian art of the same period". (p. 60).

Rostovtzeff finds that the Scythian kings, like their Iranian counterparts, believed in "the connexion of the royal power with divinity" (*khwarreh*) and in "the dualism of the Iranian religion". It is important to observe that the same subject recurs, six centuries later, on Sassanid gems. Still more interesting, that the holy communion reappears on a great many other monuments, in which the administering divinity is not the great god Ahura Mazda, but the great goddess whom we may call Anaitis" (Anahita) (p. 104), which seems to me to be in keeping with the later Achaemenian tradition. However, I must note that *the Scythians worship Ahura Mazda as Armazi,* and named a town near Yalta after this name. Rostovtzeff asserts: "The Scythian legends collected by Herodotus corroborate my theory.... The part of Herakles (mentioned by Herodotus) is played by the hero and demi-god Rostahm. The legend reported by Herodotus is confirmed by the archaeological monuments". (p. 107).

Further, the Sarmatians who also "belonged to the Iranian group" were "advancing east and west towards the Danube and western Europe" (p. 114). "The Sarmatian element played an increasingly important part in the Roman army, and we may go so far as to say, that in the third and fourth centuries some Roman corps, like that which figures on the arch of Galerius at Salonica, were almost entirely Sarmatian both in composition and in armament". (p. 119). The Sarmatians ... did not greatly differ from the Scythians. They were Iranian ... perhaps of purer blood than the Scythians". (p. 120). "The Sarmatians would seem to have been fire-worshippers". (p. 121). The objects they used are the same as the Scythians used. "But one characteristic is immediately obvious: the total absence of Greek imports which was not the case with the Scythians. "Imports are not lacking, but they are Oriental, generally Persian". *They "maintained regular relations with the eastern Iranian world, especially with the Persian kingdom".* (p. 123). They even left their mark on what Rostovtzeff calls the Irano-Celtic art. (p.139). "It is well known that he (the Parthian king Mithridates) made himself popular by marrying his sons and daughters to Scythian princesses and princes." (p. 149). Except for Nero, "more sensible (Roman) emperors saw that the Roman forces were not sufficient to conquer the Iranian portion of the world. The Sarmatians and the Parthians remained dangerous enemies, to be averted, if possible, from the Roman frontiers". (p. 153).

Rostovtzeff maintains that "the ruling family (of Bosphorus) had not a drop of Greek blood in its veins". The queen of Bosphorus, who seems to be partly Sarmatian, married a Sarmatian prince.[1] "She struck coins with her own effigy and the insignia of Mithridates". (p. 151). Sarmatian deities play a great part in the coinage of Mithridates VII, the son of Dynamis. (p. 157). The second century B.C. witnessed "the thorough Iranization of the dynasty and its increasing religiosity". (p. 159). The organization of society in all Bosphoran towns seems to have been based on "an institution of the same sort in the Iranian world". (pp. 165-166).

---

1   Op. cit., p. 151.

Rostovtzeff regrets that the part played by the Alans in the conquest of Western Europe is almost ignored. But we must not forget that the Alans long resided in Gaul,[1] near Orleans, (and) that they and other *"Sarmatian tribes never disappeared from the Danube"*. (p. 237).

Mary Boyce insists that the Shakas in ancient Khotan were Zoroastrian, as the name Śśandrāmatā they assigned to one of their goddesses is an exact equivalent of the Gathic Spenta Armaiti, "who, as one of the six Amesha Spentas, belongs to Zoroaster's own revelation." She offers her own reasoning for disagreeing with Sir Harold Bailey's views in this regard, despite his "ingenious etymologizing." She is "inclined therefore to regard the use of Śśandrāmatā's name in Khotanese Buddhism as proof that the Khotanese were in fact Zoroastrians before they embraced the Indian doctrine. There is in itself nothing surprising in the teachings of the eastern Iranian prophet having reached them," which I believe seems quite plausible in view of Darius's keen desire to have them accept his own religion. Boyce does not seem to fully trust the Greek reports that the Shakas or Scythians of the Black Sea steppes were not affected by the teachings of Zoroaster, and she qualifies it by specifying "if Greek reports are to be trusted." Boyce also provides a ready explanation for the Shakas not always following "the Persian Zoroastrianism": "The Zoroastrianism of the Khotanese has a special interest, in that they would be the only known group of Zoroastrians who lived beyond the wide borders of the Achaemenian Empire, and so, presumably remained unaffected by the special developments of Persian Zoroastrianism at that epoch." Thus, it is striking, she points out, that they called the sun Urmaysdaan, "belonging to Ahuramazda" even though by then the sun was closely associated with Mithra, as it is at present. I may note, however, that their familiarity with the very concept of Ahuramazda, which is also denoted by the use of the word Armazi for Ahuramazda by the Scythians of the Black Sea steppes, in itself reflects their adherence to the teachings of Zoroaster, who was the one who came up with the very name and concept of Ahuramazda.[2]

The Iranian influence on China in the two centuries before Christ was quite significant too. As Rostovtzeff maintains: "The most characteristic features of Chinese life, especially Chinese military life in the Hans dynasty (206 B.C.-220 A.D.) cannot be explained without assuming profound Iranian influence.... I maintain that the whole military life of China was recognized by the kings of the Han dynasty on Iranian lines. The Iranian influence reached China, not directly from Parthia or Bactria, but through the medium of the Sarmatian tribes, many of which, beyond doubt, took part in the Hunnish assaults upon China. The Huns had no culture of their own." Rostovtzeff believes that "they borrowed everything "from the Sarmatians and Alans." He adds: "But Sarmatian influence was not restricted to the military life of Hans China". He found many Iranian figures of the type found at Persepolis "regularly buried with the dead in China.... The phenomena which we have observed in the military and *religious* life of China

---

1    L. Schmidt, *Allegemeine Geschichte der germanischen Völker*, 1909, p. 41.
2    See *Journal of the Royal Asiatic Society of Great Britain and Ireland*, London, No. 2, 1983, pp. 305-6.

under the Hans dynasty show that we have no right whatever to speak of Chinese influence on South Russia, on the Scythian and Sarmatian world. The opposite is true. The Chinese of the Hans dynasty, remodeling their life and their civilization to meet fresh requirements, borrowed many features from their Central Asiatic neighbors". Such indeed was the Scythian influence on China, Eastern Europe, and South Russia.

Government of Hungary's fact sheets on Hungary (1996) at its outset states: "From the first century B.C. people on horseback – the Scythes – of Iranian extraction, and Indo-European tribes" settled in Hungary and replaced one another. Hungarians often travelled to Asia in search of their roots and history. They were interested in India too (because the Scythians, the Shakas, conquered India too) and translated 20 works of R. Tagore in the 1920's when they were very vocal and very fond of their Asian heritage, which is quite evident from Bulsara's research. However, Bulsara has only quoted them without making it his own claim. Even so, we need much more evidence for the Magyars being Zoroastrian, but we cannot know the truth by haughty denials. *It is to the credit of Bulsara that he has provided opposite views too here* (pp. 26-27). Moreover, he quotes research by various Hungarian scholars who were very enthused to claim a Zoroastrian heritage, but Z.S. seems only interested in twisting the facts and taking an easy way out by attacking Bulsara instead of challenging the Hungarian researchers he quotes. Several of my well-wishers strongly advised me to omit Bulsara's views from the AFA but that will be defeating the purpose for which they were quoted – to contrast trio's views with his – so the lay person can judge them better. Very likely, I believe, one of the triad had studied Avesta and Pahlavi under Bulsara. If Z.S. distorts my purpose, it is regrettable. Someone in my position would indeed appreciate Bulsara as a lone crusader.

According to the *Fact Sheets on Hungary*, 1997, Ministry of Foreign Affairs, Budapest, the Hungarians "came in contact and lived together with primarily Turkish and Iranian ethnic and language peoples.... Hungarians continued to preserve their memories linking them to the Orient for centuries to come.

"The interest in Hungarian-Iranian studies focused, by and large, on three major points. The first stemmed from research into Hungarian early history.

"The culture of *the ancient Persian Empire*" (italics not mine) "and its survival constitute the second major sphere of questions. Several Hungarian travelers and orientalists made pilgrimages to the ruins of Persepolis, or as it is today known Takhte Djamshid, ranging from Armin Vámbéry (1832-1913) to Sir Marc Aural Stein (1862-1943), who researched under English colors but remained a Hungarian, and whose expeditions over the territory of historical Iran, produced tremendous results for archeology. But Aurel Stein is also associated with the exploration of the written records of Baktria and Khotan *saka*.

"The exploration of Old Iranian linguistic relics and the examination of the Avesta … the ancient Persian royal inscriptions … and of the Central Iranian languages belong among the great scholarly achievements of this century. Hungarian readers could familiarize themselves with the hymns of the Avesta. Outstanding researchers of the Old and Central Iranian linguistic finds still continue their work to this very day."

Shaul Shaked traces the Hungarian loanword Kalap for the Middle Persian word, Kulaf for caps worn by non-military personnel.[1] One may wonder how such a thing came about for the word we now commonly know as Kolah (headgear), except by a Scythian connection. But it seems the Z.S. vision is too parochial and limited to dwell deeper into such relationships.

### Alans in Hungary

Greek sources often refer to the Alans as Sarmatians or Jazyges, and noted that they inhabited the territory between the Danube and modern Hungary, and the Rhoxolani occupied the Eastern Danube border. (p. 85). Some Alans/Jazyges moved to Central Hungary to save themselves from the Mongol invasion. (p. 160). Alans arrived independently in Bulgaria and settled there in the city of Vidin. A historian wrote in 1543 that "there still exists today in Hungary the people of Jazyges, who call themselves by the shortened name of Jaz and still now maintain their own ancestral and peculiar language, which is different from Hungarian … and his contemporary Archbishop of Gran lists Jazyges among the Hungarians who had his own language in his time". The territory they occupied is still known as *Jaszsag*, just a little east of Budapest. Still today there are at least two Hungarian towns of Jazyges origin – Jaszfalu. (p. 162). The Alans at first inhabited the land from Mt. Caucasus to the Caspian Gates, most of whom were the allies of the Persians and marched against the Romans and their other enemies. (p. 195).

When the Alans settled in the Orleanais they were identified with Armorica, which was a composite of erstwhile imperial troops, Gallo-Romans, fugitives from Britain, etc. The Bretons there learnt Alan tactic of feigned retreat. *Thus, in the tenth century Regino of Priim noted that the Bretons fight like the Hungarian cavalry.* Like the Alans, both practiced feigned retreat in battles and did not dismount to fight on foot. The Scythians were closely related to the Alans and are often identified as Alans in literature. As the Scythians did inhabit Hungary, they seem to be instrumental in paving the way for the tactic of feigned retreat in Hungary.

### Data Available So Far on the Religion of the Alans

The Alans may have been Zoroastrian or at least pre-Zoroastrian Iranians. Idolatry has hardly ever been recorded among the Alans. The Alans believed in a cult of seven Gods (Amesha Spentas?). Among them neither temple nor sanctuary were found, not even a straw-roofed hut is visible anywhere, which fits well with Herodotus' description of the Iranian religion. A naked sword is fixed in the ground and they respectfully worshipped it as God of war, probably Avestan Verethragna. A sword is still placed in Zoroastrian fire-temples. They gathered very straight osier twigs and separate them while reciting certain secret spells at an appointed time. The reference to "very straight osier twigs" is suggestive of *Barsom*, which is still used by Zoroastrian priests in Yasna and Baaj ceremonies.

---

1    *Irano-Judaica*, Vol. III, Jerusalem, 1994, p.171.

*They adhered to ancestral worship even after converting to Christianity. They addressed Ahura Mazda as Armazi.* Scholars find pre-Zoroastrian elements in the religious conceptions of the Alans, the ancestors of the present day Ossetians (Georgians), as also the presence of much of the ancient Iranian language in the modern day Ossetic language, as well as of ancient Iranian religious beliefs among the Ossetians today. They see beneath the Christian texts pre-Christian concepts, though distorted but discernible here and there, such as Izad, "powers" of the angels, seven Gods, and Waejing (Vayu, the God of Wind). Herodotus mentions the Gods worshipped by the Scythians in his times, but scant attention has been paid to their number, which is indeed seven. The Crimean city of Theodosia was called the city having 'seven Gods' in the Alan language. This cult of seven gods was also observed by the Ossetians, the descendants of the Alans and a shrine dedicated to *"the seven Gods"* ('Avd Dzwary') has been sighted near the village of Galiat. Since the concepts of Ahuramazda, Asha, and seven Ameshaspentas are Zarathushtra's own unique conceptions, unknown before his time, some Zoroastrian beliefs, also seem to be prevalent among the Alans.

### Three Significant Religious Concepts of the Alans

Three Iranian words signifying religious import – *Ard, Farna* and *Wac* – are used often in the Ossetian parlance associated with everyday life as well as with religion.

*Ard*, derived from Avestan *Asha*, Sanskrit *Ruta*, meaning cosmic truth, has deep religious significance for Indo-Iranians. The religious significance of the word *Ard* is quite apparent in such Ossetic expressions as "God's *Ard*", "people's *Ard*", etc.

*Farna* stands for the Middle Persian/Pahlavi word *Farnah*, Avestan *Khvareh*, which is so frequently mentioned in the Avesta, but is hard to translate for the western audience as its concept is quintessentially Iranian, if not Zoroastrian, as per which it denotes the aura or luster reflecting one's piety, every one having this Farnah. The following form of incantation is often met with in folklore: "I cognize you by your Zaed (Izad, Yazad), by your farn." According to Alan beliefs, every man has his Zaed, i.e., his deity and his Farn.

*Wac* in the modern day Ossetian usage means "news", but in the Avesta it means speech, words, holy word, often belonging to the sacred sphere. Thus, "the principle personages of the Christianized Ossetic pantheon are preceded by the epithet Wac (was): Was-Gergi- St George. I. Gershevitch, citing certain middle Iranian data, interprets Wac as "spirit", which is equally acceptable.

39. The reason for quoting Bulsara is expressly stated. If Zoroastrianism was limited only to Mazdayasnis, how can an eminent scholar such as Frye even contemplate saying non-Mazdayasnis became Zoroastrians?: "The identity of the Tokharian people is much disputed by scholars, but most agree that the "Tokharistan" was brought to Bactria by a nomadic tribe, which if not originally Iranian in speech, soon must have been Iranicized after settling down in Bactria. Some scholars believe the Tokharians spoke the Centum Indo-European language which has been found in documents unearthed in Chinese Turkistan but, as

mentioned, if this is true they probably soon afterwards adopted an Iranian tongue in their new homeland. In Sogdiana local Mazdaism, as in Khwarazm, was more important than other religions." It is thus evident Bulsara's views may not be far off the mark after all, and Marco Polo might perhaps have witnessed some Mazdean cultic practices, not just "Zoroastrian influence" as Z.S. willfully claims without buttressing it with any evidence.

37-38 & 40-43. Z.S. challenges Antia's statement that "There are evidences of non-Mazdayasnis embracing Zoroastrianism throughout the ancient times." Since AFA was written to refute the triad's claim that Zarathushtra only meant to preach to the Mazdayasnis, and since Z.S. here maintains that 'Zoroastrians did not propagate their faith among outsiders,' they take for granted the ethnical integrity and purity of Irano-Aryans when they settled in Iran. *Iran was, however, not an empty place when Iranians moved in*, and the early Mazdayasnis must have retained memories of the migrations and the ultimate fusion and integration it brought about of *Aryan tribes with the native Elamite population of Iran*. These early memories of racial and linguistic integration seems to have refrained them from limiting their religion to a particular race and nation until millennia later when they became conscious of their identity as a superior race, and began regarding others as Anaryas. Even so, Persepolis Fortification tablets clearly reveal that Elamite priests got daily food ration to worship not only their own gods but also Ahuramazda and other Zoroastrian deities. See my tractate on Elamites. As little has been written about the assimilation of Semitic Elamites into the Persian population, I have detailed it in a research paper awaiting publication.

As per Yuri Stoyanow, "In the first century of Sassanid rule and expansion, Zoroastrian worship and fire-temples were established in the newly conquered areas … such as Armenia, Georgia, and Caucasian Albania". (Recently the *National Geographic* magazine cited ruins of a fire-temple in the Georgian capital.) "The characteristic pre-Christian temple of the Bulgars (Bulgarians) and the pronounced Iranian impact on their art certainly raises the possibility of Zoroastrian or Zurvanite influences in their religion." However, my earlier work on the Bogomils suggests it may also be due to Manichaean influences. He also quotes several historians, too many to list here, tracing the Iranian origins of the Serbs and the Croats (Croatians).[1]

According to Professor Nigosian: "If someone does want to come in, there have been cases in the past of those who have been adopted into Zoroastrian religion".[2] Robert Brody expresses the same opinion even for the Islamic period in Iran and states: "It is clear that conversion was possible in the Sasanian period".[3] So does Russell as seen later.

Thus, Zoroastrianism spread among non-Iranians as long as the clergy was supported by the royalty. The Sasanian theocracy practiced proselytization mostly inside the Sasanian borders. Had the clergy somehow conspired to transcend over-reliance and in-toto linkage to royal power and attempted missionary attempts on

---

1 *The Other God*, Yale University Press, New Haven, 2000, pp. 141-144, 164, 370, 382, 383.
2 *Proceedings of the Fourth North American Zoroastrian Congress*, 1982, p. 19.
3 *Irano-Judaica II*, Jerusalem, 1990, pp. 52-62.

their own, like the Buddhist and Christian missionaries of their time, the spread of religion would have been significantly extensive and intensive.

Z.S. does not lead the reader right by lumping these together as Antia's views but they are actually quotes from the *Cambridge History of Iran* (*CHI*) which has the highest reputation in the field for its scholarship and impartiality. It is Z.S.'s arbitrary opinion versus the studied views of *CHI*. *CHI* as well as this author are familiar with Manichaeism since 1956 at least, and so conversions to Manichaeism are not confused with conversions to Zoroastrianism, as Z.S. seems to imply. The author has honestly quoted the fact that "the Chinese themselves were not allowed to participate in any foreign ceremonies," which refutes Z.S.'s allegation that Antia tries to distort quotes in order to mislead the reader. The very fact, however, that the Chinese found it at all necessary to prohibit the Chinese from participating in Zoroastrian ceremonies suggests that many Chinese were in fact doing so, and perhaps their number was swelling rapidly enough to force the Chinese authorities to crack down on them. The fact that Firoze, the son of the last Sasanian King, Yazdegard, escaped, of all the countries, to China along with his supporters suggests that the Chinese were well disposed to Zoroastrianism. If *CHI* attributes the disappearance of Zoroastrianism from China to its objection to the infiltration of non-Iranian elements, who but the Chinese can be expected to opt for non-Iranian elements. The Iranian Zoroastrians in China apparently would have no need for them. So there is little validity in Z.S's assertion that "Antia has somewhat blundered by quoting the very point that has made the religion so strongly linked to an ethnic base." Rather it is the Z.S. that is working against the universal teaching of Zarathushtra by ratcheting it down to mere ethnicity, apparently indulging in communal politics. Nobody should deny the utter and urgent need for our communal survival, but not by perverting the teachings of Zarathushtra, as ethnicity per se won't lead us to Asha and God, nor to heaven and Frashokereti. Even Tanya Luhrmann, who recently reviewed the advocacy of ethnicity by the Z.S. for survival, finds serious faults with it, as also with the cultic preachers advocating the same. The truth will, however, prevail ultimately. The true and proper Zoroastrian way is to admit the truth, instead of denying that Asho Zarathushtra preached a universal religion, as Boyce and other scholars have frankly explained it, and as we all know it well, the vicissitudes of our history unfortunately and helplessly have now turned its devoted adherents into the world's most minuscule religious and ethnic minority. And therefore it is so necessary to preserve this ethnical link as much as possible in our modern times, but at the same time we must respect the circumstances and rights of those who marry out to remain Zoroastrian. A fanatical bent on ethnicity which goes against the very grain of Zarathushtra's universal philosophy that preached mankind for the first time in human history of the consequences of human thought, words, and deeds leading all mankind of all times and climes to paradise (which itself is an Avestan word – Pairi-daeza) or hell, resurrection, etc., will seriously negate Asho Zarathushtra's own mission. The Zeitgeist, the spirit of the times, too is against the ethnicists, and ultimately they are bound to fail, but it may be too late then for our microscopic race to survive, as the damage will be done by then already. The Z.S.

leader is reported in the *Wall Street Journal* of May 27, 1982, p. 18, as serving a sad warning: "It is a great tragedy. This wonderful religion may soon die out." It seems however, that so sadly he is hastening this process by his clout over orthodoxy at the moment. Moreover, Kotwal's admission that "In the Avesta there is evidence that Zoroastrians of old used to do missionary work in India and even China" (p. 10), which not only contradicts his own Mazdayasni theory, but also the Z.S. position, though he is a known Z.S. supporter. While *CHI* asserts that the religious thought and practice intermingled from early times in Iran and Iraq, Z.S. denies it, and asserts that Neusner quoted by Antia on p. 32 supports its stand. Rather, Neusner disproves it: (The Sasanians) "did sporadically attempt to impose their religion on (Iraq) and in Armenia, to the north, these efforts went on for centuries." (p. 32). Such blatant distortion of facts is problematic, to say the least.

42. Z.S.: Surkh Kotal temple was devoted to a variety of divinities. Kushans were mainly Buddhists. Kanishka was a major sponsor of Buddhism, he was just not sympathetic. But Z.S. provides no evidence as usual, but adds: If Ronald Reagan puts on a Jewish skull cap at a prayer breakfast for his constituents, one does not go on to say that America was converted to Judaism and its President is a Rabbi. This unscholarly remark reveals not only ignorance about Kushans and Kanishka but also about the religious reality in U.S.A., which is so well known that one doubts if Z.S. is unaware of it too. It tries nevertheless to circumvent the facts as it has no scholarly research to fall back upon. Gherardo Gnoli even muses "whether there is any point in dedicating any new notes to the historical-religious significance" and "parallels between Surkh Kotal and Rabatak" inscriptions, as their religious significance has already been established by various scholars. Gnoli stresses that "In any case the Rabatak inscription lends decisive weight to the definition given by Fussman of the "dynastic sanctuaries." The presence of Sraosh, Nairyosangh, and Meher, "often associated with each other in the Avesta, as has already been pointed out, reinforces the purely Iranian (and more exactly Zoroastrian) nature of the Rabatak pantheon. However, even more may be said in order to appreciate the possible reason for their presence in our inscription. Indeed their presence is no coincidence. It is quite significant, in fact, that a sanctuary housing the images of three deceased kings and of the living one should be characterized by the presence of deities linked to the *post mortem* period, to the final judgment and the reverence owed to the souls of the deceased or to their *frauuaši*s, which is so important in the Zoroastrian tradition in all its manifestations and during the various periods of its history. Sraoša, the *yazata* of religious obedience, is the guardian of the soul after death and 'le psychopompe par excellence'; Nairyō.saŋha, the messenger of Ahura Mazda, who in Mihr Yast is associated precisely with Sraoša and Mithra (Yt. 10.52), is a *yazata* of prayer, whose various functions include that of cooperating with the future saviour Pešōtan, of helping Wištasp to carry out his journey to Paradise and to protect the *frauuaši* of Zoroaster; Mithra is the great Judge of the souls at the Činvat Bridge. It is therefore not without a specific reason that these divine images are present in a place of worship where the statues of kings are present, the *frauuaši*s of which cooperate with the divine beings in protecting the reigning emperour." Gnoli

asserts that "there is no doubt that 'Zoroastrian' is still meaningful and there is no reason to consider Kanishka's religion, as described by Fussman, as an Iranian religion, which was moreover unknown at the time, other than Zoroastrianism.... The old definition given by Stein (1887) of 'Zoroastrian deities' on Indo Scythian coins retains its validity."[1] Antonio Panaino not only buttresses Gnoli's claim in the same Festschrift (pp. 331-346), but also affirms "the Iranian religious elements in another Kushan inscription at Dasht-e Nawure." Even the *Cambridge History of Iran*[2] observes: "It is likely that Kanishka's patronage of Buddhism did not proceed from his conversion but from his tolerance," and "he favoured Zoroastrian deities as much as any." J. Duchesne-Guillemin also regards Kanishka as Zoroastrian "though he made room for Buddha," and reiterates: "Kanishka was not as some would make him, the Clovis of Buddhism.... During the Kushan period" Zoroastrianism "reappeared" and cites copious evidence for it.[3]

According to A. R. Colledge, Kanishka "promoted Buddhism ... doubtless for political ends". Many deities occurred on his coins but, "most were Iranian." Colledge states that "The obverse image on the Kushan coins, even on the post-Kanishka coins, was of a figure at a fire-altar".[4]

Another expert on the subject, Prof. David Bivar, asserts that "the Kushans must have adhered to some extent to this religion (Zoroastrianism) though they were probably not orthodox in the Sasanian sense." He too doubts that Kanishka had converted to Buddhism.[5] Just because Kanishka patronized Buddhism, there is no reason to believe that he had converted to Buddhism. If Buddha appears on some Kushan coins, many Greek deities says Colledge, "are shown on Parthian coins,"[6] but that does not make them Greek.

Iranian deities predominate in the coins of Kanishka and Huvishka, despite their remarkable tendency toward "religious syncretism", says John M. Rosenfield.[7] Not only do their coins portray popular Zoroastrian deities, but also the highly abstract Amesha Spentas" which makes their being non-Zoroastrian highly unlikely. Rosenfield compares them to the early Arsacid rulers, who despite being Zoroastrian themselves, "supported the popular cults yet permitted the Magi to maintain their holy fires and ancient traditions". (p.72). The Kushans, says Rosenfield, "modeled its dress and beliefs on those of the Persian courts". (p. 73). He gives a detailed description of the Zoroastrian deities on the Kushan coins (pp. 79-101) and asserts that the Kushans found Vohu Manah "a most reasonable coin emblem, appropriate to dynastic symbolism". (p. 80).

A Kushan dynastic temple excavated in recent years at Surkh Kotal in Afghanistan was, according to Rosenfield, centered around the ceremony of Haoma and "images of Kanishka and Mithra were erected in the temple, either as

1 See Sundermann et al., 2009, 141-159.
2 Vol. 3(2), pp. 954-5.
3 *Religion of Ancient Iran*, Tata Press Ltd, Bombay, 1973, pp. 164-5.
4 *Parthian Art*, Cornell University Press, Ithaca, N.Y., 1977, pp. 18 & 109.
5 *Central Asia*, (Ed.) Gavin Hambly, Delacorte Press, N.Y., 1969, p. 48.
6 "Ancient Peoples & Places," *The Parthians*, F.A. Praeger, N.Y., 1967, p. 104.
7 *The Dynastic Arts of the Kushans*, University of California Press, Berkeley & Los Angeles, 1967, p. 72.

two separate statues or, more likely, as one with Kanishka in the guise of Mithra. After his death Kanishka was worshipped as Mithra himself. The temple was a site of sacred fire, but not of a fire sanctuary as such". (p. 159). Rosenfield wonders whether this temple was "containing fires to perpetuate the name and benefit the souls of members of the royal family? Was there a Vaharam fire to exalt the prowess of the head of the ruling dynasty?" (p. 162). He concludes: "Granted differences in religion, geography, and historical background, the Kushan portraits reflect strong awareness of activities within the Iranian cultural sphere. Indeed, in important respects they must have belonged to that sphere". (p. 172). Sir Aurel Stein[1] made an earlier attempt to prove that the Iranian deities on the Kushan coins were Zoroastrian. Also see Louis Gray, a student of Professor William Jackson, who has made a thorough research in this regard – "The Foundation of the Iranian Religion."[2]

According to Dr. Philip Lozinski, an authority on this subject, "there is no reason to reject this record of history that the Kushan dynasty was originally Parthian."[3]

The Iranian origin of King Kanishka is upheld by the likes of Sir H. W. Bailey,[4] as well as by W. B. Henning.[5] "As usual", observes Frye, "coins provide the primary source for our knowledge of Kanishka.... Kanishka, however, inaugurated on his obverses a new type, a standing figure of the ruler in Central Asian costume with boots, and with one hand extended over a small fire altar. This consistency on the obverse was matched by a proliferation of deities on reverse of his coinage, the majority of which are Iranian rather than Greek or Indian. This change ... supports the theory that Kanishka consciously promoted a pro-Iranian policy in his empire, or perhaps ... a proclamation of a new policy of tolerance in religions, ... possibly an imitation of the Achaemenids as suggested by Fussman, but surely with strong elements of the ancient Indo-Aryan culture as preserved by local Iranians or Iranicized nomads of the Steppes, which the ancestors of the Kushans were". Even "the basic inspiration" of the Kushan's "artistic productions" was Iranian.[6] In his chapter on the Kushans, Frye finds Kanishka's "place in Buddhist tradition" "prominent but unhistorical", and he asserts that "attempts to write a history of the early life of Kanishka" "based on fanciful ... Buddhist works are unacceptable", (p. 260) which tends to reject the Z.S. hypothesis that Kanishka was Buddhist. Moreover, Frye finds a "revival of Iranian elements, both Achaemenid and Central Asian, in architectural decoration, in monumental architecture" under the Kushans. "In summary" says Frye, "the great Kushans' played a role on the stage of history in the east as the Achaemenids had done in the west" and it was "the last great Iranian empire in the east before the

---

1   *Indian Antiquary*, XVII, 1888, p. 89.
2   Published as the Ratanbai Katrak lecture in an entire publication number of the *Journal of the K.R. Cama Oriental Institute*, 1929, 15, pp. 1-229.
3   "The Parthian Dynasty", *Iranica Antiqua*, Vol. XIX, 1984, pp. 125-126.
4   "Kanishka", *Journal of the Royal Asiatic Society (London)*, 1942, 16-47.
5   "Surkh-kotal und Kanishka", *Zietschrift der Morgenlandischen Gesellschaft* (Wiesbaden), 1965, 115, 82-84.
6   *History of Ancient Iran*, pp. 257-8.

coming of the Turks and then of Islam". (p. 269). Duchesne-Guillemin also considers Kanishka to be Zoroastrian, and adds that Zoroastrianism reappeared under him, citing copious evidence for it.[1]

44 to 49. Again S.J. Bulsara's views are deliberately misrepresented as Antia's views. Z.S. comments on 47: "How Jokai accounts for this slight disparity of some twenty-five odd centuries, Antia does not inform us." Antia is merely quoting Bulsara. Yet, if one reads Jokai carefully as saying the ancient religion of Magyars was the Avestan religion, then it easily explains the disparity of 25 centuries. It is like someone saying that the ancient religion of Parsis was Mazdayasni, though at that time they were not known as Parsis. Z.S. finally admits on 49 that Antia "states that Bulsara's research 'may be rather outdated now'" and asks "why, does Antia quote Bulsara ad nauseam?" The answer indeed is there in the text for anyone who really cares to find it.

According to William McGovern,[2] *the Parthians* who ruled over Persia from 247 B.C. to 226 A.D. *are classic examples of a Scythian group, called Saramatians, and kept true to their nomadic conditions*" (pp. 7, 68 & 73), *which indeed propelled them to spread themselves over eastern Europe.* He adds: "Archaeological records show us that at a very early period one branch of the *Scythians settled far to the west in what is now Romania and Hungary....* (p. 36). Archaeological finds show that during the fourth and third centuries the Scythian kings held their courts in the steppe-lands north and north-west of Krimea.... The Scythian Empire was long able to remain overlord of many of the Greek colonies scattered along the coast of the Black Sea". (pp. 36-38).

"*The Ossetes*, the direct descendants of the Alani," a Scythian tribe, observes McGovern, "*still speak a very archaic form of Iranian quite different from but closely related to, early Persian....* In view of this vast mass of evidence, we may take it as definitely established that the Scythian and Saramatians spoke languages which ... were far closer to the Iranian than to the Indian branch of the Indo-European group". (p. 43), which also *suggests a close affinity in matters religious in view of the close interaction between race, location, language and religion in antiquity.*

Since the Scythians tended to adopt the customs and beliefs of many nations they conquered, their beliefs may have come to differ somewhat from those of the orthodox Iranians, but certain Iranian traits persisted all through their history according to McGovern's findings, such as "no use of images in their worship of the gods," (p. 57), "all persons who had any contact with the corpse were forced to undergo a ceremonial purification" (p. 56), "no pigs were domesticated, a fact which is of great interest when we remember that among many of the Indo-European groups dwelling in Europe pigs were already kept in large numbers", (p. 44), and "the Massagetae, undoubtedly due to Persian influence, worshipped only the sun god" (p. 57). I may add they worshipped Ahura Mazda as Armazi, detailed by me in my paper on the Scythians.

---

1   *Religion of Ancient Iran*, Tata Press Ltd., Bombay, 1973, pp. 164-5.
2   *The Early Empires of Central Asia, A Study of the Scythians and the Huns and the part they played in World History*, Chapel Hill, University of North Carolina Press, 1939, Reprinted in 1965.

Most important of all, as per McGovern, *"the Parthians (who were Sarmatians/Scythians) were instrumental in the revival of the Zoroastrian religion.* Not only did they acknowledge the old Persian gods and build fire-temples, but *they did something which even the Achaemenids had failed to do, namely, they exposed even the royal dead to the vultures and the dogs as strict Zoroastrian doctrine demanded".*(p. 74). This view is now universally accepted by scholars, Boyce being its strongest proponent. How can Parthians being Scythians be such staunch Zoroastrians without their Scythian ancestors being Zoroastrian or Mazdean, especially if they continued their Scythian traditions all through. They even took refuge among the Dahae or Sakas to regain power whenever they lost their throne, per McGovern (p. 73) and many others. Parthians being staunch Zoroastrians, and saviors of Zoroastrianism in many respects, may not have been comfortable seeking refuge with the Scythians if they were not Zoroastrians, especially in view of the strict observance of Purity Laws. It seems the Scythians adopted Zoroastrianism as they came into contact with the Medes and Persians. Darius I apparently seems to have encouraged them to adopt it, as he specifically rebukes them and the Elamites for thwarting his efforts for urging them to worship Ahura Mazda (though the Persepolis tablets clearly reflect that the Elamite priests did worship Ahura Mazda, along with their own gods, and even received ration for it). Boyce reports that the Scythians became Zoroastrian in Pontus in Asia Minor, and enthusiastically celebrated many Zoroastrian festivals there.[1]

Even J. Harmatta's[2] research which Z.S. cites (without however any specific quotes) to disprove Bulsara's thesis, states that Persians and Scythians "spoke language closely akin to each other and did not require interpreters" which suggests an overall similarity in their background, including religion and ethnicity.[3]

Frye also opines that the Chionites "were Iranian in that their culture and presumably language was Iranian" (p. 346). The Z.S. claims that the Chionites were enemies of the Zoroastrian religion in its early period, but not much thereafter. Z.S. needs to heed Frye's advice: "Although so little known, the eastern Iranian world must not be forgotten in any assessment of the heritage of ancient Iran" (p. 357). Colledge also asserts: "In Central Asia, however, the tenets of Zoroastrianism were seemingly influential."[4]

Frye: "It is interesting to note that *ancient Iranians* in Central Asia (*such as Scythians*) presumably extending into European Russia, *did have contacts with the Finno-Ugrian peoples".*[5]

According to Frye, *"The Medes*, in their early spreading over central and northwestern Iran, *hardly could be distinguished from Scythians"* (*HOAI*, p. 77). Scythians were known as Sakas among Iranians and Frye thinks *Rustam was "a Saka hero"* who was "later adopted by all Iranians". (p. 166), a fact that is upheld

---

1    *A History of Zoroastrianism*, Vol. III, p. 292.
2    Op. cit., p. 95.
3    *Prolegomena to The Sources on the History of Pre-Islamic Central Asia*, Akademiai Kiado, Budapest, 1979, pp. 168, 169.
4    *Parthian Art*, Cornell University press, Ithaca, New York, 1977, p. 110.
5    *History of Ancient Iran*, p. 50.

by many scholars. *Frye finds Sakas (Scythians) and Parthians "closely related to each other".* (p. 197). "Information on the origins of the Parthians", says Frye "comes from Justin (XLI, 1) who says they were originally exiles from Scythia, and Strabo (XI, 515) who says Arsaces was a Scythian man". (p. 206). Since Mary Boyce has conclusively established the fact that the Parthians and Arsacids were staunch Zoroastrians, their Scythian ancestors must have been Zoroastrians too. However, I want to make it especially clear that while the Scythians and its allied tribes were definitely Iranian and at least pre-Zoroastrian; I am not claiming them to be Zoroastrian (though some Scythians became Zoroastrians in Anatolia per Boyce[1]).

My aim is to expose the arrogance apparently arising from ignorance (and I hope from nothing else) of the Z.S. about how far and wide "the Iranian influence had spread in the antiquity, a subject that consumed my interest since my teenage years. Hopefully my findings will reveal who really is "entering the realm of historical fantasy and leaving scholarship panting far behind" as well as answer the Z.S. question: "In any case, what Parsi would dare to tread on the soil of scholarship in Hungarian or Finnic or Scythian Hun?" I have labored to point out these facts as an average Zoroastrian is so unaware of them, including Z.S., and as they represent an important but unknown saga of our history.

50. Again, Sir Harold Bailey's views are twisted around to mean Hyonas were not Zoroastrians. While Hyonas were the enemies of King Vishtaspa, they later became Zoroastrians as indeed all other Iranian tribes, without which all of Iran would not have become Zoroastrian. The Huns and Scythians migrated to Hungary long after the conversion of Vishtasp.

51. Answer is already provided in the earlier pages by Antia as to what factors reduced Zoroastrianism to an ethnic faith etc.

52 to 55. These are wrongly given under the heading of Antia instead of Prof. Neusner. It is an arbitrary and self-serving opinion of Z.S., unsupported by references, versus the well-documented evidence of Prof. Neusner and *CHI*, where his views are republished, as stated in the AFA.

54. Z.S.: "The customs of Armenians were to the Greeks, for example, completely indistinguishable in dress, religion, and even past times, from those of their Iranian neighbors. The Armenians were, therefore, scarcely a typical non-Iranian people unaccustomed to the message of Zarathushtra." *This is inconsistent with the earlier Z.S. stand that Zoroastrianism is an ethnic faith meant solely for the Iranians as Judaism was for the Jews.* If a whole non-Iranian nation could be Zoroastrian, why not a self-taught individual like Mr. Peterson? Darius' attempt to convert the Semitic Elamites, mentioned in the text of A.F.A., is yet another example of the conversion of Semitic people. While conceding all fire-worshipping Arabs among the tribes such as Tamim may or may not have been Zoroastrians, Prof. Richard N. Frye of Harvard University leaves no doubt about the fact that "*some Arabs also were Zoroastrians*, especially in areas under the Sasanian rule, such as Bahrain and Yemen.... Although Zoroastrianism was never

---

1   *A History of Zoroastrianism*, Vol. III, p. 292.

a missionary religion, *before the spread of Islam it was neither restricted to Iranians nor as exclusive as it later became*; so the existence of Zoroastrian Arabs is plausible."[1]

56. Z.S.: "Antia's citation of Neusner is selective." As a matter of fact, the evidence from five volumes is abridged into one single page, along with the note that Neusner often refutes false allegations against Sasanians. Apropos Z.S. claim: "We do not know of a case of conversion of a Jew to Zoroastrianism," the evidence gathered by Neusner and others points to the contrary. Moreover, a tenth century book obtained through H. Michael Simmons, called *Ketāb-e Tārīsk-e Qomm*, written by one Hasan bin Mohammad bin Hasan Qommī, states that the founder of Sasanian dynasty Ardeshir Babegan transported and converted to Zoroastrianism forty Jewish families and entrusted their guardianship to the Sakan fire-temple.[2] The question is not, as I have stated in AFA, whether the story is true or not, but how would one even mention such a story if it was so much contrary to the beliefs and practices of Sasanians? Originally I made a 25 page synopsis of Neusner's findings and I still have it, but it is unflattering and very critical of the Sasanians, and so I preferred to refrain from publishing it till more research was available on this subject, and I intend to publish it in a book on the Relations Between the Jews and the Zoroastrians in Ancient Times. But in 1983 mostly Neusner's work was readily available on this subject. Even so, Sasanians do not come out as tolerant as the Achaemenians and Parthians in my later research. Neusner wrote to me in a letter dated December 4, 1986: "I have no doubt at all that in Sasanian times Zoroastrianism most certainly did want to convert people to the worship of Mazda. I believe that the Kartir inscription is about as clear on that as anything. I don't doubt that there was a considerable interest in conversion at least in the 3rd and 4th centuries, because almost all of the sources are clear on that point".

CHI reports: "the extensive use of slave labor in Iran", consisted of Zoroastrians, non-Zoroastrians, as well as non-Iranians. However, a Zoroastrian slave could not be sold "to an infidel." Furthermore, a slave who embraced Zoroastrianism could leave an infidel master and become free forever. (Vol. 3(2), pp. 635-639). These laws which are spelled out in the *Madigan-e Hazar Dadastan*, (The Code of One Thousand Laws) allowed non-Zoroastrians working for a fire-temple to become Zoroastrian, thus refuting any theory that only a Mazdayasni could become a Zoroastrian.

57. This is a matter of of one's conscience. Others may have stooped much lower than the Sasanians, but they could not claim the glorious religious traditions of tolerance of the Achaemenians. Antia does concede in the text that Christians often provoked Zoroastrians by their intransigence (p. 31), but Z.S. does not recognize it.

58. Z.S.: "The issue was primarily political." This is the opposite of what Asmussen states in *CHI*, which Z.S. needs to re-read.

1    *The Golden Age of Persia, the Arabs in the East*, Harper and Row, 1975, p. 26.
2    *Bulletin of the Center for Zoroastrian Research*: Vol 1:1, Oct. 1985, p. 6.

59. Z.S. asserts "the only other faith that he (Zarathushtra) knew was the violent cult of the demons" per the Gathas. The Gathas refer ten times to the Daevas. There is unanimity among scholars that there was a split between the Gathic Aryans and the Vedic Aryans over the Daevas.[1] Thus, Zarathushtra must have been well aware of the existence of the Indo-Aryans (Hindus). While attempts have been made, rightly or wrongly, by various scholars, the renowned historian S.K. Hodivala being one among them, to identify Zarathushtra in the Rig Veda,[2] the fact that the Zoroastrians and Hindus share common deities (including Varuna as Berezo as shown recently by Boyce, a fact not well recognized hitherto) suggests Zarathushtra knew, at least, of our Hindu brethren. As Boyce has recently revised the date of Zarathushtra as 1100 B.C. or so, Judaism too must have existed in his time. Twice in the Gathas (28.5 & 48.3), Zarathushtra calls himself *Vaedemna*, "one who knows," and he often claims to have seen and perceived God (31.8, 33.6-7, 43.5). In Yasna 44.11 he says that for his mission on earth "I was set apart as Yours from the beginning." If Zarathushtra could prophecize so well about the *menoi* world, how can Z.S. deny him the right to know about the *geti* world? Z.S.'s undocumented interpretation is in stark_contrast to numerous scholarly interpretations cited in the text.

60. This is a typographical error, (30.3 instead of 31.3), which the author regrets. He knows them by heart, however; it is a typographical error that could easily be detected by even a casual reader, because Yasna 31.3 is discussed at length in the preceding pages and the famous phrase "all living ones" appears there only once in the entire Gathas. But it is so sad that the Z.S. had to resort pathetically to pouncing on a typo for running out of substantial issues instead of seeing the vision of the prophet in Yasna 31.3, as that was the main issue.

61. Z.S. "Only the Iranians of his times could have understood not only his language, but (also) the *convoluted* (italics not mine) poetic structure of hymns. Only Iranians, also, would have understood his allusions to local heroic figures, such as Yima?" The same is true about Christ, Buddha, or Mohammad. However, it is so unique in the religious history of mankind that *Zarathushtra could be referring to two peoples at the same time* – Iranians and Indo-Aryans. Yima or Yama (as also Haoma/Soma, Daeva/Deva, Ahura/Asura, Arta/Rta, Magavan/Maghavan, Hvar/Svar, Airaman/Aryaman) were as much known to the Gathic Iranians as to the Vedic Aryans. Since Hodivala even sees "references to different Vedic Rishis and other personages, namely Manu, Puru, Yama, Kavya, and Kripa" in Yasna 32, as also to Kehram (as Grehma), Dregvant and Dush-sasti,[3] it could be easily disclaimed that "only Iranians would have understood his allusions." Z.S.: "Our language, ritual, tradition and doctrine" are quite particular to the Iranians." And yet the Hindus have much in common with us in this regard, and the reconstruction of the entire Avestan grammar which was completely lost to us for centuries, was made possible mainly because of its close affinity to Sanskrit, a fact which has enabled a Sanskrit scholar, such as Insler to provide us

1    Boyce, *A History, of Zoroastrianism*, p. 184.
2    S. K. Hodivala, *Zarathushtra and his contemporaries in the Rig Veda*, Bombay, 1913.
3    Op. cit., p. 27.

with the best translation so far of the Gathas. Gathic Avesta is closer to the earlier Rig-Vedic Sanskrit than to the later Avesta. Moreover, it is regrettable that Z.S. describes the Prophet's verses as *"convoluted,"* to say the least, just to score a point even at the prophet's expense.

Z.S.: "One can be a Christian without having a Gothic cathedral." But Boyce maintains there were only hearths and no fire-temples in Iran until the Achaemenian times, and she ruled out any possibility of the fire-temple recently discovered in Russia being any older than the Achaemenian times, in a personal conversation with this author in November, 1985 in Chicago. As already explained in the text, Zoroastrian eschatology postulates universality, which is clearly spelled out in *Denkard*. Since Z.S. has often compared the Zoroastrian position with the Jewish one, in this regard the reader may find Dr. Paul du Breuil's observations helpful. "It seems that there is a confusion made between the Zoroastrian eschatology (religious destiny and end) and the Jewish one. While Jahveh the Hebraic God requests Prophet Abraham's People to return and settle for ever on the Promised Land (i.e. the Canaan country – Gen. 12.7), and that Moses' People is nothing less than Jahveh's selected humanity (predestined for the grace of salvation); on the contrary Zarathushtra's wish was to see the whole universe following the good Law of Ahura Mazda. On this point, see Yasna chapters 31, 44 and 45. Also Yasht XIII.94, 99, 100, 143; Yasht LI.19 and *Denkard* VII.10.10; IX.38.8; X.5.14. It is grave confusion, because *prophetism* happens in History for an elected People, and is opposed to the concept of *eschatology* which means the coming of a totally different world, Kingdom of God." Thus, Zoroastrianism was far more universal in its concept than at least the earlier Judaism, which I have explained at length in my yet unpublished paper on The Influence of Zoroastrianism on Judeo-Christian Traditions but *all my unpublished research will be available eventually on* www.avesta.org.

Z.S.: "There are no non-Iranian heroes of Zoroastrianism." Zoroastrians would have had many, had their missionary zeal not dampened after reaching the borders of Iran.... "If Antia believes Zoroastrianism is the only true faith ... he must concede also that Zoroastrianism should actively seek converts." Every Zoroastrian declares it too in the *Jasa Me Awanghahe Mazda* prayer. Strong objection to the Peterson Navjote on scriptural and historical grounds by the triad and others forced the issue of whether it was in accordance with our scriptures and traditions, and the ultimate truth emerging with the publication of AFA seems to be so stunning to the community. *Hence, the need felt by Z.S. among others to suppress the truth*. Even so, Z.S. admits once again in No. 61 that conversion "is extremely rare." But so is the Peterson case. I rest my case.

62. Here Antia follows Insler who, in *The Gathas of Zarathushtra*, translates "Ahmai varenai nidatem" very convincingly as "fated for this world" on the basis of a Rig-Vedic equivalent of "nidatem" in Rig Veda X 59.4c and a matching type of construction found in Rig Veda I 165.9ab. So it is hard to accept the Z.S. translation for these words as well as its interpretation of them as a statement for dualism in Zoroastrianism, about which too I am writing at length at present, which too shows the Z.S. explanation to be untenable.

63. AFA explicitly states that an extensive research was done and it was established that no requirement exists among various Christian denominations here to renounce Mr. Peterson's original baptism. Zoroastrian Confession of the Faith, which every Navjote recites, is so comprehensive in this regard that even in olden days, the Sasanians may not have needed any other abjuration formula (which is supported by the fact that none exists) than the one categorically professing in an inspiringly positive way rather than in an abjuringly negative way: "Of all the religions that have existed in the past and-will exist in future, God-worshipping Good Religion is the greatest, the best and the most excellent." "A Byzantine, Christian formula of anathema" may have existed for Christian converts to 'condemn' Zoroastrianism, in view of utter hostility between Armenian Christians and Zoroastrians, but Zoroastrians have found the above more in spirit with their positive faith.

64. Z.S. remarks are not relevant, but rather support Antia's stand as Z.S. and Antia both view wearing sudreh-kushti after converting to another faith as illogical. But Antia's focus was on answering the triad's query about renouncing baptism, which Z.S. here tries to obfuscate.

65. Again an attempt at deliberately perpetrating the myth of diluted North American Zoroastrianism. Mr. Peterson's Navjote was performed exactly as a Navjote is performed in India, as indeed are all other ceremonies here. "The Peterson Navjote has achieved nothing." Rather, it has forced us to re-examine our false assumptions about a very critical issue facing us since the turn of the century. Its non-resolution will most certainly threaten our existence in a near future, the painful initial stirrings, may be a fair price to pay. As Dr. Paul du Breuil exhorts us: "Being a most sincere admirer of Zoroastrianism ... I feel certain that the future of Zoroastrianism will depend upon the delicate matter of conversions. Not being a Zoroastrian I feel no right to give any advice on this point, but it is clear that one day or another community will have to face the inescapable facts of history."

Z.S. – If Peterson is not a scholar, then Antia contradicts his earlier contention that Peterson "has read and known everything possible on this subject". But Peterson did it for his sheer love of the religion and his website, www.avesta.org, bears testimony to it. But as Z.S. knows well, that alone does not make one a scholar.

Z.S. accuses Antia and his supporters of having fermented a bitter schism in the small community. Quite the opposite is the truth, as the Z.S. and the orthodox simply seized upon this event to buttress their one-sided, orthodox agenda and gain popularity, whereas Antia had never intended to get the Indian community involved in this issue. Z.S. jumping in the fray when Antia was only responding to the three most learned High Priests of our time mightily proves this point. The reformists even claim that this is a deliberate attempt by the orthodox to prop up its support as they have no other agenda left to engage in.

66. Compare Prof. Whitehurst's ready acceptance of Antia's response (AFA, p. 40) to the trio's contention that none of the scholars of Zoroastrianism wanted to be a

Zoroastrian, with Z.S.'s criticism of Antia. Antia apologized to Prof. Hinnells when during personal conversations with him in January 1985, he learned that he has long ceased to be a candidate for an order of monks. The error is regretted. However, inasmuch as he has, unlike Mr. Peterson, publicly denied any desire of becoming a Zoroastrian, the essence of the argument remains unaffected. Z.S.: "Antia only demonstrates his own ignorance when he decries Prof. Boyce's mention of Zarathushtra's three wives; this is the orthodox tradition, found in the Pahlavi Zand and in a Gujarati manuscript." But where is the most important evidence – Avestan? Zoroastrians are deeply indebted to Prof. Boyce for an in-depth and life-long study of Zoroastrianism. As a historian she has to study and report even controversial matters. But as Zoroastrians we are guided by what we believe to be true as Zoroastrians, and it is strange that the so-called traditionalists like Z.S. leaders do not accept the fact that the oral tradition among both the Iranis and Parsis knows only of one wife of Zarathushtra, and only her name and nobody else's; the so-called tradition of three wives of the Prophet existing only in books that are reputed to be "an interpolation" or "proved to be a forgery" as vindicated by Dasturjis Mirza and Jamasp Asa in an article in the *Journal of the K.R. Cama Oriental Institute* (1980, No. 48, 193-210). Boyce's views are based on the assumptions that the Prophet married Hvovi much later in life after establishing himself in the court of King Vishtaspa, and so his daughter Pouruchista, whose marriage he celebrates in Yasna 53 *to Jamaspa Hvogva*, cannot be by Hvovi, but by his first wife. When she repeated these views in her lecture in Chicago in November1985, the author pointed out to her that if this was so, Zarathushtra must have been 35 when Pouruchista was of the marriageable age of 15 because she must have been born before her father left for the mountain retreat of 10 years at the *supposed* age of 20 per Zoroastrian tradition. However, since he spent another 10 years preaching and finding converts before he found a single convert as per the tradition, and since he must have spent *at least* 2-3 years in establishing himself at the court of Vishtaspa, he must have been *at least* over 42 at the time of Pouruchista's marriage, and Pouruchista must have been over 27 years old, so prohibitively over the conventional lage of 15 for the marriage then. Yasna 53.3 describes Pouruchista as "young (yezivi) one among Zarathushtra's daughters," which further deepens the dilemma here. Martin Schwartz even postulates her as the youngest daughter of Zarathushtra in *Festschrift Sims-Williams*.[1] Moreover, the prophet came to know Hvogva only after his acceptance by King Vishtasp. These figures match Boyce's.[2] Boyce replied that this discrepancy in figures needs to be worked out by her, which I do not know if she ever did. If the Prophet spent ten years in the retreat after the age of 20, another ten years in unsuccessful preaching, and another unknown years in intensive organizational and missionary work without which the religion would have never taken roots, commonsense dictates that this would have left him little time to have three wives. We cannot possibly be sufficiently grateful to Boyce, however: may her soul rest in peace. I was fortunate to know of her since 1956, but she would have liked us to pursue

---

1    Op. cit., p. 429.
2    *A History of Zoroastrianism*, Vol. I, pp. 184 and 187.

her mission of inquiry, instead of regarding her work as gospel truth, which is amply brought out by her rejection of the ethnicity hypothesis on which the Z.S. and the trio so hopelessly latch on to reject my thesis. Even Amélie Kuhrt has noted that the Achaemenians did not rigidly adhere to ethnicity, and states that King Darius bestowed full Persian ethnicity upon a pro-Persian Greek citizen, and allowed him all the rights of a Persian.

67. Z.S.: "Antia places the printed crown of pure idiocy on his convoluted abortion of an argument by suggesting that Zarathushtra converted Hindu and Greek scholars' to his religion ... like so much of (Antia's) history, this is sheer fantasy for which he cannot offer a thread of evidence, and it is perhaps for this reason that the assertion stands 'badly unfootnoted,'" which is not true, since Z.S. mischievously omits the words that follow: "as seen above," as the reference is already provided in No. 15.

68. Z.S.: "Antia's summation of Christianity is incorrect." Not so if one cares to read the references cited in AFA, which are based on careful discussion with the scholars of Christianity vis-a-vis Z.S.'s arbitrary, self-serving, undocumented opinion.

69. Z.S.: "The translation by Dastur Jamaspa Asa is *here as elsewhere in this text somewhat misleading.* (Italics are ours). Curiously, Antia seems to have ignored question 46 in the same text...." Curiously, Z.S. reprimands Antia for ignoring the very translations it finds "somewhat misleading." Z.S. seems to have been laboring under some bias at least *then* against Jamasp Asa too, which is vindicated by Z.S.'s outbursts against him as reported in the Parsi Press in late 1985.[1] Otherwise, one knows that it is hard to find a match for Jamasp Asa among Parsis today as a Pahlavi scholar, which Boyce also supports.[2] As regards question 46 in the *Pursishniha*, the translator of *Pursishniha* and *Vaetha* being the same, it should be apparent that the Z.S.'s interpretation of question 46 will conflict with what is stated in the *Vaetha* and so an apparent Z.S. explanation of question 46 seems to be that a man of alien faith or a non-Iranian could not participate in the Good Religion if he is not strong and vigorous in righteousness. But logically it follows that a non-Iranian could become a Zoroastrian if he attains full righteousness. *Rivayat-e Dastur Darab Hamziar* translated in Gujarati by R. J. Dastur Meherji Ranana as also other Rivayats support such a deduction. The following is an exact English translation from *Hamziar Rivayat* (p. 425) under the sub-heading: "(We) should Accept a Juddin (non-Zoroastrian) in our Religion": "This matter is written about in the Rivayat of Kaus Mahyar. The question is: If some Durwand (non-Zoroastrian) acquires faith in our holy religion and that Durwand wants to be a member of the Good Religion, is it proper to make him a member of the Good Religion? The Answer (is) this that if he observes the laws of the holy religion real well and if no harm comes to the Good Religion by taking him into the faith, then it is permissible to make that Durwand a Behdin. It is appropriate to bring that Durwand into this holy faith."

1   *Parsiana*, September, 85, p. 14.
2   *Zoroastrianism*, p. 224.

70. Z.S. Mobed Azargoshasp (of the Mobed's Council in Iran) told James Russell that "the Pahlavi texts and the Sasanian rulers were corrupt and that Western scholars know nothing about the religion. If these are the views of a Mobed from Iran, it is difficult to regard, with confidence, the authority of a body whose members espouse ignorant and unsubstantiated opinions." One swallow does not make a summer and one Mobed does not represent the entire Mobeds' Council even if the Mobed was wrong. As this author personally discussed the meaning of Geush Urvan with Dr. Russell, he is aware of how strongly he (Russell) feels about interpreting it according to the Pahlavi texts. The world is all the better because of his learned views. However, as we know fully well, no two scholars of Iranian studies agree completely with each other. Azargoshasp's views about Geush Urvan represent the views of early Parsi scholars whom H. P. Schmidt hails as the one the Western scholars should emulate. As I told Russell, Schmidt too interprets Geush Urvan as "The Universal Soul or the Great Vision," a fact already recorded in the A.F.A. text (p. 20), and many Zoroastrians feel deeply offended when Russell and other scholars translate Geush Urvan otherwise. Few scholars interpret Geush Urvan as studiously as Insler (op. cit., pp. 134-158), who concludes: "... The figure of the cow approaches in essence the Lord-created values of truth and good thinking, whose quest for and realization on earth is the task of the righteous man (29.10, 31.4, 47.2, 51.5, etc.) and which shall bring on the defeat of deceit (31.4, 48.1, etc.). Similarly, (in) 51.5-6..., the reverence to be allotted to the cow comes very near to that of Ahura Mazda himself in importance.... This line of reasoning leads me to believe that the *cow is an allegorical figure for the vanguhi daena* 'the good vision' (51.17, 53.1, 3).... The whole outlook of Zarathushtra on these points is aptly summarized in 51.21: 'Virtuous is the man of piety. He is so by reason of his understanding, his words and actions, his conception. Virtuous is truth and the rule of good thinking. The Wise Lord created this, and I shall entreat Him for this good reward.' This verse also clarifies the content of 33.3 which states that the man serving the cow with zeal shall be on the pasture of truth and good thinking. For the person who dedicates himself to Ahura Mazda and to the values of truth and good thinking which the Wise One created, represents and sustains the one who strengthens the power of his god by granting meaning and significance to the very qualities which characterize the true nature of the Wise Lord. He is the pastor, the man of faith and piety, the champion of what is good and proper, who tends and promotes the good conception of a world governed by truth and good thinking by his own active involvement in his own world through these lordly principles conceived by wisdom and aroused by a spirit of virtue. In this way he gives life to the essence of his god on earth, whereby *the whole human condition is elevated towards a better existence.*" (Note how well Insler's remarks enhance the appropriateness of Whitehurst and S. R. Vakil's advice to the Parsis, despite Z.S.'s protestations to the contrary). "All the actions of the cow in Y.29 are equally appropriate to Zarathushtra himself. ... particular request in 31.4.... *This leaves unanswered the question of the exact choice of the image of the cow.* However, if we examine those passages in the Gathas where there are mentioned the direct benefits the cow

shall bring to the world of man, these passages seem to express a uniform theme: *The cow shall bring peace to the world*. We see in 48.6 ... 50.2.... And in the direct context of Yasna 29.10, we notice the pointed supplication for (this) rule..... Herein, I believe, lies the answer *to the choice of the cow as symbol for the rule of truth and good thinking*."

Boyce, despite her strong preference for the Pahlavi tradition, prefers the Parsi scholars' interpretation of the word Geush Urvan, unlike Russell, which R. Frye finds rather surprising in view of Boyce's proclivity to be guided by the Pahlavi texts.

Since Schmidt and Insler both disagree drastically with Russell, and since Azargoshasp's reasoning is leaning more towards that of the former as well as of the early Parsi scholars and Boyce, his opinion is in no way "ignorant." Moreover, what exactly transpired between him and Russell in a heated exchange is hard for the Z.S. to determine unless of course, Russell is somehow involved in writing this Z.S. response. Z.S. is obviously biased in favor of Russell who obviously may have had a hand in the Z.S.'s publication, the anonymity of its authors lending all the more support to it. We must respect the fact that the Iranian mobeds, despite hazardous odds, have spared nothing to preserve our traditions of which Z.S. talks about so much, and other than indulging in partiality and bitter bickering, Z.S. has not come up with any valid argument for so summarily rejecting the views of a prominent member of the Mobeds' Council of Iran and an erstwhile high priest of Iran. If Antia had done so, Z.S. would have come down with most vicious verbal attack on him.

71. Z.S.: "Why should Antia prefer the views of Iranian Moslems to those of the Parsi Dasturs?" Antia does not even remotely imply or say so. This is a mischievous distortion of what Antia says. Is it a question who holds the purse-string in California.... Rather than of those who know the tradition better...." It should be clear to the reader that it is written to allay the triad's fear of "a possible repercussion in some countries" but is obviously taken out of context. Its implication that 'purse-strings in California' control and influence religious affairs is as ridiculous as it is irresponsible. Anyone who knows the North American milieu along with its fierce individualism will not even conceive of such an accusation, especially as Antia has donated thousands of dollars to charities and has not taken a single penny for his priestly services for over the past fifty years, including Peterson's Navjote. Rather, the reports in *Parsiana* (Oct., 1985) as well as the reports of the Fifth North American Zoroastrian Congress point a finger in the other direction. Reporting on the Congress, *Gavashni* (Dec., 85, p.3) comments: "The first meeting of the delegates was one of the most acrimonious gathering ever witnessed by this author (editor). The meeting was attended by 18 alleged delegates, the credibility of some of them was echoed by the walls as well as representatives of 'Dummy Organizations'. It was interesting to note that a non-resident member (Mr. Khojeste Mistree) was a delegate representing the members of the Zoroastrian Association of California (southern). 'Power play'." Who paid for K. Mistree and his "crew" (who all raged wild against Antia there) for attending this conference? It seems, by now, Z.S. has established a trend in

representing remote associations in devious non-Zoroastrian ways, and using contributions from some sources for furthering its own agenda, according to the Parsi media, thus compromising its reputation for neutrality and integrity.

72. Z.S. has failed to respond to the legal expert, Mr. S.R. Vakil's opinion: "Lastly, although it may hurt our High Priests and half-baked scholars, it is not their function to determine now whether a person who is not a Zoroastrian by birth can profess Zoroastrian religion and wear Sudrah and Kusti". This right cannot be taken away by any alleged negative custom. Since many other Parsi legal luminaries have lately expressed similar legal opinion in the Parsi media, Z.S. needs to deal with it objectively for the sake of communal harmony at least.

73. Z.S.: "Is it not arrogance for Antia to state that it is the Parsis in India who have to come to terms with some North American Zoroastrians?" Another distortion, Z.S. style. No arrogance was meant by this rather earnest and humble plea, but if that is how it was understood, it is because his detractors are desperately trying to find any excuse to thrash him. Wisdom clearly requires that we understand each other. Z.S. should re-read the whole 26 line paragraph: "An exchange of views and facts on this subject, therefore, will be very productive, and will assure the community that a resolution of this life-threatening problem is entirely possible without in any way jeopardizing its rights or existence or religious observances.... We on our part ... love our community too dearly to harm it in any way," and so on.

Z.S.: "Antia, it would seem, want the very foundation of the religion to be changed by dismissing the need to preserve this all-important ethnic identity." Antia's message is clear, unless one deliberately twists it: North American Zoroastrians try a whole lot harder to preserve their ethnic identity, socio-religious practices, rituals, social, communal and familial ties, religious heritage, and traditions than Zoroastrians elsewhere, and certainly a lot more than the Z.S. gives them credit for. But Zeitgeist is set against them and they need their co-religionists elsewhere to understand their need for adapting to their challenging milieu in the spirit of *Shayast ne Shayast*. Even the Zoroastrian communities in the old country are not far from escaping the challenge of our times.

## Conclusion

Z.S.: "Although there have been isolated and rare examples of conversion of non-Iranians to Zoroastrianism, Antia has failed the Peterson case as an exception" which only serves to strengthen *The Argument for Acceptance*, and which means the Z.S. needs to re-read it after shedding its bias. *There would have been no need to write it, had the triad conceded the existence of such rarities*. Z.S.: "Antia seems oblivious to the particular beauty and strength of the very religion he now advertises to the world." Having initially condemned Antia and other priests who performed Mr. Peterson's Navjote, and having asked for their removal and excommunication on untenable scriptural and historical ground, Z.S. and its orthodox allies forced the priests to defend their action, but Z.S. now even accuses them of advertising the religion to the world, apparently for doing too good a job of defending the Peterson Navjote on scriptural and historical grounds. *And yet the theme that emerges as surely and unequivocally from the Z.S. response is "there have been isolated and rare examples of conversion of non-Iranians".* Whether to accept the Peterson case as one such rare example in our history is now for the reader to decide. However, *Z.S. deserves the credit for being the first orthodox Parsi group in our time, ever to concede that conversions do exist as "rarities" or "exceptions" in Zoroastrian history, as exceptions often prove the rule.*

Even the well-known Z.S. ally, James Russell concedes: "Both the religion of Zarathushtra and Judaism regard their revelatory scriptures as universally true, and consequently both religions have accepted, or even, on rare occasions, encouraged proselytes. Legends ... indicate that outsiders were sometimes welcomed". Russell even states that at times Judaism was "far more receptive to converts than the Zarathushti religion", contrary to the Z.S.'s claim of Zoroastrianism being an ethnical religion like Judaism. (*Fezana Journal*, 2009, p.33).

Z.S. complains of Antia's "air of authority and arrogance." Compare this with Antia's statements: "In view of the paucity of reference materials and time, however, it is hard to do full justice to it", (p. 1), "due to an acute shortage of reference materials" (p. 1); "an exchange of views ... will be very productive, and will assure the community that a resolution of this life-threatening problem is entirely possible without in any way jeopardizing its rights or existence or religious observations" (p. 43), "I'll humbly renew the appeal of Dasturji Dhalla...." (p. 43), "A conference ... is urgently needed to clarify ... issues" (p. 43). "Everyone must readily concede the community the right to exist and continue its traditions and cultures. However, inaction in this regard may jeopardize its very existence more than any encroachment on its right to exist. There is no way new converts will be entitled to any benefits of the Parsi trusts, etc., in view of various verdicts by the Indian Courts; however, it is distressing that mass hysteria is still whipped up by some on this issue." (p. 44).

Z.S.: "This argument for acceptance is no argument at all. The traditional ban on conversion should remain intact; the facts mitigating against conversion are plain". There cannot be a more poignant and flagrant example of "air of authority and arrogance" as well as cognitive dissonance and closed mind, more so when the matter does not pertain to the Z.S but to a continent half the world across from it where the matter has been already resolved, no thanks due to the Z.S. or its allies. To Z.S. not only what Antia maintains is wrong, but also those that he cites to support his thesis in any way are also found misleading and unacceptable: the entire Mobeds' Council of Iran, Jamasp Asa, Zaehner, Insler, Schmidt, E. Meherji Rana, Palkhiwala, Piloo Modi, Prof. Jackson, Dasturji Dhalla, *The Journal of the K.R. Cama Oriental Institute* ("an obscure journal"), *Cambridge History of Iran* (and obviously its authors and editors of relevant sections), Gibbon, Zajti, D.F. Karaka, Auriel Stein, Bulsara, and others. Even Asho Zarathushtra is belittled in an effort to deny him the unique privilege of proclaiming a universal religion for the first time in human history, an honor that no great scholar has ever denied him. However, *for every argument for acceptance that Z.S. summarily and arbitrarily presumes it has nullified, there are so many more in AFA that it has not even touched, not to speak of so many more presented in this text*. And many more are on the way or awaiting publication.

Ethnicity has its place in view of our peculiar situation and history. To have the religion revolve exclusively around ethnicity, however, is to deny the prophet's mission for preaching a universal religion first time in human history, based not on force or forces of ethnicity but on choice. An ethnicity-based or ethnicity-centered religion is a contradiction in terms, shorn of spiritual inspiration and guidelines which it cannot supplant. Ethnicity will not enable anyone to pass through the Chinvat Bridge where no divine judgments are governed by ethnicity functioning as a redeemer. It is easy to ride the tide of ethnicity for one's personal gain and popularity, but it is an ephemeral game. You hardly find a Zoroastrian family sans intermarriage today, including Mistree's, and that's just the start of the season. It seems we are engaged in an unwinnable war against the Zeitgeist. Insisting on preserving ethnicity is highly laudable, but using it to force one out of one's religion which is no one's property but the prophet's is an act of aggression against the prophet himself, and a sure stab at communal harmony in the long run. There are few cases in the world history when a Semitic country was completely absorbed into the race and religion of an invading Aryan race, such as when Persians entered and occupied the ancient Semitic country of Elam which is today only known by the name of Iran or Persia, so complete was this assimilation. Even the post-Gathic scriptures represent Zarathushtra as addressing his message to "every human being", per Almut Hintze who has succeeded Boyce, and Yasht 13.152 requires him to be worshipped by "every one of those who exist – Kahmaichit Hatam". Yasna 39. 1 & 2 venerate the souls of all human beings "wherever they may have been born – kudo-zaatanaamchit". Hintze notes: "their birthplace being irrelevant, what matters is that they are committed to truth" or the law of Asha which was at the time preached only by Zarathushtra.[1] Even a little heed to the prophet's teachings can save the community by averting the calamity it is heading forth by turning its back on the prophet by relying so exclusively on ethnicity and on the pseudo-prophets of ethnicity interested in their own power politics and game.

I sincerely hope my efforts, as well as Z.S's and the trio's, will not only enable the reader to find the truth but also provide a mine of information for our religion and history as well as for a very unique study of cognitive dissonance, denial, cognitive rigidity, and a closed mind, as a consequence of our self-interest and religious ignorance propelling us to shun all outsiders that can presumably make a demand on our charities which however, are already and happily so well secured for the Parsis by various court verdicts. So such perceived threats to our financial well-being are not even realistic. However, as an average Parsi knows so little about his/her religion that s/he easily falls prey to those who misguide them about Acceptance for their own selfish ends. I have taken pain to collect the best of scholarly opinions on this important subject, so that anyone who cares to read them with the light of his mind as the Prophet recommends in Yasna 30.2 will easily find the truth. I see no meaning, therefore, in carrying this debate further as

---

1    Hintze 2007, pp. 93, 269-270.

cognitive dissonance is degenerating into egregious religious politics, acrimony, deliberate distortions, and untenable manipulation of facts, especially as I have re- sponded quite exhaustively to all the facets of this subject, and as I do not feel at home with manipulation of facts in any way. Some die-hards may find my find- ings too unbearable to stomach, and may once again respond by distortion and the like they are so good at, but hopefully the truth will ultimately prevail, hopefully before it is too late.

Let me conclude with Yasna 60.5 (Dahm Afringan): May the Fravashis and Ahura Mazda visit and bless our abodes. May listening to our conscience over- come not listening to our conscience, may peace and harmony overcome anarchy, may generosity of spirit prevail over poverty of spirit, may good temperament pre- vail over hostile mentality, may the well-spoken word drive out the ill-spoken word, may Asha (Truth) prevail over Druja (Lie). Amen!

# Appendix I. Opinions of Scholars in 1903 on Conversion

**Note:** This collection of letters was originally published in Gujarati by an anonymous Zoroastrian in 1909. This English translation was made by Ervad Noshir Hormuzdiar and Marion Hormuzdiar in 1983.

Anjuman Atash Behram
10, Sirdar's Building
Bombay
23rd June 1903

Dear Sir:

We have the honour to submit for favour of your opinion a question of Parsee religion which has been exercising the minds of the Parsee community of Bombay for some time past. The question has arisen under the following circumstances:-

A young educated lady of French birth and parentage, having expressed a strong desire to embrace the religion of Parsees or Zoroastrianism, a High Priest of the Parsees of Bombay performed her Navjote, i.e., the ceremony of investing her with the sacred shirt and thread which are recognised by Parsees as the essential symbols of the faith of Zoroaster. All the rites and formalities observed in admitting children of Parsee parents in the Zoroastrian fold were performed and observed in the case of this lady, and in addition to these she underwent a purificatory ceremony imposed by orthodox Parsee sentiments upon those who are supposed to have contracted gross impurity or contamination. The ceremony was performed by an orthodox High Priest assisted by other High and subordinate Priests, the latter subject to the spiritual jurisdiction and control of the High Priest of Navsari, which is recognised to be the stronghold of Parsee religious orthodoxy, and several leading and enlightened members of the Parsee lay community took part in the function. The young lady made a voluntary and full declaration of her new faith and her acceptance of its fundamental doctrines and teachings.

Sometime after this event a question was raised as to whether she could be admitted into the Parsee Atash Behram or Fire Temple for prayers, and the question was taken up by the Fire Temple, on whose behalf your valued opinion regarding the question is now solicited, and which is known as the "Zartoshti Anjuman Atash Behram," i.e. Fire Temple of the Zoroastrian community. At a meeting of the Governing Body of the Fire Temple held on 22nd February 1903, six of the members present voted in favour of her admission, and eight desired to have the opinion of European savants versed in Parsee scriptures before coming to a decision, and hence this reference to you. We may mention here that there is a consensus of opinion among our Avesta and Pehlvi scholars who, on being consulted, have given their opinion on the preliminary general question that Zoroastrian religion does not forbid the admission of persons of other communities or castes into the Zoroastrian religion.

We may also inform you that about a year ago, a Parsee, older than the French lady, born of Parsee parents and brought up as a Parsee, but who had since renounced Zoroastrianism and became a convert to Christianity, was some years after such conversion re-admitted into the Parsee religion by another High Priest of the Parsees of Bombay, and that shortly before the conversion of the French lady yet another Parsee High Priest, renowned for his learning and piety, publicly admitted into the Parsee religion the children of a Parsee father by a non-Parsee mother not united in wedlock, and that several years ago another High Priest performed a similar ceremony on children of Parsee fathers by non-Parsee mothers of low castes living in concubinage, many of them so admitted being considerably older than the French lady in question. In none of these cases was a question of their eligibility to admission into Parsee Fire Temple raised, and they have been freely recognised as Parsees, and admitted to all social and religious rites of members of that community. The case of the French lady being unique and quite novel, has naturally provoked keen controversy, the *opposition resting their case mainly if not entirely on the social and material side of the larger question of conversion of members of other faiths to the religion of Zoroaster, a side which we may state is quite beyond and outside the scope of subject of the reference made to you, which is restricted solely to the religious object*. We, therefore, request that you will be so good as to consider all the above facts, and favour us with your opinion on the question of admitting the lady into our Fire Temple. The question being one of great importance to the Parsee community, we trust your opinion will be as clear and full as possible.

Apologising for the trouble, and thanking you in anticipation,

> We are, Dear sir,
> yours very faithfully
> SD.   Sorabji Rustomji Bunshah
> Sharpurji Byramji Katrak
> Honorary Secretaries

REPLIES TO THE ABOVE:-

The letter of inquiry which you did me the honor of sending was received after I returned from Persia, where I had been making an interesting journey in connection with my Zoroastrian studies. In reply I beg leave to say that if all the requirements had been complied with, as your letter indicates, I should think that the lady had become accepted as a Zoroastrian, and that any question of admission to the Fire Temple had thereby been removed. Such at least would be my understanding of the spirit of Zoroastrianism so far as my knowledge goes.

> Respectfully yours,
> SD.   A.V. Williams Jackson (New York)

If the point is raised that these religions, the Christian and the Zoroastrian, are inherently mutually too antagonistic to admit of a transfer from the one to the other; that I deny in cases where the two religions are philosophically considered, though the popular aspects of them must be worlds apart.

If it is asserted that the race of Europeans is especially alien to the Iranians, that is an error; all are Indo-germanic.

Finally, it is practically contrary to universal usage for the member of a religious community, who value their religion as helpful or necessary to salvation, to forbid any sincere person from sharing in such parts of its privileges as are thus deemed to be necessary to their eternal spiritual welfare.

I gather that you do not request my opinion as to the expediency of creating a distinction with reference to the inheritance or transfer of property in the case of converts; you simply ask for my results as above cited which I willingly afford you.

The main question which should come before us is whether the original Zoroastrian Religion discouraged the admission of proselytes. Upon this the community can then proceed to statutory action. To that point I would answer that this is to the last degree improbable as a fact, while it is positively contradictory to the letter and spirit of the original documents.

Yours obediently

SD.     Lawrence H. Mills
Professor of Zend Philosophy in Oxford
July 18th 1903

### *Evidence and Arguments in Favor of acceptance of People of Other Faiths into the Zoroastrian Religion and a Collection of other Writings Compiled and Selected from Different Sources by a Mazdayasni*

Bombay

J.N. Petit, Parsi Orphanage Captain Printing
Works Lal Baug, Parel

1909

----------------------------------------------------------------------------------------

Bombay 8 February 1903

----------------------------------------------------------------------------------------

Gracious Seth Ratanji Dadabhai Tata,

Respected Sir,

We have received your letter dated February 7. I would like to thank you for your gracious invitation to participate in this Navjote ceremony that is going to take place today. For this invitation I consider that you have kind feelings for me. Because of certain items, I am sorry that I will not be able to attend the gathering.

You have said in your letter that you had read the public sermon which we have published, and that you are planning to act accordingly. I am very happy to know this.

If a pious man or woman with firm belief is accepted into the Zoroastrian religion and taken into the community, then the Zoroastrian religion has no closed door policy. This is our humble opinion that we have expressed in our sermon.

Signed,
Dorab Dastur Peshotanji Sanjana

--------------------------------

Colaba, 8 February 1903

"If any lady or gentleman of another faith with a true belief wishes to enter the Zoroastrian Religion, are there any restrictions" is the question being asked of me. I am taking permission to inform you that according to my understanding there is absolutely no restriction.

Signed,
Jivanji Jamshedji Modi

**The following letters are the answers to the letter written by Seth Rustomji Dosabhai Sethna, Trustee as well as the chairman of the Anjuman Atash behram.**

Sir,

I have received your letter of this current month dated the 16th, and I am taking the liberty to answer the questions being asked in it.

If any person of another faith, man or woman, who with a firm belief, free will, and a desire, wishes to enter our religion to perform his Navjote and accept him into the Zoroastrian Religion.

If once an individual either born to people of another faith or born to a Zoroastrian has a Navjote performed, and has made the necessary solemn declaration in the presence of the priest thereby being accepted into the Zoroastrian Religion, from that point that person should be considered for all the rights as a Zoroastrian. This is my humble opinion.

Signed,
Ervad Shehiarji Dadabhai Bharucha

Sir,

I am taking permission to answer the question asked in your letter dated 16th of this month. Any person of another faith, man or woman, with a firm belief, free will, and a desire to enter into our religion, then to perform his Navjote and to accept him into the Zoroastrian religion, according to my thinking there is no restriction in our religion. If his Navjote is done according to the customs, and he makes a declaration of faith, then according to my opinion he should be considered a Zoroastrian.

Ervad Edalji Kersaspji Antia

Respected Sir,

I am taking the opportunity to answer in the shortest possible way the question asked in your letter of the 16th of this month. Any non-Zoroastrian, with his own understanding or with an explanation provided by a Zoroastrian, that could understand the faults of his own religion, and at the same time understands the purity, truth, and Ashoi of the Zoroastrian religion, and of his own free will openly declares and desires to become a Zoroastrian, and is deeply wanting his Navjote to be performed to enable him to be recognized as a person of the Zoroastrian religion, and this person keeps the sign of a Sudreh and Kusti on his body, then to such a person there is no restriction to accept him into the Zoroastrian religion as it is declared.* Not only that, but to accept these people into the Zoroastrian religion is the duty of every Zoroastrian. In this manner those who have become a new Zoroastrian should be given the same benefits and rights of the existing Zoroastrians.

If we create difficulties and delay in the process of initiation of these people who request to become Zoroastrian, then this is comparable to stopping someone from correcting his path of wrong deeds to changing to good deeds.

*INSTRUCTED

Signed,
K. R. Cama

Respected Sir,

I received your letter on February 16. I am taking the liberty to answer the questions you have asked.

According to the customs and rituals of our religion there is no objection to initiating into the Zoroastrian religion a person of another religion – man or woman – who because of the beauty of the Zoroastrian religion, and who with the goodness of his heart, is attracted toward this noble religion, and wants to join our own religion.

You Respected Sirs, must be aware of the fact that about 21 years ago the late Dasturji Jamaspji Minocheherji JamaspAsana had accepted into the Zoroastrian religion several Zoroastrian children with Non-Zoroastrian mothers – boys and girls – and had performed the necessary ceremonies. At that time also there were many questions and discussions. On that occasion because of the suggestions from several friends, *I had published a booklet named "Judeeno ne Mazdayasni Din Ma Dakhal Karva Rava Che Te Vishaynee Shahadato" (The Argument in Support of Accepting non-Zoroastrians into the Mazdayasni Religion)*. I am enclosing a copy of the booklet for you, Sir. On reading this booklet you will note that there is no objection to accepting into the Zoroastrian religion with great care and religious ceremony any person of another faith.

Signed,
Ervad Temurasp Dinshawji Anklasaria

Sir,

In reply to your letter of this week, I am taking the liberty to write to you. There is absolutely no objection in the religion to accepting, after the necessary rituals, people of other faiths with a true belief and noble intentions and wishing to enter the Zoroastrian Religion. However, it is my opinion that based upon today's time, place, and conditions, this particular question should not be looked at from the religious point of view – that is whether the religion says it accepts or does not accept. We should look at it through the cultural point of view. I would like to inform you that for this we have to keep some reservation and create some law and order.

Signed,
Ervad Jivanji Jamshedji Modi

Respected Sir,

A letter signed by your respected hand has been presented to this very humble servant at a very timely moment. Please allow me to thank you openly for asking a question to such a humble servant of yours.

You have asked for an answer to your question. I would not try to take your valuable time by explaining in detail the examples cited in the sacred writings of Avesta in our religion. I take the satisfaction of explaining in short that any non-Zoroastrian, man or woman, who with heart-felt feeling, and of his own free will with great faith and dedication, who wishes to join the Zoroastrian religion, then to accept him and give him all the rights of the Mazdayasni Zoroastrian is the sacred duty assigned to a true Zoroastrian. And, as this duty of great, strong importance has been given by the religion, those who wish to stop or oppose this person from entering are judged guilty by the religion.

You must have read *a very informative publication full of examples* regarding the religious history, written by my revered and honorable teacher Ervad Temurasp Dinshawji Anklasaria.

This particular publication deals with the subject of accepting the non-Zoroastrian children into the Zoroastrian Religion and *was published 20-25 years ago. During the same time the late Pestonji Sanjana had written and published in opposition "Nirangeh Javit Deenan".* To answer this the late elder Dasturji Saheeb Dr. Jamaspji Minocheherhomji had written "Pasokhay Nirangeh Javit Deenan", and had published this with examples and arguments. You, Respected Sirs, must be aware of this. Both these publications point out with examples and arguments from the religious books which you must be aware of, and hence this humble servant should not write any more about it. If you, Respected Sir, are not in possession of these books, and if you ask this servant to send you a copy for your work and if you order me to do so, I will be very glad to kiss your feet and present it to you, Sir.

You, Respected Sirs, are so much experienced and knowledgeable about this subject matter as well as much informed about the details of the religion and its implications on the long-range planning and its implications on the whole community, that this poor servant with limited knowledge cannot venture to advise you anymore.

In the end, there is a humble request from your servant to Your Excellencies. Once a person of another faith is accepted into the Zoroastrian religion after the sacred Navjote ceremony, then this particular person cannot be stopped from entering the Atash Kadhey (Fire Temple) to say his or her prayers. This person is free to enjoy all the rights of a Zoroastrian.

Signed,

Ervad Nosherwanji Burjorji
Desai

**The opinions of the Dasturs sought by the sub-committee which was appointed by a committee chosen by the Zoroastrian Anjuman Council on the question of the non-Zoroastrian being accepted into the Zoroastrian Religion.**

September 14, 1903

Sir,

You have asked our opinion of whether or not to accept people of another faith into our religion, according to the teachings of our religion. You want to know whether this is acceptable or not. I am taking the permission to reply to you that according to our religion there is absolutely no restriction against accepting a non-Zoroastrian into the Zoroastrian religion. This is what the religion says. In the daily prayers of the Zoroastrian such as "Khurshid and Meher Niyayesh", the person prays that "May the Mazdayasni religion be spread on seven continents. (Hafta Keshvar Zamin)". In the olden times, the Athornan (Priest) class did not only pray this and sit around, but they went into far off countries in order to spread the Mazdayasni religion or the religion of Ashoi. (See Yajashne Ha chapter 41 paragraph 6). In several instances tyrannical people used to create problems when these Athornans went out to spread the religion. (Yajashne Ha 9 paragraph 24). We would like to point out above instances only; from the instructions or the ruling found in the Zoroastrian religion we can say that it is perfectly alright to accept non-Zoroastrians into the Zoroastrian religion.

*We agree completely with the second publication of the booklet by Ervad Temurasp Dinshawji Anklasaria with the necessary proof for accepting non-Zoroastrians into the Zoroastrian religion.* (Judeen No Ne Mazdayasni Din Ma Dakhel Karwa Rava Chhe Te Vishaynee Shahdato). In this, the learned Ervad points out examples from Avesta, Pahlavi, and Farsi books.

*Also, our late respected Dastur Jamaspji has pointed out in the book "Pasokhay Nirangeh Javit Deenan" published in 1252 Y.D. that to accept non-Zoroastrians into the Zoroastrian religion is perfectly alright, and he has given examples.* From the examples of the above booklet by Ervad Temurasp, as well as our late Dastur Jamaspji, one can say that for any new student there is nothing left to search for. For this reason we are pointing you to the examples in these booklets, and are presenting them to the sub-committee.

Signed,
Kaikushru Dastur Jamaspji

September 22, 1903

Respected Sir,

Received your letter on September 18, 1903 in which you write, "Please give your opinion at your earliest with examples and arguments of whether it is alright to accept people of another faith into the Zoroastrian religion according to the teachings of the religion".

For this I am writing you, Honorable Sir, in short, that on reading attentively the Sacred Books of our religion, it appears that if any person who is on the wrong path, and if by staying on that path he is committing sins, that person should be informed of the good teachings of our sacred religion, and should be brought onto the noble path, so that he might stop performing other acts of sin.

From history one finds that our Iranian kings made the best efforts from their hearts in order to spread our sacred religion. Also, after the holy prophet Zarathustra spread his religion, Gushtasp sent his son Esphandiar to foreign countries. Gushtasp accepted the Zoroastrian religion and kept on his body the sacred signs of our religion, the Sudreh and Kusti. This writing is found in detail in the *Shah-Nameh*. Also our ancient kings had married ladies of other religions, and had brought them back, and had them made to accept the Zoroastrian religion.

In the sacred writings of Avesta such as in the Gathas, Vendidad, etc., wherever it is written to bring a bad person (darvand) onto a good path, the purpose of this seems to be that one should give good advice to those on the path opposite to righteousness, and those who spread evil in this world, by showing this person the path of the religion and improving him. On reading the writings of the Gathas very carefully, one finds many instructions to that effect. At the same time in the 19$^{th}$ Pargared (chapter) of the Vendidad there are sentences, as well as in the 2$^{nd}$ Pargared of the Vendidad in the final sentences, that *one finds clearly that a person who has faith in our sacred religion, and who wishes to join happily with free will, should be accepted. From the same 2$^{nd}$ Pargared of the Vendidad in the 1$^{st}$ paragraph it is written to such an extent, that if a non-Zoroastrian even on his death bed wishes to join and makes a declaration of this, he should then be accepted.* Also, if by staying in another religion he is committing acts of sin, then he should be made to turn away from that path.

Our ancestors, the pious Dastur Saheebs who have gone to heaven, have left us in writing that any person of another faith who with deep rooted feelings has faith in our religion and wishes to join us, then that person should definitely be accepted. *If any individual does not accept this person into the Zoroastrian religion, this individual is considered a big sinner.* When the Dasturs of previous years have left behind such writings, it is perfectly clear that this must have been written according to the sacred instructions of our religion.

Since there has not been acceptance of people of other religions into our religion for a long time, this appears very surprising to our people, and they say that a person of another faith should not be allowed to enter into our sacred religion. The people who think in that way are making a big mistake. Since we came to India, and after that when our Rivayat (book of customs and laws) was written, the writing of that period notes acceptance of people of other faiths into our religion. This particular writing is found in the Rivayat of Dorab Hormuzdiar.

After we came to India and for a long time, the Sudreh and Kusti has been offered to the children of Parsi women but having been born to women of other faiths. These children have been accepted into our sacred religion. There are many of these children born in the villages surrounding the far-off cities that have been accepted in our religion, after having their Navjotes performed. Their numbers are many, and they come and go in our sacred Dar-e-Mehers and Atash Behrams.

They also participate in the sacred rituals of our religion. *Such cases are in our city of Surat.* My strong opinion is that when children are born of such illicit acts, and their Navjotes are performed, it is the equivalent of encouraging illicit, lusty acts. Instead of performing such Navjotes, it is better to accept a good person of a noble family and of a higher caliber who has devotion and a great belief in our religion, and who wishes to be accepted into our sacred religion. To accept such a person into our religion is a meritorious act. Instead, the efforts are being directed to increase the Zoroastrian population by performing the Navjotes of these children of illicit acts. Such acts of accepting these children have not put up a good show, but have brought disgrace on our religion.

The present day Dasturs, learned Ervads, and learned Zoroastrian people knowledgeable of other faiths, have expressed their opinion that there is no restriction to accepting people of other faiths into our religion. However, within these people, some have expressed that they don't know which rituals should be performed for acceptance, and that accepting people of other faiths might create cultural problems. For this, I believe that all these learned individuals should get together and try to resolve this minor matter. They could then accept into our religion the people of other faiths, as well as the children born of a Zoroastrian father. In doing so the entire issue which has been discussed for a long time can be resolved, and the discussions going on in the other communities will die down.

Sir, you have written that I should answer with examples and arguments about this particular question; but, *there are so many examples available on this situation that if I try to point them all out the entire thing will become very lengthy. This is why the famous Ervad Saheeb Temurasp Dinshaw Anklasaria has compiled such examples and has published a booklet recently on this subject. I have read this and I completely agree with several of the examples expressed in it.* It is my opinion that if it appears necessary to accept a person of another faith or children of a Parsi father into our religion, that any Dastur or Mobed should take the authoritative permission from the Panchayat, and should accept them into our religion. This must be considered very authoritative and correct.

Signed,
Dastur Framji Jamshedji Suratwala


January 3, 1904
Navsari

Received your letter in which you have written, "Kindly express your opinion at your earliest with examples and arguments on the question of whether according to the teachings of our religion is it alright to accept people of other religions into the Zoroastrian religion". I am taking the liberty to answer this question. According to the writings of our religious books, any person of another faith with a true belief, and who is anxious to enter our noble religion, has no restrictions shown him. There are certain proofs in favor of acceptance as found in:--

Yajashne Ha (Chapter) 30 Paragraph 11
Yajashne Ha (Chapter) 43 Paragraph 6

Yajashne Ha (Chapter) 46 Paragraph 13
Yajashne Ha (Chapter) 45 Paragraph 1
Yajashne Ha (Chapter) 8   Paragraph 7
The final paragraphs of the Vendidad Pargareds, etc.

We must also inform you that in the customs of our area, the last 100 or so years, not a single incident has taken place, and that our respected elders, the elders of our Anjuman, as well as we ourselves, have always respected our customs. You must be aware of this.

Signed,
Dorabji Dastur Maheeyarji

Sir,

In your letter dated September 5, 1903, "Whether to accept or not accept people of other faiths into our religion according to the teachings of our religion," you have asked the opinion of this humble servant to this question. I am taking permission to express my thoughts.

There is only one answer to the above question. This answer can also be given by a person with a simple knowledge of the Zoroastrian religion and without a deep knowledge of the religious books. The answer is that there is no objection if a person of another religion or a person who follows another religion other than the Zoroastrian religion, who with a great belief and devotion wishes to enter our religion. He should then be allowed to do so. To ask the question whether to accept a person of another faith into our religion is the same as asking the question whether a Zoroastrian can stop a person of another faith from speaking the truth, or from performing a noble deed. Our simple religion is created for the prosperity and upliftment of the whole world. Its basic laws were set hundreds of thousands of years prior to the Prophet Asho Hazrat Zarathust. These laws will stay in existence even after the end of time. It is not the religion of one era. It has been created for the immemorial (Zavraneh Akarneh) and for the laws of the seven continents (Hafta Keshvar Zamin). The Zoroastrian religion is the word of God. This word was in existence before God created the skies, before He created the land, before He created the animal kingdom, before He created the water, before He created the fire that cleans, before He created this world, and before He created all the good things full of Ashoi. The Mazdayasni religion, along with Ahura Mazda, is omnipresent and infallible. With such a religion, that was in existence prior to any creation, and which has no end, *How can anyone with any common sense say that this religion was created only for a handful of Parsis in the 20th century.* With a simple common sense, the teaching of the holy Avesta declares that this bright, noble religion is open for any virtuous and honest person. In our holy Gathas it has been said, "Oh Ahura, everyone will recognize you as the Protector (Khavind) and will come to you". Asho Zarathust prays to Ahura Mazda, "Give me strength of words to help others have a firm belief in this noble religion". With pious prayers one can give a true belief to a sinful person. These sinful people, because of the teachings of evil, spoil the land of Ashoi. For them our religion has created prayers.

This particular religion is created to spread righteousness in the whole world and in the Kingdom of Dadar Ahura Mazda. For those who are anxious to spread this religion, our religious books give them hope of a suitable reward. According to Arda-Viraf, the souls of persons like Gayomard, Spitama Zarathustra, Kai Vistasp, Jamasp, Esadvastar, who were the originators of the Mazdayasni Religion, and who were given the responsibility of bringing the message, and who were given the title of Dasturan Dastur (highest form of priesthood), and who were given the responsibility of teaching and spreading the religion, their souls were found to be the closest to Ahura Mazda in the highest form of heaven (Garothman Behesht). Not one or two, but numerous paragraphs can be pointed out from our religious books. From these paragraphs it can be correctly proven that our ancient, pure religion has been perpetuated from the beginning of time til the end, to bring light into the hearts of mankind, and to show the path of righteousness in this world and the world beyond (Meenoy). THE MAZDAYASNI RELIGION IS PURITY. Any person can purify his soul with the help of Manashni, Gavashni, Kunashni. This means that any person can become Mazdayasni. This religion is supreme among all the religions, and it has control over all other religions. Its boundaries are compared with the ocean of Vourukash. Its spread is considered as the force of Mohari. Its greatness is like the picture of a very huge tree which can cover all the trees in this universe, and which can increase its spread, and its position is comparable to the sky. It can hide innumerable solar systems within its vast interiors. The real meaning of all this is that the Mazdayasni religion is a storage of Ahura Mazda's laws from which other religions with little differences are born based upon the time. This religion is the root of all religions, and ultimately it will unite in the ocean of religions with all other religions. If we may say in the mysterious words of Avesta, The River Ardivisur originates from the invisible peak of Mt. Hakhairea and flows into the ocean of Vourukash. In the same way all religions do this. The original stream of Akeedavo, with the help of Ahura Mazda's spiritual prayers on the path which Ardivisur flows, brings prosperity to its riverbanks. One of its brooks reaches the seven continents of this earth (Hafta Kesvar Zamin). In winter or summer it equally fills all needs. This means that it is the knowledge of the divine path, which is declared by God for the benefit of mankind through prayers. Whichever person acquires this knowledge is bathed with the waters of patience and bravery equally for happiness or sadness, hope or despair. The branches of this knowledge are spread all over this world, and this collection of knowledge can also be found within the people whom we recognize with the label of Juddeen (people of other faiths). We find the real Mazdayasni within them. Our Asho Zarathust has remembered and revered with great respect such real Mazdayasnis of other faiths. From this one can clearly see that our religion does not intend to keep its magnificent teachings from others in this world. The religion does not wish to hide its light under a cover. Its bright beacon shines like a lighthouse in the middle of an ocean, trying to help all of mankind, which is caught in the center of the storm. It is trying to save them from evil, and take them on the other side of the ocean. For this it is kept open, so that every man with its help can take his sacred boat away from the rocks of bad thoughts, bad words, and bad deeds, and safely reach the shores. It is the duty of every Mazdayasni to keep that light shining and open in all four directions, and to make sure that no one should come in between them. If someone does come in between them, the right thing to do is to try and keep that person away. By doing this, we Zoroastrians will be fulfilling one of our duties. Not only this, but we would also be making the soul of our Holy Prophet happy. He has given the choicest blessings to the person who is an expert in the knowledge of the religion, because that person would show love to the people of this world, declare openly the laws of Ahura Mazda, and openly teach happiness, truth, and the lessons of immortality to others. The amount of happiness and pride that we can feel by the spread of this noble religion, by the same amount this religion can become useful to the world. This is the religion that helps to stop fighting. It helps toward disarmament. It makes you unselfish, and it is righteous.

In short, in my simple thoughts and according to our religion, the following principles can be proven:--

1)    Our religion is established for the entire world.

2)    You should spread the religion in this world as much as you can. It is perfectly alright and useful for mankind.

The above thoughts that I have expressed on this delicate question are only from the religious point of view. In order to do this I have taken the help of our holy Scriptures. However, the same subject can be discussed from the point of view of culture, community, and politics. Because the Anjuman Committee has asked the question from the religious point of view, I haven't taken this opportunity to discuss it in other ways.

Signed,
Khorshed Dastur Behram

# Appendix II. The Status of Women in Zoroastrianism

By Dr. Kersey H. Antia

Parsi traditionalists often belittle the importance of the Gathas and even of Prophet Zarathushtra, in order to justify their views. One such view is that men and women are not equal or are equal only in the spiritual (Menog) world, after death, and not during their lifetime in this physical (Getig) world. Such a view is untenable, and an unforgivable insult to the greatness of our Prophet, who had the courage and the vision to say in those prehistoric days that his message applies equally to men and women (Yasna 53.6).

If they have not attained an equal position in this world, it can only be attributed to human frailty, and not to the Prophet's teachings. He advises us to bring about Frashokereti by our actions (Yasna 30.9) and Frashokereti is not possible without women working as hard for it as men. For this reason, he included women in the initiation ceremony of Navjote, though such may not have been the practice among the Indo-Iranians, because to this day, the Janoi (Hindu initiation) is reserved for men of certain higher castes alone. Even the Jews had Bar Mitzvah only for men and not for women, until the American Rabbi Mordecai Kaplan in 1922 "invented" the modern-day Bat Mitzvah, in which 12 year old girls accept the religious responsibility of adulthood. But the orthodox branch of the Jewish faith still does not accept this reform.[1]

## Men and Women are Equally Required to Make the Right Choice

Women played an active role in the spread of the religion and Farvardin Yasht (paragraph 141) venerates sixteen married women and eleven maidens who did so. To be godlike, men and women have to imbibe the qualities of the seven Amesha Spentas, three of whom are female, which would postulate equal status for both in this very world where such an authority is to be emulated. Moreover, Zarathushtra emphasizes that God has granted us Free Will (Yasna 31.11, 30.2, 45.2, etc.), and each person has to make his or her own choice. If so, how could women be reduced to an unequal status in this world, when both men and women are equally required to make a choice, leading to right thinking and right actions, which in turn lead us to Frashokereti? The Ahunawar prayer,[2] which embodies the importance of serving the needy, in my opinion, includes the principle of righting any wrong done to a helpless woman.

Spenta Armaiti, the Beneficent Right-Mindedness, is a feminine attribute of God Himself, and the word for religion is Daena, a feminine noun. The Yenghe Hatam prayer venerates both good men and women still living on this earth because of their piety. In Yasna 51.22, which apparently is the origin of Yenghe Hatam, Zarathushtra venerates such souls "who have existed and still exist" by their name. The prayer Airyamana (Yasna 54.1) also includes men as well as women. In fact there is not a single derisive statement or sentiment about women

---

1   *Wall Street Journal*, January 29, 2010, p. WII.
2   *FEZANA Journal*, Summer 1994.

in our ancient Avesta. Rather, Yasna 41.2, which is closest to the Gathic period in its composition, unequivocally states: "May good ruler, man or woman, rule over us in both (Getig and Menog) existences." Yasna 41.3 and 41.6 also embody the importance of both the worlds. Even the word for our Lord, Mazda, has a feminine root. When even today girls are unwanted in some cultures, the Avestan blessing for good progeny refer to 'Frazantin' – children of both sexes. The *Shahnameh* reflects this belief: "If the child is well-behaved and thrives splendidly, then hold it dearly no matter if boy or girl." In *Women in the Shahnameh,* D.K. Motlagh vindicates that they enjoyed "a certain degree of independence" in various spheres.[1] Roman records reveal that Persian women fought along with men against the Romans.

Maria Brosius refutes Ernst Herzfeld's comment: "In Achaemenid sculpture no woman is pictured, and evidently it never became a normal subject."[2] His view was primarily based on the absence of female representations on the Persepolis reliefs, which Brosius observes "has no bearing on the status of royal and high-ranking women at the Persian court or their relevance as artistic subjects in Achaemenid art."[3] The PFT seal PFS77 depicts an enthroned lady with a maid and lady visitor, and many more such seals are presented in this book. According to Herodotus (7.69.2), Darius had a statue of gold made for his wife Artystone. Brosius maintains that archaeological findings from the Achaemenid satrapies prove that the artistic representation of women was not exceptional at all, though such women were wrongly interpreted as representing goddesses. "Yet," she notes, "there is no evidence that the Achaemenids built temples in which to worship their gods; on the contrary, they performed religious rites in open-air sanctuaries, and in front of fire altars." The relief plaque from Egypt depicts a crowned Persian lady, and four crown Persian ladies are also depicted on the carpet from Pazyryk while standing before a fire altar. Brosius also believes the royal women assumed responsibility to act as mediators between the king and the members of the Persian nobility. She also points out the artistic objects depicting women that have already been documented by other historians. More examples of the representation of women in the art of the Achaemenid period have been presented in the same publication for the eastern region of the empire as well as for Asia Minor.[4]

Din Yasht reveals that a wife aspires to be equal to her husband in carrying out her moral and religious duties. Gah 4.9 extols a pious woman as comparable to Spenta Armaiti. Yasna 5.27 adores female holy persons along with male ones. Moreover, Yasna 1.16, 14.7, 8.3, 16.9, and 61.10, among other Avestan texts, speak of pious women along with men in the same breath. Fravardin Yasht 15.4 depicts a wife trying to excel her husband in gaining spirituality.

### *Zoroastrian Persia had More Queens than Perhaps Any Other Nation*

It is not surprising therefore that Zoroastrian Persia had more queens than per-

1   Costa Mesa, CA: Mazda Publishers, 2012.
2   See Herzfeld, *Iran in the Ancient East*, London, 1941, p. 325.
3   See, "The Royal Audience Scene Reconsidered," in *The World of Achaemenid Persia*, edited by John Curtis and St John Simpson, London: I.B. Tauris, 2010, pp. 141-152.
4   Op. cit. pp. 153-176.

haps any other nation in the world in ancient times. Zoroastrian women braved sailing to India with their men, and later braved living with them in hiding on Bahrot Mountain when Muslims conquered Sanjan. And once again, they braved fighting the locals who wanted to take advantage of the absence of their male rela- tives, as the legend of Jange Variav goes. Today, they rank almost invariably as the first among Indian women to compete with men for any and every profession, in- cluding the arts and sports.

Aerpatistan 37 will further bear out the priestly role played by them in the ear- lier days. In Yasna 46.10 Zarathushtra declares: "Whoever, be it man or woman, would grant to me those things which thou dost know to be the best for existence." Elderly women continued to perform rituals of a secondary nature in Iran, as late as a few decades ago.[1] Insler interprets "existence" as "this world." How can women offer their best for this world if their hands are tied down with inequality in this world? In Yasht 13.143-151 pious men and women of all countries are ven- erated.

### Equality of Men and Women Essential for Frashokereti

Zarathushtra is firm in his conviction for gender equality because women's equal status forms such an integral part in his divine vision and message, that the very basis of it falls apart if it is compromised or undermined in any way, for whatever reason, may it be for justifying ethnicity, patrilineality, or denouncing in- termarriages, and safeguarding the benefits of the Parsi trusts, which are already legally safeguarded by court verdicts.

### Women in Zoroastrianism

The evidence for the equality of sexes in Zoroastrianism is so abundant, it is hard to cite them all. So one can gather a few instances which could prove suffi- cient enough to establish this fact. Visperad 3:4 declares: I want to appoint the woman whose good thoughts, good words, and good deeds prevail, who is well taught, who is an authority for rites, and (who is) truthful. (We worship) Spenta Armaiti (a female Amesha Spenta) and (all) your noblewomen, O Ahura Mazda!

Yasna 13.1 addresses the Ratu of the women along with troops of heroes. Vis- perad 2.7 invites the worship of women, and Visperad 1.5 even venerates the women "of various varieties." In Yasna 35.8, Ahura Mazda grants the best salva- tion for everyone who follows Asha in the Getig (physical) as well as the Menog (spiritual) world.

Yasna 38.1 venerates females along with "this earth" and implies the similarity between the two in bearing fruits and fertility. Indeed the earth – Spenta Armaiti – is represented as a female Amesha Spenta (Bountiful Spirit) throughout the Aves- ta. Yasna 39.3 venerates both male and female Amesha Spentas – Spenta Armaiti, Haurvatat, and Ameretat being female, and the other three being male. Yasna 38.1 makes it clear that both of them are equal in goodness. Thus, being female does not carry any stigma or sense of inferiority in the Avesta, but rather represents un- precedented gender equality.

---

1    See *Fezana Journal*, Fall 1994, p. 36.

Yasna 35.8 represents Zarathushtra as addressing his message to "every human being" per Almut Hintze (p. 93) and others. For that reason, Yasht 13.152 wants him to be praised and worshipped by "everyone of those who exist" (Kahmaichit Hatam).

In Yasna 39.1-2 the worshippers venerate the souls of all human beings "wherever they may have been born" (Kudo-Zatanamchit), who as pointed out by Almut Hintze "are explicitly described not as coming from the worshippers' own local community or land, but as possibly having been born anywhere." (Hintze 2007, pp. 269-270.) "Their birthplace being irrelevant, what matters is that they are committed to truth." Thus, Yasna 39.2 "encompasses, in a universal manner all truthful (Asho) human beings" who follow the law of Asha as expounded by Zarathushtra, who was the only one in his time to preach such an intricate doctrine of Asha. According to Hintze, *hakhemān* in Yasna 40.3 implies "the 'fellowship' within the worshippers' own families and communities. In Yasna 40.4, that 'fellowship' is characterized as one which the worshippers hope to join. Hintze and Narten suggest that the request for the latter could refer to a situation of mission, in which Zarathushtra's followers approach other communities in order to win them over to the religion preached by him. According to this interpretation, the worshippers ask that all the qualities in Yasna 40.3-4 desired for their own communities at home may also be present in those groups which they hope to persuade to become adherents of Zarathushtra." (p. 303). If Zarathushtra's mission was merely to restore the so-called "Mazdayasni" religion, there was no need to go in search of "fellowship" anywhere else. Yasna 41.2 declares that a good ruler, either man or woman, would govern us in both the worlds, (corporal and the spiritual).

Fravardin Yasht depicts Fravashis, the female beings, as the ones who first showed their paths to the heavenly waters, the heavenly bodies, sun, moon, stars, and the plants. They also helped Vohu Mana and Asha Vahishta when Angra Mainyu tried to enter Ahura Mazda's domain in order to stop waters from flowing and plants from growing. If these female angelic beings can thwart the evil attempts of Angra Mainyu so successfully, how can women be an instrument or embodiment of evil? And since Fravashi seems to have Fravarti (an element of choice) at its etymology, women, along with men, cannot be branded as evil unless they choose to be so. While noting that the Parsi priests do not consider the children of a non-Zoroastrian wife as entitled to any share of the paternal property, Dr. Martin Haug contends that "there appears to be nowhere in the Avesta texts extant any direct prohibition of intermarriages between Zoroastrians and non-Zoroastrians."[1]

### Women in Ancient Persia

Zoroaster's emphasis on gender equality was reflected in ancient Persia. Maria Brosius has written a book, *Women in Ancient Persia: 559-331 B.C.*, (Clarendon Press, Oxford, 1996) to denote the high status of women in the Achaemenian court and to counteract the negative impression depicted of them by Greek writers. Nu-

---

1    Haug, Martin. *The Parsis: Essays on Their Sacred Language, Writings, and Religion.* New Delhi: Indigo Books, 2003, p. 46.

merous texts found at Persepolis refer, among many women, employers, Irdaba-
ma, whose workforce consisted of various work-groups ranging from three to several hundred workers. She had her own seal to authorize business transactions.
Brosius also adds Artystone to this list. (p. 181). On the Greek view, Brosius says,
women are not part of, and do not belong easily in, the male dominated Greek society. It was not at all so in the Persian society: "We cannot overestimate the implications of the action royal and nobles wives could take. Their independence can
be observed in the (Persepolis) Fortification texts. Royal women enjoyed a position which allowed them free disposition of the produce of their estates, reflected
in their ability to give their own orders to officials, to use their own seal, and to
employ their own bureaucratic staff to execute their affairs. These women had
their own centers of manufacture, and their own workforce – and engaged the
same officials as the kings." Women in no other society are known to have enjoyed such independence and gender equality 2500 years ago, and it is natural that
such equality trickled down to all strata of the Persian society. As a matter of fact,
Damascus and other historians claim, on the basis of the remarks of Nicolas of
Damascus, that the credit for the formation of the first and foremost Persian empire goes to Persian women, who shamed King Cyrus's defeated soldiers back to
the battle for a fight to the finish, which ultimately led to their victory against the
Medes. In appreciation of it, King Cyrus even decreed that any Persian King visiting their town should award one gold coin to each woman.[1]

Youtab, along with her brother, Ario-Barzan, organized 2500 soldiers to stall
Alexander's assault on Persepolis. Sura, the daughter of the Parthian king Ardavan
V, commanded a Parthian army as she was very skillful in military maneuvers and
strategy. Shapur I's wife, Azad-Dokht, advocated women's participation in war
maneuvers for helping out in war times. She played an important role in establishing the university city of Jondi-Shapur. Azad-Dailami was at the forefront of the
army fighting the Arab invasion. Banu Khorramdin, an excellent archer, joined her
husband in battles, and started the Khorramdinan movement to fight the Arab
domination. The Parthian king Ardavan IV appointed Arta-Dokht as director of
the Treasury, because of her accomplishments in the economic and administrative
spheres. The list can go on.

A relief from the fifth century B.C., carved in the Greek style, depicting a Persian woman on horseback, has been found in Phrygia which is in modern Turkey
(Dandamaev and Lukonin, op. cit. p. 299). Women are often reported to ride horses in ancient Iran, especially on royal hunts. Archaeologists working in the northwestern Iranian city of Tabriz have identified the skeletons of female sword-wield-
ing warriors by DNA analysis. Other such female skeletons have also been found
in the Caspian Sea region.[2]

They also found that Parysatis, wife of Darius II, had her own cities and villages.[3] Herodotus[4] reports that the Persian queen owned the city of Anthylla in

1   M. A. Dandamaev, Vladimir Grigor'evich Lukonin, Philip L. Kohl, and D. J. Dadson. *The culture
    and social institutions of ancient Iran.* Cambridge: Cambridge University Press, 1989, p. 120.
2   See http://www.cais-soas.com/News/2004/December2004/06-12.htm, accessed May 13, 2015.
3   Op. cit. p. 136.
4   *The Histories,* II, 98 and I, 192.

Egypt, which had to supply shoes to her. "The villages (of Parysatis) were the sovereign private property of the queen." "Even the wet-nurses of the royal children and the palace ladies (for instance, the Persian women Artiya and Atragata) owned fields and orchards in Babylonia."[5]

Credit for the spread of the world's first monotheistic and creedal religion also goes to women, as Boyce surmises from what evidence we have that "It was probably through his wife that the king (Vishtasp) was converted."[1] And when Zarathushtra himself welcomes any assistance from "be it man or woman" in Yasna 46.10 so that "with all these I shall cross over the Chinvat Bridge," who are we to deny equality to women unless not intent on passing the Chinvat Bridge ourselves?

The equal status assigned to both men and women in the Gathas is also reflected in later Avestan texts. For example, a University of Zurich dissertation,[2] found only thirteen female names in the *Rig Veda*. But the Avestan female names swelled primarily by the list of twenty-seven female names in the Fravardin Yasht (Yasht 13, 139-42) alone.

Touraj Daryaee brings out a point that I have mentioned elsewhere: "The non-Zoroastrian women, especially the Jews and Christians, did marry Zoroastrians, particularly the nobles and the King of Kings as well. For example the mother of Wahram V was Jewish and the favorite wife of Khushro II, the mother of Queen Buran, was Christian. This may have made the situation of their respective communities safe, as such women would represent their concerns."[3] Thus, even the non-Zoroastrian women married to Zoroastrian noblemen and kings were able to exercise their influence to assert the rights of non-Zoroastrian women in Iran. Moreover, "By the fifth century of the religious minorities and attempted to co-opt them into a system of governance where according to legal precepts, all would be considered simply as *nard/zani* (*iran*) *shahar* – men/women citizen (of the Empire)."[4] This must have enabled even the non-Zoroastrian women to assert their rights in the political domain of Iranshahr.

Even though Pahlavi Videvdat 18 is in many ways harder on women than on men regarding their culpability for sin, nevertheless, in reply to the question: "(Is) man (a) more grievous (sinner), or a woman?," its response is: "Both (are) equal." Thus, even the post-Gathic texts celebrate the role of women in Zoroastrian Iran.

### Women's Legal Status During Sasanian Period

Professor Yaakov Elman asserts that "the legal status of Iranian women improved dramatically during the Sasanian period (224-657 C.E.) as demonstrated by the legal debates preserved in the Middle Persian *Book of a Thousand Decisions*, namely, *Mādayān ī Hazār Dādestān* . Although it was written around 620 A.D., he maintains that it contains various rulings from earlier times. According to this text, an Iranian woman "was permitted to manage the family estates, and thus

---

5    Op. cit. p. 137.

1    *History of Zoroastrianism*, Vol. I, pp. 187-9.

2    As reported in *the Journal of the American Oriental Society*, 2008, pp. 397-8.

3    *Sasanian Persia*, I.B. Tauris, 20, p. 56.

4    Ibid, p. 56.

represent the estate in court, give testimony, alienate her husband's property, inherit a double-share from her husband and a half-share from her father, and sometimes choose her own mate. If a childless widow, she could remarry to provide
offspring that would be considered the child of her deceased husband." However,
he wondered "how such women managed all this while observing the Zoroastrian
laws of menstrual impurity, which could include an up-to nine day period of isolation from her family in a windowless hut called Dashtanistan." He believes a de-
mographic crisis was brought on by constant wars with the Byzantine as well as
by the Black Plague that raged over Iran and Byzantium for centuries from 542
A.D. onwards. As the plague bacilli do not affect women as adversely as it affects
men, it led to the shortage of adult males, and to the employment of women for
economic as well as religious purposes. He points out that "various Avestan passages in the Herbedestan text assume the possibility that women could run the
family property alone." As they are not constricted as the Vendidad in defining
women's roles, they provided "proof-texts for the new policy." On the basis of the
Avestan Herbedestan 5.1 and 5.3, 5.4-5, he shows that the wife can go forth to
pursue religious work if the husband can take care of the possessions, and "it is
clear that it is possible for a woman in particular, to supervise the (sacred) fires,"
especially "her own fire, ... but not a public fire." *The Cambridge Ancient History*[1]
reports that even the Elamite women "had won a large measure of equal rights for
themselves," and *only* the sons had to care for the mother after the father's death,
to be able to inherit his property, but "mother and daughter remain privileged, as
they "will inherit in any case." Almut Hintze in the same *Sims-Williams Festschrift* co-edited by her in 2009, and Maria Macuch in the same Festschrift, wonder how to reconcile it with men being the Ratu (guardian; overseer) over women
in those days. My own intuitive answer is, this Ratuship was not as rigidly enforced in real life as it was in the priestly manuals, as can be gleamed from Mary
Boyce's *Zoroastrians*, etc. and from the progress made by modern Parsi women in
every conceivable field. "The Nerangistan," she adds, "has a number of provisions
allowing for women to recite the liturgy even while menstruating – something that
contemporary Zoroastrianism does not allow even for women who are not menstruating." While their rights in this regard are limited in contrast to males, the
very fact that even menstruant women could officiate is quite amazing and beyond
belief. Elman tries to show that this "liberal" tendency even "predates the demo-
graphic crisis of the sixth century – not to mention the Avestan texts themselves,
which must be dated to 1000-1400 years earlier." He does quote Dastur Kotwal's
opinion that "these statements seem improbable in view of what is known about
general Zoroastrian attitudes regarding menstruation; modern Zoroastrian women
are not allowed to pray at all at such times."[2] These findings sounded as much unthinkable to me as to Dastur Kotwal, because as classmates at the Cama Athornan
Institute we shared the same orientation in religion for many years. However, I de-
tect in them a flexibility, nay, a concession even on a very fundamental principle

---

1    Vol. II, Part 2, pp. 286-8.
2    For more details, see Yaakov Elman, "Scripture Versus Contemporary Needs: a Sassanian
     Zoroastrian Example", 28 *Cardozo Law Review* 153, Volume 28:1, 2006, pp. 153-169.

of the religion when crucial times demanded it, even as I pray we may never have to face them again. However, the bitter truth is, such a crisis is staring us right in our face with our women marrying out due to the Zeitgeist, but we are not heeding the advice of these ancient texts, recognizing the pivotal role of women in contin uing our race, religion, and heritage. Even the latest Zoroastrian texts of ninth century maintain that there will be fifteen male and fifteen female helpers of the Saoshyant who will come to usher us into Renovation – Bundahishn 34.16, indicating a high status for women, even when our very last texts were written in the Dark Ages.

What Touraj Daryaee observes is worth noting here: "Women of high rank such as the queen and the mother of the king were much freer in the scope of their activity and decision making. Their seals demonstrate their presence in the royal 'bazms.' As mentioned before, they engaged in hunting, drinking and feasting with men, wore elaborate costumes, and two women were able to rule in the sev-enth century CE. Although by all accounts Queens Boran and Azarmi (g) dukht were the only legitimate surviving members of the Sasanian family in the seventh century, the acceptance of their rule and the benevolent remembrance of them by the Sasanian sources suggest that they were accepted by the clergy as well. The other queens remembered but who did not rule were Ardashir-Anahid, Wahram II's sister and wife, and later Shabuhrdukhtag, his other wife who is the only queen whose portrait was on the coins beside Wahram II." However he observes, "since male priests wrote them," (scriptures) "it was their opinion that is known." Common women did not therefore fare well in the Sasanian society, since most of the religious injunctions against women firmly allied to women of non-noble cate-gory, (which goes against the grain of gender equality emphasized by the prophet in the Gathas.)[1] as well as against other findings quoted earlier. Daryaee also states that "The chase of the hunt was another favorite activity of the nobility in which women participated also." (p. 51). We know it from several Greek and Byzantine writers that Persian queens, princesses, and even queen-mothers accompanied the kings to the battles.

Despite living under the strict Islamic rules about gender, as Janet Amighi[2] makes it copiously clear, Zoroastrian women in Iran have also succeeded in ensur-ing their equal status with men despite confronting many obstacles for achieving it.

### Recent Research Challenging Equality of Women

Of late attempts have been made to attribute malevolence to the female and benevolence to the male in Zoroastrianism. J. K. Choksy[3] attributes such a di-chotomy to the dualistic tendencies latent in Zoroastrianism, which, however, was not so latent and pronounced until the ninth century A.D. Such an attribution to dualistic tendencies in Zoroastrianism is fraught with danger and can lead to un-

---

1    *Sasanian Persia*, I.B., Taurus, 2009, p. 59.
2    *The Zoroastrians of Iran: Conversion, Assimilation, or Persistence.* New York: AMS Press, 1990, pp. 239-244, etc.
3    Choksy, Jamsheed K. *Evil, Good and Gender: Facets of the Feminine in Zoroastrian Religious History.* New York: Peter Lang, 2002.

tenable conclusions. For example, in his tractate on "Madjus" (Magi, Mobed) in the *Encyclopedia of Islam*, second edition, M. Morony points to the dualistic tendencies without providing reliable data when he claims: "Material wealth was equated with the virtue and goodness inherent in the upper classes", whereas, "sin and evil were inherent in the lower classes", which contradicts all the tenets of Zoroastrianism, starting with the status of *Dregubio* (the poor) in the most important prayer of Ahunawar. James Russell has severely criticized Morony's views in an article in the *Journal of K. R. Cama Oriental Institute*. One wonders what more theories will show up based on such false notions of dualism, a subject which I have challenged in a separate essay, and the learned Shaul Shaked has maintained the same opinion long ago. However, as "There can not be doubt of the Iranian origin of the Muslim Waqf" (charity foundations) as per the *Cambridge History of Iran*,[1] Morony, who has great expertise regarding the history of Arab conquest of Iran, should be expected to be more discrete in his attributions to dualistic principles in this regard. The same could be expected of Choksy, whose expertise on Zoroastrianism is so well established. As I have explained at length in my paper on dualism, this rigid dualism, though always nascent, appeared first time in full force in our history as a consequence of the conquest of Iran by Arabs, who insisted on their form of monotheism being a superior one over that of Zoroastrians, who did not regard their God as the author of both the good as well as the evil as the Arabs did. The Magis therefore had to apply every means they could in their hapless condition to prove the superiority of their mode of monotheism by pointing out that an all-good God cannot be the author of evil, a role they attributed to Ahreman. However, in building up a strong case, perforce they had to resort to all they can, and had to add or devise many ideas about cosmogony and cosmology theretofore not espoused in the Avesta, thereby rendering their dualism in collision at times with the one preached by the prophet, as they had little recourse to it in those trying times, and had a fight for their very life on hand against their hostile conquerors. Choksy himself has more-or-less acknowledged this fact in the past, as I have explained in my treatise refuting this type of dualism (forthcoming).

Instead of finding fault with these Pahlavi writers, it is to their credit they were able to discern and debate a subject that the Kerderites and Mu'tazilites also favored during the Abbasid period, along with most writers on this subject, as detailed in my forthcoming treatise on dualism in Zoroastrianism. After perusing the chapter on the Mu'tazilites in the *Formative Period of Islamic Thought*, by W. Montgomery Watt,[2] I suspect that the Zoroastrian ecclesiastics, ever so fearful of offending the religious sentiments of their alien rulers, found it safer to follow the lead already espoused by the Mu'tazilites, which is apparent from the over-emphasis they had to place in this process on dualism in order to counter the absolute monotheism of their rulers, a fact recognized by Choksy himself, as pointed out by me in my forthcoming essay on dualism. Such a surmise is supported by the fact that "discussions" were held between "the chief of Zoroastrian clerics" and Dirāz ibn-'Amir who "did more than any other single thinker to make possi-

---

1    Volume 3 (2), Cambridge University Press, 1983, p. 664.
2    Edinburgh: University Press, 1973, pp. 209-250.

ble the flowering of the Mu'tazila."[1] Although Watt attributes Greek influence to the Mu'tazilite views,[2] he himself notes, "some groups seem to have accepted certain Persian ideas, such as free will, and emphasized the words 'we do not fix evil upon God' In a way that might link up with the Zoroastrian dualism of good and evil."[3] There is little surprise "the Mu'tazilites were regarded as heretics, however by the Sunnites"[4] later on.

### Radical Evil Not Attributable to Women in Zoroastrianism

Radical evil cannot possibly be attributed entirely to the feminine gender in its origin, nature, or prevalence, as Choksy does. In Zoroastrianism, as in the Judaeo-Christian traditions, the origin of evil is assigned to the masculine, be it God or Satan. The word Mazda for the Zoroastrian God, however, contains a feminine component in its grammatical composition, which is strong evidence for the equality of men and women in the eyes of God Himself. Pious male as well as female adherents and their souls were eulogized as Ashavan, as in the Fravardin Yasht, and the word Dregvant includes both male and female adherents that strayed away from the path of Asha. Druz is regarded as applicable to both masculine and feminine, as can be attested from its use in the Achaemenian inscriptions or in the Pahlavi texts or in the Parsi parlance. Thus, "Druz-Taromaiti" is translated by Parsi scholars as "hatred, arrogance or haughtiness."[5] and Nasus as "putrefaction."[6] Any proper disposal of Nasus renders a blow to the male demon (Druj) but a demoness is not even mentioned.[7] Vendidad 15:7 pronounces a man worthy of death who copulates with a menstruating woman, and holds the man responsible for such behavior. It is difficult to ascertain the exact basis on which certain evil spirits were assigned feminine names and why they often got transformed into masculine beings later on. Thus, *khshnathaiti* first stood for sexuality, lewdness, and later came to represent idolatry, which is hard to explain on the basis of the scriptures, though it could be explained away by making assumptions. Jennifer Rose raises the same gender issue.[8] Moreover, even when certain vices were attributed to feminine beings, these vices or evil tendencies were evinced by both males and females and were not the exclusive domain or qualities of women. Later myths as expounded in *Bundahishn* regarding Mashya and Mashyana, the first human couple, was apparently an attempt to provide a Zoroastrian version of the story of Adam and Eve, but, unlike it, *Bundahishn* does not blame the first woman, Mashyana, all by herself, for disobeying God. However, how much we should rely on what the learned B. T. Anklesaria called *dantkatha* "folklore", as noted in my tractate on Dualism. Mashyana is later depicted as indulging in an irreligious ritual act but that seems to be an attempt to attribute to her the inadequacies inher-

---

1    Ibid, pp. 189-90.
2    Ibid, p. 249, etc.
3    Ibid, p. 34.
4    Ibid p. 249.
5    See *K. R. Cama Oriental Institute Golden Jubilee Volume*, Bombay, 1969, p. 87.
6    Ibid, p. 79.
7    Ibid, p. 84.
8    See the *Journal of K. R. Cama Oriental Institute*, No. 56, 1989, p. 16.

ent in all of us – man or woman. Except perhaps for some myths in the Pahlavi literature of ninth century, there is no scriptural evidence for portraying women as weak in combating or resisting evil but strong in promoting or advocating evil. Rather, a Pahlavi marriage contract requires a husband to "keep his wife well and honored".[1] Even Rev. J. H. Moulton regards "Druz as the opposite of Asha – falsehood, against Truth, chaos against Order, wrong against Right. This is the Enemy with whom we have to fight perpetually on the battleground of our own soul."[2] Even when the *Bundahishn* (14a:l) goes out of the way to portray Ohrmazd as musing about His utter inability, (a highly unlikely possibility for an omniscient God and very un-Zoroastrian and un-Avestan to the hilt, but quoted quite often), to replace womankind with a better species because He could simply think of no better alternative to it, instead of interpreting it in the negative way, it could and should be interpreted in many positive ways, e.g., even God could not better his own creation of womankind, and so it must be inherently good, as good as God could fashion it, especially as he created the Getig world first in the Menog world, etc. As seen later, De Jong rejects Zaehner and Choksy's interpretation for it and maintains "it specifically mentions the fact that woman helps Ohrmazd by producing men", even though "The passage, it is true, describes this abhorrence in offendingly misogynist terms". (p. 36), which unfortunately seems to be a common male reaction to women, for instance, a Greek complaining to Zeus: "If you wanted to sow a mortal race, you need not to provide it from women but men could have deposited a sum of bronze or iron or gold in your temples and brought the seed of children".[3]

It seems, more often than not, female names denote the feminine quality of the vices they represent rather than the gender of the one possessing the vices or evil, as can be seen from the way the Parsis conceive and speak of them. The Ahreman has a host of assistant spirits who take active part in the cosmic war. As S. Shaked explains, these spirits "designate both human qualities (virtues and vices respectively for each of the major spirits) and independent spiritual entities." For example, a man whose body is inhabited by anger makes it impossible for others to talk to him, "when people talk to him he does not listen, when they report to him even a small fault he is offended and does not discipline it. He tells many lies to people, and inflicts much chastisement on an innocent person." (*Denkard*, Book VI 78). As Shaked explains, "the spirits settle inside the body of a man and induce him to do their desire." Since man is endowed with free will, Yasna 30.2, 45.2, 31.11, etc., the spirits cannot do what one does not choose to do as ultimately he, and not the spirit, will end up in hell. Evil spirits thus play their role in the freedom of choice in their own medieval ways, as otherwise the very fabric of Zarathushtra's theology will fall apart. Moreover, the *Denkard* here does not attribute radical evil to the feminine gender in its origin. Male and female evil spirits work the same way as a rule and any digression from it in Pahlavi literature is a veritable digression from Zoroastrian theology. As many of these references cited here are con-

1   Ibid, p. 107.
2   Ibid, p. 156.
3   See *Women's Life in Greece and Rome*, Mary R. Lefkowitz and Maureen B. Fant, Baltimore: The John Hopkins University Press, Second Edition, 1992, p. 29.

tained in a single text, much more such evidence is easily available from other sources too, but I have very limited resources and time as a self-funded non-academician to include them all here, vis-a-vis well-funded academicians.

The distorted image of Persian queens and noblewomen in Greek writings, as I have explained elsewhere, is indeed polemic and self serving, and therefore, any unfavorable opinion about Persian women based on Greeks, Persia's bitter rival, is not valid. Even if the Greek criticism of them is somehow right, the condition of the Greek woman was pathetically worse than the condition of the Achaemenian woman, lay or royal.[1] Anyway Greeks hardly had any direct access to Persian queens and royal women and tended to project their own hostility onto them, mostly out of jealousy or pride.

The Zoroastrian Sogdia too had a queen even after the Arab conquest of Western Iran. Hugh Kennedy notes:[2] "The local historian of Bukhara, Narshakhī, gives (an account) of the court of his native city shortly before the Arab conquest in the time of the lady Khātūn (c. 680-700), of whom it was said that 'in her time there was no one more capable than she. She governed wisely and the people were obedient to her'. This tribute is particularly striking in contrast to the generally hostile attitude to female rule encountered in early Muslim historical sources. Every day she used to ride out of the gate of the great citadel of Bukhara to the sandy open ground known as the Registan. Here she would hold court, seated on a throne, surrounded by her courtiers and eunichs.... she enquired into affairs of state and issued orders, giving robes of honour to some and punishing others.... In the evening she came out again and sat on her throne while the landowners and princes waited on her in two lines."

Such an elevated status of woman is incompatible with the demonic qualities assigned to woman in some Pahlavi texts. Moreover, as these texts were written in the tenth and eleventh centuries, much after the Parsis left Iran, the Parsis could not have been even cognizant of it, which is attested by the fact that the crucial requirement for the performance of Vendidad for the Maratab ceremony was not even known to the Parsis in India until they were made aware of it by the Rivayats, which initially started in 1478 A. D.[3] This scenario is further attested by the fact that Dastur R. E. Sanjana, whom John Hinnells (rightly) regards as "the most orthodox" among all Parsi authors of his time, and applauds as "the only author known to me who preserves the doctrine of the resurrection of the body," *nevertheless* "considered Angra-Mainyu to denote nothing but the evil spirit or thought of man. I can find no twentieth-century Parsi writer who believes in an evil BEING which might correspond to the Middle-Persian Ahriman."[4] This may be partly due to the Parsi psyche not being exposed to the Pahlavi texts written after they had already left Iran.

1   Mary F. Lefkowitz and Maureen B. Fant, op. cit., pp. 28-29.
2   Kennedy, Hugh. *The Great Arab Conquests: How the Spread of Islam Changed the World We Live In*. Philadelphia, PA: Da Capo, 2007, p. 231.
3   See Philip G. Kreyenbroek, Societas iranologica europaea. *Transition periods in Iranian history: actes du symposium de Fribourg-en-Brisgau, 22-24 mai 1985*. Paris (Institut d'études iraniennes): Association pour l'avancement des études iraniennes, 1987.
4   *Journal of Mithraic Studies*, Vol. III, Nos. 1 & 2, 1980, pp. 134-5.

Sarah B. Pomeroy implies[1] that his exposure to Persian culture led Xenophon to accord Greek women an equal status with men, at least to the upper-class Greek woman. He narrates how a Greek woman excelled her husband in running his estate, and even imposed fines and punishments on him for failing in his duties, even though Plato (Meno, 71e-73b) confines women's expertise to running a household, and Pomeroy quotes Aristotle's view that "the husband's rule over the wife is fundamental" even for running a household.[2] Thus, what the Greek philosophers did not accomplish, the Greek exposure to Persians did.

There is no tendency whatsoever in mainstream Zoroastrianism to regard women as weak in their denial of evil and strong in espousing wickedness, as J. K. Choksy posits. It is not difficult to find disparaging remarks against women in any society at any time, even by a President of Harvard University in our own times due to the male domination in all societies and sciences. If Mithraism admitted slaves but not women in its fold, as held by Choksy, it has absolutely nothing to do with Zoroastrianism, as Mithraism was Iranian only in its name, as already established by John Hinnells and others.[3] If certain evils were assigned to female beings, it did not mean those evils happened to be feminine only as men were not free of these very evils, and many evils were assigned to male demons too. There is nothing in Zoroastrianism that corresponds to the ancient Greek mythology which describes sirens as women – creatures who lure sailors to their death with sweet songs. The *later* Pahlavi literature, especially *Bundahishn*, relates that Ahreman set up his own team of male and female evil spirits to compete with Ohrmazd's own, which in His wisdom also included both male and female beings. What even the *Cambridge History of Iran* notes,[4] escapes Choksy's consideration or attention: "according to the *Bundahishn*, Ohrmazd bears in himself, as a mother her child, the ideal form of the 'world'!" Ohrmazd is thus no more partial to men than to women. Pollution caused by the Corpse demoness is the same in man and women, and if pollution is said to attack the corpse of a pious soul more virulently than that of an impious one, as per the Pahlavi lore, it is not known to attack the corpse of a pious woman any less than that of a pious man. *Naso* (for *nasush*), pollution of any kind in Parsi parlance has always been regarded as masculine, as the feminine will be *nasi*, which is never heard among them. If parting of the blood from a female's body during menstruation renders her impure, so does parting of blood, skin, saliva, etc., renders even a priest impure and unqualified to practice priesthood. Choksy's claim that "the religion *implied* that two female demons and all mortal women unite to violate male ritual purity and render men unfit for resisting evil" (p. 62), goes entirely against the spirit of the Avesta and relies, *if not entirely*, mostly on the ninth-century texts of doubtful validity and reliability – "folklore "as the learned B. T. Anklesaria calls them. Compare, rather contrast it, against Aiwisruthrem Gah, Yenghe Hatam, Gathas, etc. Choksy relies

---

1   *American Journal of Ancient History*, Vol. 9, Issue 2, 1984, pp. 98-108.
2   In footnote 33, Pomeroy notes that "Aristotle, unlike Xenophon, consistently refers to the leaders as male."
3   See Mithraic Studies, *Proceedings of the First International Congress of Mithraic Studies*, Vols. I and II, USISBN0874715571.
4   Vol. 3 (2), Cambridge University Press, 1983, p. 899.

on mostly post-Sasanian evidence, but even the Sasanian evidence does not support it, because a female Yazata, Anahita, had a temple at Stakhr, which was served by Papak and by King Ardashir and his successors, probably until Varhran II. She invested Shapur I, Ohrmazd-Ardashir, Varhran I and II, Narseh (on the Naqsh-I Rustam relief), Varhran IV, and Peroz. A fire was dedicated to Anahita under Shapur II. Shapur III's crown imitates hers. It was in her temple at Stakhr that the last Sasanian king was elected. If the Sasanians also had female queens, any denigration of females can hardly be possible or plausible. Despite the obvious fact that the Sasanians were a male-dominated society like most ancient societies, women were still entitled to some inheritance, such as the portion brought by a wife (her "daughter's portion", *bahr I duxtih; vaspuhrakan*) and, if the mother of the head of the family was alive, her "widow's portion" (*bahr I katak-banukih*) of the inheritance left by her deceased husband, as well as the portion of any unmarried sister. A *woman* disposed of income if she was either in co-partnership with her husband or brother or *if she had been specially accorded this right.*[1] Since the Herbedestan (5.1, 5.3, 5.4-5) allows the wife to pursue religious work if the husband is busy taking care of the family possessions, as well as to supervise the sacred fires, how could radical evil, etc. be attributable to women even in Sasanian or post-Sasanian times? The real problem here is, as pointed out by Shai Secunda, "Iranists often treat Pahlavi literature as a continuous unified expression of the religious practices and beliefs of Sasanian times" and "rarely focus on the development of ideas *WITHIN* Pahlavi works," (which gets very complex in the case of *Bundahishn* as noted here).[2]

As Zurvanism did not actively intervene in the struggle of the good with the wicked, its adherents did not affect the essential Zoroastrian moral and spiritual goals or even the manner of regular Zoroastrian rituals and worship. But it contradicted Zarathushtra's strong emphasis on good and evil being utterly separate and distinct by origin and nature, as Mary Boyce has often emphasized. Zurvanism also reduces the greatness and unique status of Ahuramazda, the All-knowing, Omniscient God and Creator who exists eternally, the only being worthy of worship, and "it confused the clear teachings of the faith with tedious speculations and *ignoble myths*" (italics mine) and "obscured the basic Zoroastrian doctrine of free-will with the power of each individual to shape his or her own destiny through the exercise of choice. Indeed, so deep is the doctrinal gulf separating Zurvanism from orthodox Zoroastrianism."[3]

This, it is apparent that "the ignoble myth" about Jahi is very un-Zoroastrian, as it arbitrarily deprives the women of the right to make their own choice, which is so firmly laid down by the prophet (Yasna 30.2, 45.2, etc.), as the very basis of his teachings. Even if Jahi represents woman and not whore, but is regarded as a demonic species because it is plagued with menstruation, that will be tantamount to setting aside the principle of Free Will that the prophet had so ingeniously laid down as central to his mission. Women, like men, have the right to choose to be

---

1   See *Cambridge History of Iran*, Volume 3 (2), p. 666 for more details.
2   *The Talmud in Its Iranian Context*, Tubingen, 2010.
3   *Cambridge History of Iran, The Achaemenid Period*, p. 307.

good or evil, and no evil can be thrust upon women without their making a choice for the same on their own, and not by Jahi or Ahreman. It goes against the very grain of Zoroastrianism to regard someone as evil without that person actually choosing to be so, as no one is born evil according to the prophet.

The Zurvanites held that it is woman as such who deserts Ohrmazd for Ahreman, whereas in the *Bundahishn* this part is played by the 'whore.' However, she is soon forgotten, and the human race is depicted as arising "not from her union with the Righteous Man, but from the emission of the latter's seen into Mother Earth out of which he had himself been formed. From the earth, too, the first human *couple* would also arise who, through their offspring, would carry Ohrmazd's fight against Ahriman and the Lie."[1]

Albert de Jong provides evidence from the fifth century B.C. for speculations on the division of time, in the form of millenarian schemes. While this division of time, based on astronomical observations on the course of stars and planets was greatly influenced by Mesopotamian speculations, de Jong explains that they were applied to Zoroastrian beliefs regarding the story of creation and *frashegird* (Av. *Frashokereti*) in the Pahlavi texts. But these notions are not found in the Avesta, even though various Avestan ideas are interwoven into them. They have "certainly been influenced by Babylonian speculations, and must therefore be connected with Western Iran," and not in the Eastern Iran, the original homeland of Zoroastrianism. However, as the latter "was never dropped from the tradition" it continues to be part of our beliefs. Thus, these notions are not inherently or originally Zoroastrian, but are a result of alien influences, and should be recognized as such.[2]

For other instances of the influence of alien ideas on the *Bundahishn* and *Zadspram* see Ph. Gignoux's article in French (pp. 59-72) and on the very concept of *paymān* (the Mean) in the *Denkard* (III, 297, III, 68, 429, B335), see Shaul Shaked's article in *Transition Period in Iranian History.*[3]

Alien influences in the Pahlavi tests thus are not rare.

We can find statements even from the Pahlavi texts that would run counter to what Choksy writes, such as from the *Greater Bundahishn* (16.1-12): "Ohrmazd by the act of creation is both father and mother to creation; for in that he nurtured creation in unseen menog form, he acted as a mother, and in that he created it in material form, he acted as a father." Citing *Arda Viraf Nameh*, Choksy states that pain-filled afterlives were believed to await women who practiced idolatry and sorcery, committed adultery and sexual profligacy, violated ritual purity, etc. (p. 68). However, this would be equally true for men per *Arda Viraf Nameh* (Chapter LXVIII) or the prophet (Yasna 53.6). It is hard to find any Avestan, much less Gathic, evidence for Choksy's claim of "a ritualistic, gender-differential, act when

---

1    Zaehner, R. C. *The Dawn and Twilight of Zoroastrianism.* New York: Putnam, 1961, p. 247.

2    "The Contradiction of the Magi" in Curtis, Vesta Sarkhosh, and Sarah Stewart. *Birth of the Persian Empire. Volume 1 Volume 1.* London: I.B. Tauris in association with the London Middle East Institute at SOAS and the British Museum, 2005, pp. 94-95.

3    Deutsche Forschungsgemeinschaft, Istitito italiano per il Medio ed Estremo Oriente, Association pour l'avancement des études iraniennes (Paris, France), and Societas Iranologica Europaea. *Transition Periods in Iranian History: Actes Du Symposium De Fribourg-En-Brisgau (22-24 Mai 1985).* Leuven (Belgique): Association pour l'avancement des études iraniennes, 1987, pp. 217-240.

weakness, imperfection, and suffering in both life and afterlife were linked to feminine disorder and disharmony." (p. 73). While almost all the Rivayats recommend the adoption of a male, apparently due to the Moslem milieu, the earlier ones such as *Dadestan-e Dini* allow females to be adopted too for managing religious rites for the departed adoptive parents.

S.B.E. XXXI (p. 193) praises the righteous women who champion the cause of not giving in to man's effort at luring them. "The female Yazata Ashi (Yasht XVII, 47-60) complains bitterly against this vice. She says that it 'is the worst deed that men and tyrants do,' when they seduce maidens from their path of virtue.... In the Pahlavi books, this vice (by women) is personified as 'Jahi,'" but they don't criticize men as Ashi does.[1] "An adulterer or adulteress is, as it were, an opponent of Gâo, the good spirit. of the Earth, ... the idea being that such a person comes in the way of the progress of the world (Vendidad XXI, 1). The progress of the world in the different spheres of activity, physical and mental, acts against the influence of this class. (Vend. XXI, 17). *Eredhat Fedhrî* is the name of a good pious maiden, who is considered as a prototype of maidenly virtue, and whose guardian spirit is invoked to withstand the evil machinations of Jahi, the personification of this vice (Yt. XIII, 142). In the Pahlavi *Bundahishn* (Chap. III), this Jahi is said to be an accomplice of Ahriman himself. Her work is said to be 'to cause conflict in the world,' wherefrom the distress and injury of Aûharmazd and the archangels will arise."[2] As atonement, the adulterer was required to pay for and bring about the marriage of four poor couples, help poor children, etc.[3] Thus, man cannot escape his responsibility for yielding to such temptations.

### *Modernity Versus Status of Zoroastrian Women*

Thanks to modernity, Choksy posits, "the feminine is no longer feared as a source of deceit, discord, lust, weakness and imperfection" (p. 110), but how can modernity alone make this happen if the problem lasted for millennia, and why did not modernity make it happen for other communities *at the same time*? Same holds true for Choksy's observation that westernization led to "gradually attenuating negative aspects which had previously been attributed to the feminine, female and women," (p. 119), which is hard to accept as the prophet's own words and the Avesta point quite to the contrary and as such a negative attitude to women was not firmly ingrained in the Parsi psyche except as an external Hindu or Moslem influence which was easily discarded in the British milieu. Even harder to accept is the very last line in his conclusion: "But changes from modernity notwithstanding, the feminine, female, and women still remain a source of potential danger in the minds of those orthodox individuals who conservatively adhere to the religion's older precepts – especially within traditionalist towns in the Gujarat province of India and in the Yazd region of Iran. Most importantly, ... the concept that the demonic feminine was more powerful than the divine feminine shaped the day-to-day lives of many Mazda-worshippers, especially women, for over three

---

1    Modi (1937), p. 46.
2    Modi, loc. cit. See S.B.E., Vol. V, p. 15.
3    Modi, op. cit. p. 47.

and a half millennia," which includes the prophet's and the Avestan period which is quite untenable. And it is not true for any period except perhaps under the Arab occupation. As someone hailing from a highly traditional town of Gujarat as well as very well trained in Zoroastrianism and its priesthood, this is the first time I ever learned of such a state of affairs and my friends from Yazd also shared my bewilderment. Even the non-Zoroastrians in Gujarat and Yazd readily acknowledge equality among Zoroastrian men and women over the years more than among non-Zoroastrians. Bravery spontaneously displayed by Parsi women by posing as armed males during the well-known Jange Variav centuries ago in an isolated Gujarat village belies Choksy's assertion. Moreover, more problematic is Choksy's conclusion that Parsis' belief in the demonic aspect of women was overcome only by modernity in Bombay but not in Gujarat and Yazd even though, I would say, these Zoroastrians were more westernized than any other communities there. I do not recall any one else reaching such a problematic conclusion. Rather, most historians have observed that the latent note for women's equality in Zoroastrianism enabled them to free themselves easily from the centuries of gender centric Hindu influence. This could be a subject by itself as so much is written about it. See also my review of Gould. In the archetype, the unconscious collective mind, of Zoroastrians hangs, not the consciousness about women's demonic susceptibility, but rather women's equal status with men. They are entitled to everything men are entitled to if they follow the precept of the prophet and nothing less, a fundamental clear-cut principle which forms the very basis of the third most important Zoroastrian prayer of Yenghe Hatam. *Various data cited earlier in this paper would bear it out*, and so I see little need to repeat them here. Nothing mentioned here, however, takes away anything from Choksy's reputation for broad and eminent scholarship which his other publications will forever attest to.

### A Review of Ketayun Gould's Work

Even though Gould herself was initially not sure of being a suitable candidate for writing on this subject as she was not a historian of religions, and even though she has examined this subject from a blended "feminist" perspective, she has succeeded in examining social and political factors which are often ignored by authors on this subject.[1] Her views on the status of women in *early* Zoroastrianism differ little in essence from what has been observed by me already, as the *Introduction* (pp. 25-6) basically supports it. According to Ketayun Gould, "with Zoroastrianism came more feminine symbolism. Although Ahura Mazda is *a male supreme deity* often called 'father'." (Ahuramazda, as seen already, regards Himself both as Father and a Mother, and the word Mazda has a feminine word component, a phenomenon so unique in human history, especially as it originated in pre-historic times and has never been surpassed to this day!) "He first created six beneficent divinities – the Amesa Spentas or bounteous immortals – three of whom were females, to help him fight Angra Mainyu. Other female divinities called yazatas, some of whom once belonged to the Indo-European pantheon, were incorporated overtime into the pantheon to protect earth, water, and plants.

---

1    Sharma, Arvind, ed., *Religion and Women*. Albany: State University of New York Press, 1994.

In the list of the names of former men and women who are worthy of veneration, the wife of Vishtaspa (Zoroaster's patron) is mentioned among the first hearers and teachers of the doctrine. Like men, women were eligible for salvation. According to Gould's summary of the sources of Zoroastrianism, women were included in the main religious activities. They were formally initiated into the religion with the investiture of sacred shirt and girdle. They were educated in religious schools. They participated in *all* rituals and acted as priests in minor ones. Women's (and men's) role was to banish evil. Publicly spreading the message of Zoroastrianism, they functioned as *teachers*. Since morality was the means to salvation, moreover, it made the pursuit of salvation attractive to ordinary women who viewed their roles as wives and mothers. Marriage and procreation were sacred duties: husband and wife were viewed in their complementary roles as master and mistress of the household. Although marriage was generally arranged, a relationship based on mutual affection was encouraged. "The begetting of children for the propagation of the race and the spreading of the faith," says Gould, was "a religious function – to further the kingdom of Ahura Mazda and cripple the power of Angra Mainyu." As in India, sons were preferred and necessary for the death ritual. But because the religion was based in the home, importance was given to women's activities. (In fact, housework was said to sweep away dirt and decay, the weapons of Angra Mainyu, and was viewed as prayer.)

"Zoroastrian women had social, economic, and legal rights. There was *no* seclusion or veiling; women frequented social and religious events with men. They owned and managed property in their own right and could legally manage the affairs of their husbands. It is noteworthy that they could seek redress for mistreatment by a husband in a court of law and be the legal guardian of a son disinherited by his father. Finally, they could give evidence in court and *be judges.*"

Gould acknowledges that Zoroastrianism "represented a significant step up in the recognition and appreciation of the *traditional* (Italics original) roles of women – an improvement in patriarchy in the Indo-Iranian context." (p. 148). Nevertheless, the prevailing patriarchal system later on undermined the equality of women initially endorsed by the prophet, a phenomenon which occurred frequently in other religions too. Even so, she submits, women "did enjoy some independence." (p. 157).

She attributes the decline in women's status due to the political milieu prevailing during the Sasanian and Islamic periods. But unlike Choksy, she provides logical explanations for it (pp. 157-8): Survival under a very oppressive alien rule led to "male patterns of dominance towards women," (who) "are the most powerless members of a victimized group," "so often becoming targets of rape and abduction," I may add, unfortunately upto our own times. Unlike Choksy, Gould emphasizes the social and political factors also playing a role in compromising the prophet's teachings on the equality of women.

### Gould's Arguments Closely Follow Choksy's Opinions

However, following Choksy, she relies on what she herself calls "Legends" (and so does even the *Encyclopaedia Iranica*, etc. but they have little basis in reality in the prophet's Gathas or even in Avestan literature except perhaps in the Vendidad which itself is a late composition), in order to prove that they "display strong ambivalence toward women", (p. 159). "Here," she claims, " the female as the *source* (italics original) of impurity, pollution, and *temptation* (italics mine) is portrayed vividly." (p. 160). In reality, *it is not the female but the female fiends of Ahreman that are the source of impurity and temptation*. The word, 'temptation' bears this point out well – Ahremanic forces present temptations to man (and woman) as they enjoy freedom of choice. As I have mentioned in my article on Dualism in Zoroastrianism, there were many dualistic beliefs prevailing in Iran at the time and to lean on such legends has pitfalls, though they may have some merits if interpreted correctly, as myths quite often have some underlying meaning. However, to maintain, as she does, on the basis of Choksy (1988, p. 78) alone that "menstruation caused in a whore demoness is replicated as a pollutant in all mortal women" during the period of Gumezishn when a mixture of good and evil will prevail in the world, is, to say the least, an overstatement since even if such outlandish fables happen by some chance to be true, "all mortal women" are not menstruating all the time and observing the purity rules for menstruation is itself a fight against Ahreman as per the scriptures. How can women so vigorously observing Zoroastrian purity laws expressly in order to fight the so called demonic aspect of Jeh come to be conceived as a pollutant herself only on the basis of a myth that Ahreman had introduced menstruation first to Jeh by kissing her, especially as it runs counter to what the pre-Vendidad Avesta holds? If the Getig world was first made in the image of the Menog world, even such Pahlavi beliefs make this untenable. It also militates against the evidence from the earlier Avesta. The hidden message here is mankind has to constantly combat evil. But (wo)men is born pure, unlike in Gnostic beliefs. Gould's stand verges on Gnosticism that Zoroastrianism abhorred and rejected vigorously. Gould relies on Choksy and Simmons to bring out the fact that Jeh, the whore demoness is not identical with women, as claimed by R. C. Zaehner, but is the primordial Whore Demoness that scuttled into creation along with Ahreman. If so, this demoness like all other demons and demonesses, belong to the Ahremanic retinue that all the time tempt men as well as women away from the path of Asha.

As I have stated in my papers on Dualism and Free Will, dualistic tendencies in the Pahlavi literature are but distant, and at times, not so distant, echoes of the principle of Free Will propounded by the prophet millennia ago. To her credit, unlike Choksy, Gould comes close to seeing this connection, though not without contradicting herself: "Jeh can be perceived in the context of Spendarmard, and thus, antithesis of good woman. Jeh defiles women and Spendarmard blesses them". In the just order of the world created by Mazda, nobody could impose defilement on women (or men) without their asking for it in some way or the other, nor is any good accruable without working for it, in both cases making the right choice being a crucial factor, as the prophet advises us again and again. If the myth of Jeh and Ahreman have any meaning for us, it consists in resenting temptations to us (even as Ahreman tempted the prophet himself) and testing our willingness and resilience to make the right choice in life. But as the Getig world was first designed and blessed in the Menog world by Mazda, there is not even remote possibility for women (or for that reason man) to be born with inherent, inborn, or external impediment or adverse condition spiritually. And to inflict such a condition on the entire womankind is clearly a Gnostic or Zurvanite concept bitterly opposed by Sasanians and utterly against what the prophet had taught long ago.

As a Jewish historian, Lawrence A. Hoffman contends, "the Rabbis made Judaism inseparable from the male life-line. Like it or not, they had no idea of a female life-line." (p. 24). Through the Middle Ages circumcision was a synagogue-based ritual which came to be performed without the presence of the mother.[1] As the advocate of an egalitarian Judaism, he suggests turning to a gender-neutral liturgy when initiating all children into a covenant with God. As Zoroastrianism has offered such gender-neutral initiation ceremonies to both male and female initiates from prehistoric times, it was miles ahead in the race for gender-equality than most, if not all, other religions. Even early European travelers, e.g., de Jong (p. 141), as seen later, have not failed to note that "sleeveless shirts and cords must be worn by women as well as men, and without wearing them, women can no more act than men."

Avesta regards men and women equally responsible for sexual misbehavior, and often blames men for enticing maidens, e.g. Ashi, a female Yazata, regards it as "the worst deed that men and male tyrants do" when they seduce maidens and lead them astray (Yasht XVII, 47-60). Vendidad XXI, 1, includes both – the adulterer as well as adulteress – as compromising the creation, and thus neither of these texts single out the female species for it. Rather, Yasht XIII, 142, invokes the Fravashi of Eredhat Fedhuri, who is a prototype of womanly virtue, to counter the evil designs of Jahi.

Gould again echoes Choksy: "women are believed to be inferior to man who although also susceptible to pollution and deception by the forces of evil, are not afflicted by a pollution which periodically manifests itself," (p. 161), but in reality men are also afflicted by semen, skin, discharges, etc., as also afflicted much more than women by cruelty, violence, greed, anger, lust, etc. The whole idea of making women more susceptible to pollution and even deception because of the un-Avestan myth about Jeh is a deduction that is not supported even by the Pahlavi literature which quotes Ohrmazd as being both the Father and Mother to mankind, as already noted. The proper observance of menstruation rules, moreover, were deemed to control pollution. Men too suffer from pollution by losing skin, blood, semen, spit, skin lesions, leprosy, etc., and male priests have suffered even much more because of these conditions as they could not practice priesthood, often for life, leading them at times to commit suicide. Such restrictions were strictly enforced up to our times as can be seen in Dasturji Erachji Meherjirana's book

---

1    *Covenant of Blood: Circumcision and Gender in Rabbinic Judaism*, University of Chicago Press, Chicago, 1996.

translated in English by Dastur Kotwal and James Boyd, *A Guide to the Zoroastrian Religion* (1982), as also by my own citation about them in my article on Dasturji Dabu in a recent *Fezana Journal* issue (Winter 2010), as also by the utter sadness all my schoolmates observed when a father of one of my dear schoolmates jumped off from the upper floors of Masina Hospital circa 1951 and committed suicide instantly for not being able to bear the pathetic helplessness and unemployment that follows such purity rules regarding skin lesions. The hardships imposed on priests by the purity laws coincided in time with the hardships placed on women by them, but was often much severer and longer in duration, if not permanent, on priests, and did not end entirely with modern times as in the case of women, this being one of the reasons for the utter paucity of higher level priests among Zoroastrians today. As Choksy himself states, "if nocturnal pollution occurs at any time during the purification prior to a *nawar* ceremony, the candidate is deemed unfit for the priesthood, as his act has polluted the world."[1] The purity laws make the priests well neigh house (or fire temple) confined and placed various restrictions on them that non-menstruating women were not subjected to. If they failed to observe them, priests had to redo their prayers, or even undergo Bareshnum for nine nights for purification. There are so many restrictions on the priests, for instance, even food restrictions such as any consumption of prohibited foods like honey resulting in the instant annulment of their ritual purity,[2] that it is hard to list them all here. It is thus not just the patriarchal system that led to stringent menstruation rules, but also the very basis of purity laws itself which hit the priests, all male, hardest of all. (This is what Mary Douglas observes about the priests in Judaism, whose purity laws are so similar to ours, as detailed by me elsewhere.)

From the viewpoint of Zoroastrianism, Gould comes closer to the Zoroastrian view than Choksky. "A woman is not inherently evil; she is always a part of the good creation", (p. 61), though it contradicts her main thesis which is, however, more-or-less uncritically based on Choksy. But her penchant for ascribing responsibility in this matter to the patriarchal system of society is belied by the fact that the same patriarchal order and customs were even harder, rather, far too harder, on the (male) priests who formulated them in the first place, except that their story has never been chronicled and is completely overlooked by her and other feminists.

Gould relies on Choksy's belief that "perhaps the influence of Nestorian Christianity on Iranian society reinforced Zoroastrian misogyny", because of its "view of the woman as an instrument of the devil, both inferior and evil." (p. 163). First of all, this is Choksy's own belief based on "perhaps" and nothing that we know of the history of the Nestorian Church in Iran would confirm such an assumption, especially as it bordered on Gnosticism vehemently denounced and rejected by Sasanian theologians. This is further confirmed by King Khusrau II, so very fond of Saint Sergius, unwittingly offending his Christian host at Edessa "by insisting that the hostess serve wine to their foreign guest by her own fair hand –

1    Choksy, *Purity and Pollution in Zoroastrianism*, University of Texas, Austin, 1989, p. 51.
2    See *Persian Rivayats*, 268, II, 4-10.

as he attested, was the Sasanian custom."[1] This incident, well recorded in many Christian chronicles, rules out the Nestorian hypothesis. As seen later, De Jong also questions any Nestorian influence here. Moreover, it is even hard to conceive of such a belief ever taking hold in the Sasanian period when it was the female Yazata, Anahid who conferred the crown on Sasanian kings (who in turn consecrated so many fire-temples to her) and did not hesitate to crown their princesses if no male heir was available. Gould is however, quite justified in interpreting the medieval pronouncements against adultery by women as also various restrictions placed on women in the context of male property rights, (p. 164). But she overreaches her mark when she generalizes from these facts: "It appears all these negative views of women seemed to ultimately find their justification in the fact that women were the physical source of menstruation pollution – a major source of impurity that is, evil – in the material world. Women, by extension, then, became inferior, sinful and evil." This will be tantamount to heresy to the fundamental teachings of the prophet. The source of menstrual pollution, according to her own views borrowed albeit from Choksy and Simmons, is Jeh, and not women. Women, as she herself states, were regarded along with men, as Mazda's agents for ever fighting the forces of evil and the medieval mind somehow came up with purity rules and customs for *both* women and men to fight them in medieval ways. If indeed women could successfully fight the forces of evil by following these purity rules, however harshly they may be affecting them, that did not and could not by itself render them "inferior, sinful, and evil", but quite the contrary – brave warriors trying to defeat the evil of impurity supposedly created by Ahreman. Men too were subjected to restrictions and isolation if they were regarded as having chronic skin diseases, lesions, discharges, etc., etc. It seems many of the Zoroastrian beliefs about impurity have passed on into Judaism or somehow are shared by the Jews. As I have written extensively about how men and women both are equally affected by impurity in both faiths, I see little need to expand on this subject here, except pointing out close similarity between the Vendidad, chapter 16 and Leviticus 12, 15:19-28, 18:19, and 20:18.

Gould defends her position by pointing out that a menstruant must distance herself from the "righteous man" and sacred elements, but this applied equally to men polluted by various impurities in both Zoroastrianism and Judaism, and in some cases, e.g., priests, pall bearers, or lepers, restrictions on them were much more severe. Even today, all-male corpse bearers are subjected to more severe and long-term restrictions by the purity laws than women ever were.

Gould rightly holds that "the subject of women in Zoroastrianism has to be approached much more critically than it has been upto now," but not on the basis of Choksy's rather logically contradictory opinion she cites on page 165, as also not on the basis of her overwhelming reliance on Choksy's opinions which makes one wonder whether she would have arrived at the same conclusion had Choksy's work been not yet available, especially as she has been quite critical of his earlier

---

1    Elizabeth Key Fowden, *The Barbarian Plain, Saint Sergius, Between Rome and Iran*, Berkeley: University of California Press, 1999, p. 166.

work on this subject:[1] "Women came to be regarded, in religious doctrine, as dual faceted: God-created, yet periodically polluted, easily tempted, and untrustworthy. Although essential for the victory of good over evil, and the direct antagonists of the Whore Demoness, women were believed to have been afflicted with this demoness's characteristics: menstrual pollution and carnal temptation."[2]

Men and women *both* represent therefore a dualistic mould and *both* are therefore dual faceted, susceptible to pollution, and easily tempted – even Asho Zarathushtra was tempted by Ahreman as described in the Avesta. It is problematic to conceive of women as essential for the victory of good over evil and as direct antagonists of the Whore Demoness, and yet afflicted with her characteristics of menstrual pollution as also with carnal temptation, to which indeed men are known to be much more prone and are condemned equally in Zoroastrianism with women when they succumb to it. This is supported by the fact that post-menopausal women in Iran can carry out priestly functions after undergoing the Bareshnum ceremony for purification, (p. 181), which male corpse-bearers can also undergo. So there is nothing inherent in women that can possibly make them evil. However, Gould somehow realizes the ambivalence towards women despite her extensive reliance on the unidimensional views of Choksy, perhaps because few such un-Zoroastrian works could be found, and posits that even the male ecclesiastical authorities perceived this ambivalence and therefore eased some restrictions on women, which, however, may turn out to be irreconcilable with Chosky's contentions. Gould's hypothesis appears to have some validity as the memory of gender equality apparently survived in the archetype of Zoroastrians, so that when modernity finally arrived, they were the first to cast off practices that the prophet would not have approved. This archetypal phenomenon is very revealing because "even in North America, Sikhs from the Punjab have often rejected women's requests for equality"[3] whereas the Zoroastrians in North America and Iran *now* allow even women to be assistant priests, a fact that may be unknown to Gould as it took place after her research came out. Numerous early European travelers have often noted the Parsi women's outgoing and assertive nature, unlike others in the country. W. de Jongh even called them "greedy and covetous in all respects." Whatever this means, it all implies they were not passive and submissive like other women.[4] De Jongh is often relied upon by other historians. He also notes they "have more freedom than almost any Banyan girl", (p. 143). However a lot still needs to be accomplished to remove ambivalence towards women among the Parsis and therefore Gould can validly contend that Choksy's statement that women are now "regarded as the religious equals and partners of men is misleading", (p. 171), as she provides ample evidence for it (pp. 168-181), which is of course common knowledge to the Parsi historians.

### *Purity Laws As the Basis For Menstrual Rules*

Unfortunately, women are hit hard over the centuries by the beliefs and

1    *Parsiana*, November, 2002, pp. 44-47.
2    Choksy 1988, p. 80.
3    P. 35 in the same text as Gould's.
4    See *Kisseh Sanjan*, by H.E. Cama, Oriental Institute, Bombay, 1996, p. 144.

customs regarding menstruation, which precede even the period of the Pahlavi scriptures by far as they are also mentioned in the Vendidad (chapter 16). No wonder they still have their hold on them and on the orthodox, and the cultists still go at length to support them though modernity makes it nearly impossible to observe them at least in *toto*. Nevertheless, the menstruation taboo is so intricately involved with purity laws, and purity laws are so intertwined with religion and so overemphasized that the line between the two is often obfuscated – whether purity laws exist for religion or religion exists for purity laws, though all religions do recognize the importance of purity. Nowhere is this dilemma more obvious then in the case of Gould's heroine, Dosebai Jessawalla who had crusaded against various inequalities but insisted that "her daughter had to spend forty days, "lying in", after her second baby, as it was the custom." (Her first one was born in England.) Dosebai had had "eleven child births" and so she herself must have done the same, and so must have observed some, if not all, menstruation requirements, especially as she was "critical of those who learnt English, and on the strength of that knowledge ignored their household duties, disregarded religion, or the performance of rituals.... There is an inevitable acceptance of certain practices."[1] I for one can however, understand her pious inclinations as she hailed from a religious family that had even built the Shroff Agiary whose fire now resides at the Agiary in Jamshedpur and as I knew Dosebai's relative, Behroze J.M. Cursetjee well, and she even gave me some religious utensils from her household for my usage. Even though she was the first lady executive in India and even though she always talked with me and even with her live-in cousin, Miss Amy Rustomji only in English, she always covered her head even at home and practised Loban and other rituals, observed religious occasions, etc. So Dosebai was apparently influenced by her religious strain, which suggests that menstruation observances may *not* be due *solely* to male domination as Gould hypothesizes but are intertwined with deep seated religious convictions, especially as religion and rituals were then regarded as twins, or equated with each other. Even setting aside the dilemma about the example of Dosebai strengthening or weakening Gould's thesis, at least regarding menstruation in view of the above, it is harder to set aside the dilemma and problems arising from the millennia old purity laws that often, though not always, fit like a square peg in a round hole in our times. Most Zoroastrians do not or even can not observe them all, but few admit it and fewer still want to amend this situation. As Judith Wegner contends, "menstrual taboos existed in many ancient churches, including the early Church, and persist in some Christian rites to this day: the Greek Orthodox Church still forbids women to go to the sacrament of confession during the menstrual period." She finds it puzzling that "the period of cultic impurity incurred for a baby girl (a total of eighty days) is twice that incurred for a baby boy (forty days)" in Leviticus [15:19-24], unlike in Zoroastrianism.[2] One's own cognition and understanding of one's problem tend to program how one would react to it, according to Cognitive Psychology and, as

---

1    See *Journal of the K. R. Cama Oriental Institute*, Mumbai, 1997, p. 6.
2    Newsom, Carol A., and Sharon H. Ringe. *The Women's Bible Commentary*, London: SPCK, 1992, p. 40.

Boyce asserts, Zoroastrian men and women both were led to perceive overcoming impurity as the requisite part of the constant struggle against evil and so women did not perceive menstruation rules adversely. Gould perceives it as a projection on the part of Boyce "who is very strongly identified with the religious tradition and the living faith" which may question Boyce's objectivity as a scholar. By the same token, Gould herself admits projecting her own feminist views in this debate (p. 140), but they are indeed an inevitable sign of the times. Unlike many scholars, Gould studies this subject from social and political angles besides religious. I may add that economic factors stemming from Parsi charities may at least in our own times be playing as equal a role at least in India as the patriarchal factors she so often hints at. This may explain why Acceptance is such a big issue in India and not elsewhere, not even in Iran. The issues of impurity and evil are not just confined to women but to all mankind, as all mankind is encouraged to banish impurity and evil from the world so as to bring about Frashokereti (renewal of the world; resurrection; renovation) by always making the right choice, as I have explained at length in my thesis on Free Will. The proof that Zoroastrian women have been consciously or unconsciously, making such a choice over the millennia comes readily from Gould's own assertion that "Zoroastrian women are not so naive that they would suffer severe damage to their self-concept by buying some priestly assertions that women are carriers of the "sin" of menstruation", (p. 181), though this may contradict her own earlier statements. Her work indeed should remind us that much more needs to be done in the social and political sphere to bring to full realization the prophet's insistence on gender equality. However, as it should be evident by now that purity laws affected not only women but also all men as well as all-male "caste" of priests, often more seriously and grievously, a fact hardly recognized so far. Her argument and reasoning, therefore, for ascribing gender inequality entirely to the patriarchal structure of Zoroastrian society, though partially valid, needs to be reexamined and more attention needs to be given to inquiring about the very basis for the purity laws which lies at the very root of this problem, that is, if it is at all now possible to do so. If not, modernity threatens to challenge such practices which hail from pre-Zoroastrian times and beliefs. As Boyce explains: "These strict customs probably represent elaborations of ancient restrictions inherited from Iranian paganism, of a kind widespread among the peoples of the world; and again, given the Zoroastrian premises, the line of thought is logical, the practice consequent. Zoroastrian women have suffered much under them, yet the orthodox observe them voluntarily, with both resignation and stoic pride. The rules are stern, to observe them is often a struggle, but they are part of the fight against evil, and so to be strictly kept. This attitude of mind enables self-respect to be maintained in spite of humiliating restrictions. The menopause marks a welcome cessation, however; and still in the orthodox Iranian villages a pious old lady will then sometimes undergo the *barašnom* purification annually three, six or nine times, year after year, and will keep her purity as strictly as a temple priest, rejoicing in being wholly and perpetually clean at last, and able thus to prepare herself for eternity." In a footnote, Boyce adds "In general women have a dignified position in the Zoroastrian community, as men's partners in the common struggle against evil, and this appears due to Zoroaster's own teachings.... As in other religions, however, the attitude of the male tends to be inconsistent. The Christian has considered women now as sisters of the Virgin Mary, now as the tribe of the temptress Eve. So the Zoroastrian looks on woman now as *ašavan*, the creature of Ohrmazd, and now as corrupted and suborned by Ahriman to be his impure ally," which is very un-Gathic. "Thus the Creator is once represented as saying to woman: 'Thou art a helper to me, for from thee man is born, but thou dost grieve me who am Ohrmazd', GBd. XIVa (BTA, 137; transl. also by Zaehner, *Zurvan*, 188). There is no reason, however, to regard this as a general or standard Zoroastrian attitude, still less (*pace* Zaehner, op. cit.) to consider it as typically Zurvanite, or on the grounds of the whole passage in question to identify the *ašavan* woman with the whore, who is specifically said there to be her Ahrimanic opposite." Later Pahlavi texts regard child-birth as polluting; Boyce comments: "Here again the purity laws produce a seeming anomaly, for, as Darmesteter observed, one might think that a woman just delivered of a child 'ought to be considered pure amongst the pure, since life has been increased by her in the world, and she has enlarged the realm of Ormazd. But the strength of old instincts overcame the drift of new principles' (SBE IV, lxxix)."[1]

Here again it should be pointed out that the purity laws applied equally to men, and even to priests who would become impure by anything parting from their body, say, skin or nightly discharges.

### Purity Laws Adversely Affect Not Just Women, But Pall-Bearers Too, As Well As Mobeds

As in Judaism, purity laws affect all those who come in contact with the dead matter in any way. The plight of the pall-bearers has been well depicted in a recent novel, as well as amply brought out by a *Parsiana* editorial:[2] "We have ensured the otherness of our Dakhma workers by inflicting a vile ostracism upon them and their close kin. We may well strive to forget this apartheid of disallowing them from temples, Jashans, Gahanbars, Navjotes and weddings. We further imposed the repeated tedious cleansings they are forced to undergo (with rancid bull's urine and naught else than water). Not content, with that they ... publicly at least, cannot hold any other occupation." It also complains of "a noxious apartheid culture," "the creation of a socially inferior sub caste", "social outcasts," etc. However, regrettably it too fails to connect this tragedy with the stringent, out-dated, highly restrictive purity laws that are hardly observed (or are often not even fully observable) in our times. This is not to suggest doing away with them all, as most have already done on their own, but rather trying to bring them in tune with the Zeitgeist to retain their real essence and meaning in our times so that they will not lead any more to uncalled for hardships to others, including on the priests who devised them in the first place.

---

1    Mary Boyce, *History of Zoroastrianism*, Vol. I, Leiden: E.J. Brill, 1996, p. 308.
2    June 21, 2012, p. 2 and subsequent editions.

### Priests Hit Hardest By Purity Laws

The purity laws, however, affect the most those who designed them in the first place, namely, the priests, (which Mary Douglas said of Israelite priests too), but they faithfully abided by them because they believed in their veracity as instruments of spiritual attainment and growth. The four questions translated from the text of *Emet I Ashavahishtan* – 9-12 by K. M. Jamasp Asa[1] clearly reflects the severe punishment meted out to a priest for failing to observe the purity rules, though such a list of priestly failings is almost inexhaustible. It disqualifies a priest who "goes to battle against thieves and enemies" from performing priestly duties because of sustaining bodily injuries and wounds, whereby he gets defiled and in turn defiles rituals he performs – "his (is a) grievous sin like the (sin) deserving death, – the worship he performs (is) akin to demon-worship." If such a soldiering priest "is seen moving on the seas," he commits the sin deserving death and is not fit for any priestly duties "even if he performs much repentance and penitence." And it is a grievous sin if a priest performs the ritual of purification without knowing it "perfectly", deserving *at least* 300 sters (whips). Much more could be written about how severely purity laws affected the priest but the above should suffice for our purpose. In our own times, even Sir J. J. Modi was prohibited from performing higher-level priestly rituals for disregarding the ban on sea travel by sailing to Europe, as sea travel leads to water pollution. H. T. Anklesaria's book, mentioned in the next paragraph, confirms this fact on page 10. All the priests who sailed to Aden for establishing an Agiary there were also not allowed to perform inner ceremonies, which implies that, by the same criterion, the Agiary they established did not conform to the rules about pollution of water voiding a priest's Bareshnum. However, the issue here is how much these priests must have suffered by being prohibited from performing inner ceremonies, ultimately though, modernity prevailed over such bans and led to their withdrawal.

How harshly the purity laws dictated the life of at least the Yozdathregar (higher category) priests can be gleaned from the book written in Gujarati by the learned H. T. Anklesaria, *Pursesh-Pasokh* (The Fort Printing Press, 1941), all the more so since the book maintains that rituals and religion are twins that can never be separated (p. 17), thus requiring strict observance of rituals. Any error, emphasizes the author, even unintended on the part of the priest or others or even birds in observing the infinite number of rules regarding ritual purity, results in the vitiation and cancellation of the ceremony, Bareshnum, etc., requiring performing the ceremony all over again or the priest, again undergoing the nine-nights of Bareshnum in a secluded section in a fire-temple where he cannot touch water or any other person or object and has to take Baj before eating or relieving himself, cleanse himself only with bull's urine all nine days, etc. All these in addition to losing work and income for nine days. It is difficult to explain them all, as the modern Zoroastrian is hardly even cognizant of these purity requirements. No wonder therefore there are few priests willing to undergo such arduous requirements and hardships, though they are now significantly less severe than in 1941 when the book was written. This problem could be resolved if we keep the dictum

---

1    *Acta Iranica*, Leiden: E.J. Brill, 1975, pp. 435-443.

of *Denkard* (581, 11. 4-6) in mind: "Pollution of the body is easier to expunge than that of the soul."

### Bundahishn At Variance With Many Zoroastrian Beliefs Because of Gnostic and Zurvanite Influence On It

Zurvanism was quite prevalent during Sasanian era and was closely related to Gnostic beliefs. Zoroastrian doctrines rather stood in contrast with both these movements. As noted by the *Cambridge History of Iran* (3, 1983, p. ICVii), "The Gnostic movement essentially espouses a rather pessimistic view of the world.... It envisages the redemption of the soul from the shackles of matter or worldly existence by a divine or divinely inspired redeemer through illuminating knowledge (gnosis). It is true that such views differ in outlook from Gathic Zoroastrianism and the optimistic view of the world reflected in known Zoroastrian writings. Therefore, a number of scholars have emphasized the non-Iranian, particularly Greek, ancestry of Gnostic ideas. On the other hand, some historians of religion have drawn attention to the close relationship of Gnostic doctrines with those of the Zurvanites." Strong Zurvanite influences on Pahlavi writings, especially on the Bundahishn, have unfortunately tended to undermine the role and importance of women, which is not at all compatible with what all Zoroastrian texts had hitherto exhorted. It is not surprising therefore that Martin Haug who lived among the Parsis in India claimed that the Dasturs did not regard *Bundahishn* as a canonical work. Nor is it generally included in the priestly education at various Madressas.

As the eminent scholar G. Widengren has noted long ago regarding *Bundahishn*, "The text exhibits very clearly the *Gnostic* attitude of contempt for the female sex and for everything appertaining to sexual life and procreation."[1] He sees the need to study *Bundahishn* anew because "it is of great importance for the Iranian background of Gnosticism in general and not only for the mythological elements of Manichaeism". In this endeavor he compares the Indian *Bundahishn* with a corresponding passage from the Syriac writer Theodore bar Konai, which has been reviewed also by R.C. Zaehner.[2] Both point out the discrepancies between the two texts:

(1) In *Bundahishn* the female protagonist is Jeh, the Whore, but in Theodore, it is women or women in general.

(2) In *Bundahishn* Ohrmazd knows that Ahreman could give what Jeh would ask, as he would have great profit from it, whereas in Theodore, Ohrmazd fears that the woman might have intercourse with the righteous who would be punished.

(3) In *Bundahishn* Ohrmazd exhibits a 15 year-old young man to the Whore, whereas in Theodore this young man is said to be the god Narsa who is exhibited naked to the women. It seems Narsa may have played a prominent role in Zurvanite Pantheon.

---

1   "Primordial Man and Prostitute: A Zervanite Motif In the Sassanid Avesta," in *Studies in Mysticism and Religion*, Jerusalem: Magnes Press, The Hebrew University, 1967, pp. 337-352.
2   Zaehner, *Zurvan, A Zoroastrian Dilemma*, Oxford, 1955, pp. 355-60.

(4) In *Bundahishn* the Whore asks for the desire of man that she might have union with him in her house, whereas in Theodore, the women ask for Narsa without specifying what they want him for.

Widengren agrees with Zaehner (p. 185) that "Theodore is faithfully repeating a version of the same myth from which the *Bundahishn* account is derived. Zaehner concludes that Theodore has preserved the true Zurvanite myth regarding the first but *Bundahishn* has emended it." Widengren posits that Jeh was the term applied to woman in the Zurvanite myths from the outset. But the Avesta represents Jahi as "the companion of Mairya, the young man, the member of men's societies". Adducing another passage from the *Iranian Bundahishn*, Zaehner,[1] according to Widengren, "has shown conclusively that Ohrmazd, according to Zurvanite tradition, had no high opinion of women.... *It is obvious that something is wrong in the text as it is transmitted now.* Zaehner (p. 189) observes, with regard to woman: '*Between her and 'her adversary the whore-species' her creator seems to see little difference.* (Italics mine). It is obvious that a later transmitter of the text took offence at this depreciation of women and tried to diminish the effect of Ohrmazd's words' by making certain changes."

Widengren observes that the Zurvanite texts "suffered from the treatment given to them after the great purge, when Zurvanism was relegated to a more obscure existence on the fringe of Zoroastrianism". And yet "the astonishing fact is that so much of its literary tradition has been preserved", which demands caution by scholars while interpreting *Bundahishn* as also calls for the need for sifting Zurvanite elements and beliefs from Zoroastrian ones.

"Zaehner has shown", observes Widengren, "that in Zervanite opinion there is no real difference between Zan and Jeh, women and whore. His observation has been more accentuated by my text analysis, leading up to a reconstruction of the text in question." He notes that even the text, in which Ohrmazd complains of having had no option to creating woman, even though he wanted to, has been exposed to some tendentious cuts because it was thought improper that woman could be characterized as "the Demon-Whore species, the adversary of the righteous man." He further notes that all the three Zurvanite texts, that is, the Indian and Iranian *Bundahishn* and Theodore's text, "thus give us insight into those Zervanite portions of the Sassanid Avesta which have later been lost." He states that Pahlavi Zurvanite texts, often fragmentary and partly revised, are still extant, mainly in *Bundahishn* and *Zadspram* (especially in XXXIV, 30-31), which requires discretion on our part for detecting the Zurvanite anti-woman attitude in *Bundahishn* as it runs against the very grain of Zoroastrian theology. A. Hultgård sees a "growing tendency, to argue that Hellenistic, Jewish, and Gnostic ideas have influenced anthropological, cosmological, and apocalyptic ideas of the Pahlavi books."[2] Philip Grignoux too in a brief article in French, "Un Témoin Du Sycrétisme Mazdéen Tardif," sees Greek, Indian, Nestorian, Manichean, and Babylonian influence on *Bundahishn*, *Zadspram*, and *Denkard*, and points out sentences from the Pahlavi

---

1    Pp. 107:14 ff, which I have quoted earlier.
2    McGinn, Bernard, John J. Collins, and Stephen J. Stein. *The Continuum History of Apocalypticism.* New York: Continuum, 2003, p. 59.

texts to prove it, and also refers to *Studia Iranica* 14, 1985, pp. 267-269 for the same. He concludes: "Sans dout ne puis-je prétendre avoir relevé tous les points de comparaison possibles, ni me justifier d'avoir omis les rapprochement avec les sources indiennes et babyloniennes, si ce n'est pour la raison que j'ai signalée au début, à savoir que l'influence de la Grèce a joué plusieurs fois et de manière profonde en Iran, et qu'il fallait d'abord mettre cela en évidence." The emphasis placed in *Mēnōg ī xrad* on "refraining from the material world and concentration on the spiritual world (e.g., 2.98-103) and references to the significance of fate, predestination, and the role of the stars in the destiny of man (8.17-21, 24, 38.5, 47.7, 51) have led some scholars to believe that *Mēnōg ī xrad* reveals Zurvanite influences and to brand it as a semi-Zurvanite work (Zaehner, pp. 117, 181, 206)."[1]

I could submit extensive evidence on this subject, but it may form a chapter or a book by itself. However, it is not necessary to brand the entire *Bundahishn* as Zurvanite as Zaehner and others have done, but it will prove fruitful to disavow Zurvanite or Gnostic influences lurking therein. Similarly, one has to be cognizant of the Biblical coloring such as in the story of Mashya and Mashyane, the first couple in the Pahlavi myth, who committed sin like Adam and Eve. Daryaee assigns early Islamic influence to this story, but does not deny Jewish influence, as claimed by Shaked.[2]

### Albert De Jong's Views Negating Choksy's and Gould's Theses

After painstakingly collecting the above data, I found an excellent tractate on this subject by Albert De Jong.[3] Had I read it earlier, I would have adjudged the findings of De Jong (who is taking over Mary Boyce's work) too profound to see any need for me to respond to Choksy or Gould, especially as he too examines Choksy's *earlier* thesis and pronounces it unviable and unacceptable. "More recently," observes De Jong, "J. Choksy has suggested that both Jeh and Jahika are intimately connected with menstruation, and that the Avestan Jahi in Vd. (Vendidad) 18.61-65 should already be interpreted as the "Whore Demoness" (suggesting in passing that the misogyny evident in some Zoroastrian sources arose under influence of Nestorian Christianity)." He astutely points out that "No explanation, however, has been offered for the growth of the *mythos* (italics mine) of Jeh or for the presumed negative view of women in some Pahlavi books. Nor has a serious attempt been made to establish the connection between the Avestan and the Pahlavi views of Jahika/Jeh (-dev)." (p. 18). Here De Jong is responding only to Choksy's views expressed in *Purity and Pollution in Zoroastrianism: Triumph Over Evil*, Austin 1989, pp. 94-103, 154 note 38, and one wonders how much more he would reject Choksy's views reviewed here, than Choksy's 2002 views which were published much later. As the debate over gender equality is raging hot among the Parsis at present, I found it imperative to address this issue raised by

---

1   *Encyclopædia Iranica*, http://www.iranicaonline.org/articles/dadestan-i-menog, accessed Mar 31, 2015.

2   Op. cit. ff.56, p. 173.

3   "Jeh the primal whore?" in Kloppenborg, Ria, and Wouter J. Hanegraaff. *Female Stereotypes in Religious Traditions*. Leiden: E.J. Brill, 1995, pp. 15-41.

Choksy and Gould to leave no doubt about the equal status of women in Zoroastrianism.

De Jong concludes that the Pahlavi word Jeh is a descendant of the Avestan word Jahi. Its usage in Yasht 17.54 suggests "a neutral meaning 'women'" which "definitely rules out the possibility of the word referring to a prostitute." (p. 28). See also p. 31 for his conclusions about Jahi and Jahika. However, in the Avesta Jahi stands for "an adulterous married woman, who endangers the legitimacy of her husband's offspring. This usage, for which the translation 'whore' is only valid as term of abuse, not as an indication of what makes jahi a jahi, can also be traced in Middle and New Persian. Next to this, however, the Middle Persian books also know of an hypostasized mythological figure, Jeh, who is the counterpart of Spandarmad in all respects." (p. 41). He maintains that "Zoroastrianism generally accords a dignified place to women is certain" and cites the Avestan evidence for the same (pp. 23-5), more or less the same as I have quoted earlier. He also holds that "it is well worth exploring the negative view of women in Zoroastrian *texts* (italics mine) as being part of the same tradition", (p. 41), but here I differ from him as they are not part of the same tradition and *TEXTS* but of myths which contain external influences such as Zurvanism, Manichaeism, Gnosticism, Islam, etc., as well as the universal tendency toward male dominance, since the prophet, as De Jong maintains, on this subject, is so very clear about the gender equality even in prehistoric times. "Zaehner's identification of woman with the JEH obscures the point in an unacceptable manner, as does Choksy's suggestion that 'women are created by Ahura Mazda as opponents of The Whore Demoness.' The species of the JEH-DEW is created by Ahreman to be sure – as opponents of the virtuous woman," that I have propounded earlier, a view that, directly or indirectly, under a medieval garb represents the Gathic emphasis on making the right choice and fighting the evil. In light of these findings it is also questionable if Gould's conclusions in so far as they so heavily and uncritically rely on Choksy, can have much validity either.

Philip G. Kreyenbroek notes in the *Encyclopædia Iranica*[1] that some speculative Zurvanite teachings about the cosmogony "occur in" the *Greater Bundahishn* and *Selections of Zadspram*. He also notes that the explanation of death as a result of the onslaught of Ahreman "rendered meaningless older myths about the origin of death, in which Yima played a central part." While the Pahlavi texts often reflect the Avesta or older beliefs, awareness of alien influences that crept in over time can lead us to right conclusions.

### Ruta-Druh in Rigveda

The ethical dualism implied in beliefs about the opposition between Asha and Druj has its antecedent also in Ruta-Druh (Rigveda I, 133, 1-2), Asha-Druj in Avesta, a role it continued to play in the Iranian lore. To this day the Hindus too observed the same menstruation practices as the Zoroastrians do, though they are less exacting in practice and are of shorter duration as well as are far less elaborate or intricate in theory. But there is little trace in Hinduism about the role of Druh in

---

1    Volume VI, 1993, pp. 304-6.

deprecating womankind (though it may be attributed to other narratives) as in the Pahlavi texts, which is all the more revealing as the Pahlavi evidence for it stands in stark contrast to the Avestan, a fact well noted by Gould herself. Therefore, the post-Sasanian Pahlavi evidence for it appears to be a much later development, possibly indicating alien influences. Moreover, it is improbable that lay Zoroastrians at any time took this myth seriously, and there is little evidence that they did, the laity being mostly illiterate, or, uninterested in theological matters or too preoccupied with their survival in very tough times after the Arab conquest to come to know about it even. Furthermore, the later Pahlavi texts were written in the tenth and eleventh centuries, probably, if not certainly, long after the Parsis migrated to India and had enough knowledge of Pahlavi to interpret them. Lastly, as brought out recently by Kreyenbroek, the fact that the Parsis were not even aware of basing the Maratab ceremony for the priesthood on the Vendidad until the period of the Rivayats, may confirm this impression.

### Conclusion

Mary Boyce observes that Greeks characterized Zoroastrianism as the "Persian religion, … as if it was an ethnic faith like the others which they encountered; but (however true this had become in part) it was in fact a credal religion, the oldest known in history. A person was not born a Zoroastrian, nor did he enter the religious community through a physical rite (such as the Jewish one of infant circumcision); but he became a Zoroastrian on attaining maturity by choosing to profess the doctrines taught by Zoroaster."[1] This finding works against any claim that one had to be born into the religion to follow it, or those born of Zoroastrian mothers (and not of Zoroastrian fathers) could not be Zoroastrians, though unfortunately they could not be Parsis according to the Parsis' self-defined rules. Modernity is changing things so fast that unless we keep up with the changes, the changes will overwhelm and overcome us. But fortunately our prehistoric religion and precepts are our eternal guide if only we shed off our myopic and parochial views, especially as we belong to, what Mary Boyce asserts, the world's first proselytizing and credal religion. The penalty for going against the prophet's own precepts will be gloom and doom. And I have based my views entirely on scripture and historical evidence, which far supersede any court verdicts or eco-social-political arguments, which may have their place, but not when they stand in stark contradiction to what the prophet himself exhorts. I pray the Parsis awake to their prophet's precepts, rather than to the ones who blatantly violate them for their own selfish or political ends. May the prophets eternal wisdom prevail over them. *Aedun Baad*: May it be so.

---

1    *A History of Zoroastrianism*, Vol. III, E.J. Brill, Leiden, 1991, p. 363.

# REFERENCES

Amighi, Janet Kestenberg. *The Zoroastrians of Iran: Conversion, Assimilation, or Persistence.* New York: AMS Press, 1990.

Anthony, David W. *The Horse, the Wheel, and Language: How Bronze-Age Riders from the Eurasian Steppes Shaped the Modern World.* Princeton, N.J.: Princeton University Press, 2007

Bailey, Harold Walter. *The Culture of the Sakas in Ancient Iranian Khotan.* Columbia lectures on Iranian studies, no. 1. Delmar, N.Y.: Caravan Books, 1982.

Barr, Kaj. *Illustreret Religionshistorie*, Copenhagen, 1968.

Baum, Julius, and Joseph Campbell. *The Mysteries: Papers from the Eranos Yearbook.* New York: Pantheon Books, 1955.

Bharucha, Sheriarji Dadabhai. *Zoroastrian Religion and Customs.* Bombay: D.B. Taraporevala Sons, 1979.

---, *See also* Hoshang.

Bianchi, Ugo. *Mysteria Mithrae.* Leiden: E.J. Brill, 1979.

Bivar: *See* Hambly (ed.).

Boyce, Mary. *A History of Zoroastrianism / 3rd Imp., with Corr. V.1, The Early Period.* Handbuch der Orientalistik, 8. Leiden: E.J. Brill, 1996.

---. *A History of Zoroastrianism V.2, Under the Achaemenians.* Handbuch der Orientalistik, 8. Leiden: E.J. Brill, 1982.

---. *Textual Sources for the Study of Zoroastrianism.* Textual sources for the study of religion. Totowa, N.J.: Barnes & Noble Books, 1984.

---. *Zoroastrians, Their Religious Beliefs and Practices.* Library of religious beliefs and practices. London: Routledge & Kegan Paul, 1979.

Boyce, Mary, Frantz Grenet, and Roger Beck. *A History of Zoroastrianism Vol. 3, Zoroastrianism Under Macedonian and Roman Rule / by Mary Boyce and Frantz Grenet with Contribution by Roger Beck.* Leiden: E.J. Brill, 1991

Boyd, James W: *See* Meherjirana.

Brody: *See* Shaked and Netzer.

Browne, Edward Granville. *A Literary History of Persia from the Earliest Times Until Firdawsi.* London: T. F. Unwin, 1902.

Cambridge, University of: *See* University of Cambridge.

Choksy, Jamsheed K. *Purity and Pollution in Zoroastrianism: Triumph Over Evil.* Austin, Tex: University of Texas Press, 1989.

Colledge, Malcolm A. R. *Parthian Art.* Ithaca, N.Y.: Cornell University Press, 1977.

Cook, J. M. *The Persian Empire.* New York: Schocken Books, 1983.

Dabu, Khurshed S., Wadiaji Atash Beheram. *A hand-book of general information containing significance of Zoroastrian terms pertaining to religion, customs, rituals etc. and answers to some important questions.* Bombay: P. N. Mehta Educational Trust, 2001.

---, *Message of Zarathushtra: A Manual of Zoroastrianism, the Religion of the Parsis.* Bombay: New Book Co, 1959.

---, *Zarathushtra and His Teachings (a Manual for Young Students).* Bombay:

R.M.D. Chamarbaugvala, 1966.

Darmesteter, James. *The Zend-Avesta. Part 1, The Vendidad. Sacred Books of The East*, Vol. 4. Delhi [etc.]: Motilal Banarsidass, 1980.

Daryaee, Touraj. *Sasanian Persia. The Rise and Fall of an Empire*. London [u.a.]: Tauris, 2010.

Dhabhar, Ervad B. N. *The Persian Rivayats of Hormazyar Framarz and Others : Their Version*. Bombay: K. R. Cama Oriental Institute, 1932.

Dhalla, Maneckji Nusservanji. *Dastur Dhalla, the Saga of a Soul: An Autobiography of Shams-Ul-Ulama Dastur Dr. Maneckji Nusserwanji Dhalla*. Karachi: Dastur Dr. Dhalla Memorial Institute, 1975.

---. *History of Zoroastrianism, Oxford University Press*. Bombay: K.R. Cama Oriental Institute, 1963.

---. *World's Religions in Evolution*. Karachi: 1953.

Dodgeon, Michael H., and Samuel N. C. Lieu. *The Roman Eastern Frontier and the Persian Wars (AD 226-363): A Documentary History*. London: Routledge, 1991.

Duchesne-Guillemin, Jacques, and K.M. Jamasp Asa. *Religion of Ancient Iran ; English Translation of La Religion Del'iran Ancien*. Bombay: Tata Press, 1973.

---. *The Western Response to Zoroaster*. Oxford: Clarendon Press, 1958.

Frye, Richard Nelson, Abu Bakr Muhammad ibn Ja'far Narshakhi. *The History of Bukhara: Tr. from a Persian Abridgment of the Arabic Original by Narshakhi*. Cambridge, Mass: Mediaeval academy of America, 1954.

Frye, Richard Nelson. *The Golden Age of Persia: The Arabs in the East*. New York: Harper & Row, 1975.

---. *The History of Ancient Iran*. München: C.H. Beck, 1984.

---. *See also Orientalia* (1984)

Ghirshman, Roman, *Iran: From the Earliest Times to the Islamic Conquest*. Harmondsworth, Middlesex: Penguin Books, 1978.

Grabbe, Lester L. *Judaism from Cyrus to Hadrian*. Minneapolis: Fortress Press, 1992.

Gray, Louis H. "The Foundations of the Iranian Religions," *Journal of the Cama Oriental Institute* 15, 1929.

---. "Zoroastrian material in the Acta Sanctorum", *Journal of the Manchester Egyptian and Oriental Society*, 1913-14, pp. 37-55.

Hambly, Gavin (ed.). *Central Asia*. New York: Delacorte Press, 1969.

Harmatta, János. *Prolegomena to the sources on the history of pre-Islamic Central Asia*. Budapest: Akad. Kiadó, 1979.

Hartman, Sven S. *Parsism, the Religion of Zoroaster*. Iconography of religions, fasc. 4. Leiden: Brill, 1980.

Haug, Martin. *The Parsis: Essays on Their Sacred Language, Writings, and Religion*. New Delhi: Indigo Books, 2003.

Henning, W. B. *Zoroaster, Politician or Witch-Doctor?* London: Oxford University Press, 1951.

Hinnells, John R. *Spanning East and West: Unit 26*. Milton Keynes [Buckinghamshire]: Open University Press, 1982.

Hintze, Almut. *A Zoroastrian liturgy: the worship in seven chapters (Yasna 35-41)*. Wiesbaden: Harrassowitz, 2007.

---. *See also* Sundermann.

*The Dastur Hoshang Memorial Volume: Being Papers on Iranian Subjects, Written by Various Scholars, in Honour of the Late Shams-Ul-Ulama Sardar Dastur Hoshang Jamasp*. Bombay: Fort Printing Press, 1918.

Humbach, Helmut. *Die Gathas des Zarathustra 1 Einleitung, Text, Übersetzung, Paraphrase*. Heidelberg: Winter, 1959.

Humbach, Helmut, and Kaikhusroo M. Jamasp Asa. *Vaeθā Nask; an Apocryphal Text on Zoroastrian Problems*. Wiesbaden: O. Harrassowitz, 1969.

---. *Pursishniha: Zoroastrian catechism*. Wiesbaden: Harrassowitz, 1971.

Hume, Robert Ernest. *The World's Living Religions, With Special Reference to Their Sacred Scriptures and in Comparison with Christianity; an Historical Sketch*. New York: Scribner, 1959.

Insler, Stanley. *The Gāthās of Zarathustra*. Leiden: E.J. Brill, 1975.

Jackson, A. V. Williams. *Persia Past and Present; A Book of Travel and Research, with More Than Two Hundred Illustrations and a Map*. New York: Macmillan Co, 1906.

---, *Zoroaster, the Prophet of Ancient Iran*. Columbia University Press, New York, 1898.

Jamasp Asa, Kaikhusroo M. *See* Duchesne-Guillemin and Humbach.

*Judgments – Petit vs Jeejeebhoy 1908, Saklat vs Bella 1925 – Reprint of original judgments with explanatory articles* published by Parsiana Publications in 2005.

Kotwal, Firoze M. P.: *See* Meherjirana.

Kuhrt, Amélie. *The Ancient Near East, C. 3000-330 BC. Volume Two*. London: Routledge, 1995.

Luhrmann, and David L White. 1998. "The Good Parsi: The Fate of a Colonial Elite in a Postcolonial Society". *The Journal of Asian Studies*. 57, no. 2: 578.

Madan, Dhanjishah Meherjibhai. *The complete text of the Pahlavi Dinkard*. Bombay: [s.n.], 1911.

Malandra, William W. *An Introduction to Ancient Iranian Religion: Readings from the Avesta and Achaemenid Inscriptions*. 1983.

McGovern, William. *The Early Empires of Central Asia, A Study of the Scythians and the Huns and the part they played in World History*, Chapel Hill, University of North Carolina Press, 1939, Reprint 1965.

Meherjirana, Erachji Sohrabji, Firoze M. P. Kotwal, and James W. Boyd. *A Guide to the Zoroastrian Religion: A Nineteenth Century Catechism with Modern Commentary*. Studies in world religions, 3. Chico, CA: Scholars Press, 1982.

Menasce, Jean de: *See* Baum and Campbell (1955)

Mills, Lawrence Heyworth. *The Gâthas of Zarathushtra (Zoroaster) in Metre and Rhythm: Being a Second Edition of the Metrical Versions in the Author's Edition of 1892-94*. Leipzig: F.A. Brockhaus, 1900.

Minns, Ellis H. *Scythians and Greeks; A Survey of Ancient History and Archaeol-*

*ogy on the North Coast of the Euxine from the Danube to the Caucasus*. New York: Biblo and Tannen, 1965.

Mirza, Hormazdyar Dastur Kayoji. *Outlines of Parsi History*. Bombay: Mirza, 1974.

Modi, Jivanji Jamshedji. *Lectures and sermons on Zoroastrian subjects*. Bombay: Duftar Ashkara, 1902.

---. *The Religious Ceremonies and Customs of the Parsees, by Jivanji Jamshedji Modi,... 2nd Edition*. Bombay: J. B. Karani's sons, 1937.

*Monumentum Georg Morgenstierne I*. Leiden: E.J. Brill, 1981.

Moulton, James Hope. *Early Zoroastrianism: Lectures Delivered at Oxford and in London*. The Hibbert lectures, 1912. London: Williams and Norgate, 1913.

---. *The Treasure of the Magi; A Study of Modern Zoroastrianism*. London: H. Milford, Oxford university press, 1917.

Nasr, Seyyed Vali Reza. *The Shia Revival: How Conflicts Within Islam Will Shape the Future*. New York: Norton, 2006.

Neusner, Jacob. *A History of the Jews in Babylonia*. Studia post-Biblica, v. 9, 11, 12, 14, 15. Leiden: E.J. Brill, 1965.

O'Donnell, James Joseph. *Augustine: A New Biography*. New York: HarperCollins Publishers, 2005.

Olmstead, A. T. *History of the Persian Empire*. Chicago: The Univ. of Chicago Press, 1970.

*Orientalia J. Duchesne-Guillemin Emerito Oblata*. Leiden: E.J. Brill, 1984.

Pangborn, Cyrus R. *Zoroastrianism: A Beleaguered Faith*. New York: Advent Books, 1983.

*Proceedings of the Second North American Zoroastrian Symposium*; ZAC, 1977.

Rosenfield, John M. *The Dynastic Arts of the Kushans*. Berkeley: University of California Press, 1967.

Rostovtzeff, Michael Ivanovitch. *Iranians & Greeks in South Russia*. New York: Russell & Russell, (1922 &) 1969.

Rustomjee, Framroz. *Daily Prayers of the Zoroastrians (in English) 1*. Bombay: Nirnaya Sagar Press, 1959.

Schmidt, Hanns-Peter. *Zarathustra's Religion and His Pastoral Imagery: Rede Uitgesproken Bij De Aanvaarding Van Het Ambt Van Gewoon Hoogleraar in Het Sanskrit Aan De Rijksuniversiteit Te Leiden Op 6 Juni 1975*. Leiden: Universitaire pers, 1975.

Schmidt, Ludwig. *Allegemeine Geschichte der germanischen Völker bis zur Mitte des sechsten Jahrhunderts*. Munich and Berlin, 1909.

Shaked, Shaul. *From Zoroastrian Iran to Islam: Studies in Religious History and Intercultural Contacts*. Aldershot, Great Britain: Variorum, 1995.

Shaked, Shaul, and Amnon Netzer. *Irano-Judaica. I, Studies Relating to Jewish Contacts with Persian Culture Throughout the Ages*. Jerusalem: Ben-Zvi Institute for the Study of Jewish Communities in the East, 1982.

---. *Irano-Judaica II: Studies Relating to Jewish Contacts with Persian Culture Throughout the Ages*. Jerusalem: Ben-Zvi Institute for the Study of Jewish Communities in the East, 1990.

---. *Irano-Judaica III: Studies Relating to Jewish Contacts with Persian Culture Throughout the Ages*. Jerusalem: Ben-Zvi Institute for the Study of Jewish Communities in the East, 1994.

Sharma, Arvind. *Religion and Women*. Albany: State University of New York Press, 1994.

Speidel, Michael. *Mithras-Orion: Greek Hero and Roman Army God*. Leiden: Brill, 1980.

Spiegel, Friedrich, and Jivanji Jamshedji Modi. *Spiegel Memorial Volume: Papers on Iranian Subjects Written by Various Scholars in Honour of The Late Dr. Frederic Spiegel*. Bombay: British India Pr., Byculla, 1908.

Sprengling, Martin. *Third Century Iran, Sapor and Kartir*. Chicago: The Institute, 1953.

Stoyanov, Yuri. *The Other God: Dualist Religions from Antiquity to the Cathar Heresy*. New Haven: Yale University Press, 2000.

Sundermann, Werner, Almut Hintze, and François de Blois. *Exegisti monumenta: festschrift in honour of Nicholas Sims-Williams*. Wiesbaden: Harrassowitz, 2009.

UNESCO. *Race and Science*. New York: Columbia University Press, 1961.

Vakil, Shiavax R. *Parsis and Conversion – An Objective Study*. Bombay, n.d. (ca 1985).

Walker, Benjamin. *The Hindu World; An Encyclopedic Survey of Hinduism*. New York: Praeger, 1968.

Williams, A. V., and Bamanji Nasarvanji Dhabhar. *The Pahlavi Rivāyat Accompanying the Dādestān Ī Dēnīg*. Copenhagen: Det Kongelige Danske Videnskabernes Selskab, 1990.

Yarshater, Ehsan. *Cambridge History of Iran: Volume 3, I [-3, II]. The Seleucid, Parthian and Sasanian Periods*. Cambridge: Cambridge University press, 1983.

Zaehner, R. C. *The Dawn and Twilight of Zoroastrianism*. New York: Putnam, 1961.

---. *The Teachings of the Magi: A Compendium of Zoroastrian Beliefs*. London: Allen & Unwin, 1956.

---. *Zurvan, A Zoroastrian Dilemma*, Oxford, 1955.

# INDEX

Made in the USA
Middletown, DE
31 July 2023

36020854R00115